THE WASTED NATIONS

THE WASTED NATIONS

Report of the International Commission of
Enquiry into United States Crimes in
Indochina, June 20–25, 1971

EDITED BY

FRANK BROWNING
DOROTHY FORMAN

Harper & Row, Publishers
New York, Evanston, San Francisco, London

CONTENTS

Preface: On the Necessity for an American Catharsis: Gunnar Myrdal

War crimes are recognized in early formal decisions by the United Nations to concern, not only the nations involved as the transgressors of international law and the victims of such transgressions—in this case the United States and the several nations in Indochina, but the entire world community. Basing itself upon this established principle of international law, the Swedish government at the last meeting of the United Nations General Assembly expressed its concerned opinion that it was a serious deficiency in the constitution of the United Nations, that it did not, as yet, contain provisions for a regular court, to which cases of war crimes and crimes against humanity could be brought for trial.

As a first step toward creating such a judicial order for the prosecution of war crimes and crimes against humanity, the Swedish government proposed the establishment within the United Nations of an imperial agency authorized to receive, investigate, and report on complaints of such crimes committed against international law. When even that less far-reaching proposal had no chance of leading to a decision in the General Assembly, the explanation was, of course, the present power situation in the world. The main transgressor of international law in this humanitarian realm at present is the United States. By its several military alliances with other governments all over the globe, and by its financial hold over even many nonallied states, it could prevent a majority of states from supporting the Swedish proposal. It can also be assumed that, even apart from pressure from the United States government, many governments, particularly of big states, would not like to be brought under the discipline of a supranational judiciary—or even something like it—in regard to this type of crime against international law.

In this situation of a faltering international order, it falls upon private individuals and organizations to establish the true facts of the grave war crimes against humanity committed by the United States in Indochina. In my opinion, to try to do this is a moral duty for every informed person. To keep silent about the horrible acts that have been committed, and are continually committed every day, amounts to becoming a conspirator, hiding the crimes. This is the moral principle upon which this Commission has been instituted, and upon which it has proceeded and will proceed. It does not pretend to be a court. It is not elected or appointed by the world community but only by an international conference of concerned private individuals and organizations from many countries. It has thus no power, except the power of revealing and publicizing its findings. There are no sanctions available to it. It is merely an investigating agency, trying to establish the true facts and view them in the light of international law. We shall conduct our hearings in public, and will meet in private only to decide upon procedures and when confronting our findings of facts with international law in order to draw conclusions.

There are other investigating agencies, and we intend to continue to cooperate with them in our fact-finding activity. The major difference is that we are elected by an international conference and contain members from different nations.

In the desperate moral and political world situation brought about by the United States's aggressive military actions in Indochina and the inconsideration and reckless way the United States has been, and is, carrying on its war, the one tremendously encouraging thing is that its government has from the beginning met criticism and resistance at home. This protest movement has been rising and is bound to rise even more as long as this cruel war is continued.

It should be readily recognized that very much of the primary fact-finding upon which this Commission has founded its work is done by American journalists, authors, scholars, and voluntary witnesses, many from the Army. On this basis there is a fight for American consciences carried on by big newspapers like *New York Times*, by political organizations like the ADA (Americans for Democratic Action), religious groups like the Quakers, and so on. This fight has had, and will continue to have, its repercussions in the political parties, in the Congress, in the churches, and in the courts.

As I have often pointed out, it is not enough that the United States stops its aggressive war in Indochina, leaves its military bases there, and completely withdraws all its troops —however important and urgent that is. Probably a majority of the American people are now becoming prepared to do this. They see that the war cannot be won against the determined defense on the part of the peoples in Indochina against the foreign intruders.

But as great a majority as possible in the American nation must also be brought to recognize that this war has been— and is—illegal, cruel, and immoral. They must go through an intellectual and moral catharsis and clearly see, understand, and even confess the war crimes committed under the order of their government. It is thus not enough to get out of Indochina as rapidly as possible and thereafter just live on and forget about the war as an unfortunate political and military failure.

The United States will not regain the confidence and trust of people abroad—that once it earned by contributing so decisively to the defeat of Fascist dictatorships and thereafter to the economic reconstruction, particularly of Europe —without going through that intellectual and moral catharsis of seeing clearly the wrongs it has done to innocent people.

More importantly, and even more primarily, it will otherwise not be possible for Americans to regain peace with their own consciences. Without such a catharsis, the nation will not be able to avoid this war from becoming a break in its history, a break against cherished national aspirations and ideals.

By the accidents of life and work, I have come near the American nation, perhaps nearer than any other foreigner in this generation. America has almost become my second homeland. I have become deeply identified with these aspirations and ideals—what I once, almost thirty years ago, called the "American Creed." I am certainly not speaking as an enemy of America, but as a very long-time friend—even when I am severely criticizing American policies.

And so I felt the whole time from the beginning of this war, even at the time when it was a French colonial war carried on with American support. I always pointed out that there were millions of Americans who shared our views. In an important sense it is a primary purpose of this Commission to support those Americans who have been fighting, and are now fighting, for the American conscience.

Introduction: Richard Falk

These reports from the war zones of Indochina make grim, macabre reading. Ample statistics are provided in this volume that show the persisting magnitude of America's criminal conduct. The ordinance totals, the daily averages of sorties flown, the acres of cropland and forests destroyed, the civilian casualty totals are reported in precise numerical detail. These abstractions of suffering are made poignant by specific descriptions of what single individuals have seen and heard at a given point in time in Vietnam, Laos, Cambodia —the concrete instances that need to be multiplied by millions to breathe life back into statistics. For instance, in a medical account by Claire Culhane, a Canadian volunteer worker, these words are found: "I have seen patients so disfigured from napalm as to make it impossible to verify whether they were men or women. I have seen skin and bone sizzling on a child's hand from phosphorus burns for 24 hours resisting any treatment." Such a single assertion puts in focus the long accounts of the arsenal of antipersonnel weaponry, routinely used for years by American forces, that sears and pierces human flesh in the cruelest fashion imaginable.

These grotesque realities that have tormented the peoples of Indochina during all these years must be attributed to the policymakers in Washington whose cool calculations and decisions have been definitively unmasked by the publication of the Pentagon Papers. For it is these men of influence who bear the primary responsibility for the policies that have been implemented each day with napalm and phosphorus. Since the war has turned out to be such a military and political fiasco, some of the more "flexible" members of this policy-making elite have started to tell the public some of their misgivings about the course of the war, but always in the pious rhetoric of "a lost crusade" (to invoke the title phrase of one prominent insider's book about why "the sacred cause" did not succeed). There is a lethal discrepancy between what these self-righteous men in Washington appear to feel when putting their policies into effect and what their military subordinates in Indochina do. Or is there? Daniel Ellsberg has spoken of "the need *not* to know" on the part of the high elite that induces government officials to wear self-imposed blinders that keep the barbarous tactics outside the field of vision. Albert Speer, the most repentant of the German leaders convicted at Nuremberg, writes in his *Memoirs* about his deliberate avoidance of knowledge of the brutal side of the early Nazi reign: ". . . not to have tried to see through the whole apparatus of mystification—was already criminal. . . . For being in a position to know and nevertheless shunning knowledge creates direct responsibility for the consequences—from the very beginning."[1] We are still without a leading government official who is prepared in public "to see through the whole apparatus of mystification"; such refusals are indeed criminal, especially when the policies persist, the prospect of deadly reprisal is virtually nil, and the evidence of criminality is so overwhelming.

Clearly this gap between the policymaker and the battlefield needs to be closed by making those who decide upon

1. Albert Speer, *Inside the Third Reich* (New York: Macmillan, 1970), p. 19.

aggressive war policies also assume responsibility for the genocidal ways in which a high-technology society wages counterinsurgency warfare against low-technology societies. The men in Washington persist in their ways, apparently oblivious of battlefield criminality, not because the information is unavailable or controversial, but because it has been removed from the agenda of legitimate concern by implicit consent. In the published accounts of the war by Roger Hilsman, George Ball, McGeorge Bundy, William P. Bundy, Dean Rusk, Chester Cooper, Townsend Hoopes, W. W. Rostow, and Eugene Rostow, there is no indication whatsoever of concern about the massive suffering imposed on the peoples of Indochina by American military tactics and technology. Shall we regard this remarkable failure to acknowledge what has been done a matter of moral numbness, racism, crass self-interest, or alienation from reality? Undoubtedly it is a combination of many factors, but no phenomenon is more significantly discouraging and revealing about the official interpretation of the Vietnam experience. It means, above all, that our rulers (the bipartisan elite that circles in and out of power) have learned nothing except that Vietnam was the wrong place to fight so strenuously and that American public opinion will stand for just so many *American* deaths and just so much dollar outflow over just so many years. It means, furthermore, that the logic and apparatus of counterinsurgency has been maintained, alas, with more success, in other parts of Asia, in Latin America, and in Africa. It means that "the Laos model" of counterinsurgency is one positive image for Washington policymakers of the future: namely, maximum covertness, maximum reliance on non-American mercenaries and equipment for ground combat, and unpublicized, but massive, U.S. strategic bombardment as needed. It also means that we adopt "the Prague model" from the Soviet Union and intervene, as necessary, with so much force so rapidly as to make popular resistance virtually impossible. And, finally, it means the "electronic battlefield" enabling death and destruction to be inflicted without spilling American blood in the battle zone. American money, equipment, and guidance is being used throughout Latin America to help repressive governments stay in power. We are involved in training death squads to kill suspected civilian opponents of such repressive regimes as those in Brazil, Guatemala, and Argentina—that is, the Phoenix Program has been generalized as a trademark of American guidance. The weaponry of counterinsurgency—such items as napalm and herbicides—has entered into the international arms flow and has been introduced, for instance, by the Portuguese in their colonial wars in Mozambique and Angola.

It is essential that the depraved realities of war crimes be brought home to Americans as part of the struggle to repudiate counterinsurgency once and for all as a mainstay of American foreign policy. These reports to the Oslo Commission of Inquiry make clear that counterinsurgency in Indochina also constitutes the crime of aggressive war. The client governments in Saigon, Vientiane, and Phnom Penh are facades that disguise from scrutiny the real nature of the war as a struggle between the United States government and the people of Vietnam, Laos, and Cambodia. The American role is not one of helping bad foreign governments remain in power; it is establishing and then using these governments as agents of a grand geopolitical design that amounts to a new form of imperialist control. As large a portion of the domestic population of the target country as possible is corrupted and conscripted into this mission of serving the interests of foreign domination and provides both "the cover" for imperialist operations and the mercenary base of the "in-country" armed forces and bureaucracy. Colonial policies have traditionally been based upon notions of "indirect rule" and "divide and rule." The policy motivation for counterinsurgency warfare is the same whenever, as in Indochina, a popularly-based revolution has taken hold. It is in this context that the imperatives of imperial control induce recourse to aggressive war, i.e., nondefensive war by a foreign country. The evidence before the Oslo Commission makes clear that the governments in South Vietnam, Laos, and Cambodia are client regimes with no prospect of being able to survive a genuine American withdrawal of presence and support; that is, including foreign mercenary troops and massive infusions of modern arms.

Finally, this evidence presented at Oslo establishes that *the battlefield tactics* of high-technology counterinsurgency warfare plus the aggressive war character of the enterprise add up to the most grotesque crime of all, that of genocide. The enemy is enlarged to include the foreign population; the tactics of warfare are savage in their impact upon this population and seek to make the surviving rural population choose between a position of active combat and refugee status. "Free-fire zones," "search-and-destroy missions," "harassment and interdiction fire," "crop denial programs," and large-scale death squads trained to torture and assassinate civilian suspects are the ingredients of such a genocidal enterprise. The population is virtually deprived of the countryside despite the rural character of the culture and the economy. The dehumanizing impacts of excessive urban migration, mass prostitution, war profiteering, and pervasive corruption are clearly predictable outcomes of such a war effort.

The evidence given at Oslo confirms, then, the major outlines of the analysis suggested here:

(1) The massive use of cruel tactics directed indiscriminately against the civilian population in flagrant viola-

tion of the minimum rules of war;

(2) The aggressive intention of imposing by force a regime on the population to serve the primary interests of a foreign power;

(3) The genocidal character of seeking to accomplish the pacification of entire population groups by active military struggle.

The Nuremberg tradition makes it clear that those who commit war crimes should bear personal responsibility. The present realities of power in the United States make the direct prosecution of this leadership class responsible for carrying on the war policies impractical. However, it does not seem impractical to set forth this evidence as part of an effort to educate the American public and to discredit the men who have been committing the country to this deplorable set of policies. The political importance of the war crimes issue is to draw a boundary line beyond which there is no basis for arguing "good faith," "honest mistake," and "in the line of duty." By depicting the criminal character of the Indochina enterprise, the whole counterrevolutionary posture of American foreign policy is exposed for what it is—a part of the wider criminal enterprise of using military technology and terror to impose oppressive political conditions on foreign populations. To end the wider pattern of criminality requires, then, nothing less than a new foreign policy and a new group of foreign policymakers.

Beyond this kind of education and enlightenment arises the moral imperatives of doing our best to rectify past wrongs. American society as a whole bears a responsibility to the peoples of Indochina for allowing our government to inflict such death and destruction over such a long period. We must—out of an inward necessity—make available the resources needed for the rapid reconstruction and rehabilitation of Indochina. This task may require as much as $50–75 billion over a five- to ten-year period placed in an international trust fund for use by the postwar governments of Indochina. This money could be collected from two sources: earmarked annual reductions in the defense budget, ideally achieved by eliminating counterinsurgency hardware and operations from the concept of "national security" and a one percent Indochina War surtax that allowed all Americans to participate in the redemptive process. (The regressive features of this tax could be offset by other needed tax reforms.)

Of course, it should be clearly understood that the overriding priority remains that of ending altogether America's direct and indirect combat role in Indochina. Nothing, not even a concern with postwar rectification of wrongs to the Indochinese peoples, should be allowed to divert our attention from the urgent need to end the bloodshed in these ravaged lands.

The persisting criminality of the war is being turned inward to fight dissident groups in American society. The police are being equipped and trained to carry out counterinsurgent missions. Many opponents of the war policies are being gradually, and reluctantly, drawn across the boundaries of official "law and order" and defined as "criminals" and "enemies of the state." The Harrisburg trial of Phillip Berrigan, Eqbal Ahmad, and other antiwar leaders involves carrying the idea of "pacification" into American civic life; Daniel Ellsberg is being prosecuted for lifting the veil of spurious secrecy that had been imposed on Vietnam warmaking so that the public and the Congress might remain ignorant of the deceit that was used to gear up the war machine for battle in Vietnam. Obviously, one consequence of the overwhelming demonstration that the Indochina war is an ongoing criminal enterprise is to place those who oppose it by radical means in the position of citizens who are resisting the commission of crime. Young Americans who chose prison, exile, insubordination to military superiors, or desertion rather than contribute actually or symbolically to the war effort deserve exoneration and some acknowledgment of their public service. This is not a matter of amnesty—for there is nothing to forgive. On the contrary, the issue of amnesty might genuinely be raised in relation to the main "war criminals"—those who could be prosecuted and would almost certainly be convicted by a war crimes tribunal that operated impartially and with a professional respect for the facts, the evidence, and the rules of international law. Since there is no prospect of bringing such an apparatus into being and since reasonable apprehensions exist as to whether the punishment of criminals is ever a beneficial form of social education, it makes moral and political sense to seek amnesty for our "war criminals" and belated exoneration for our "peace criminals."

Let us make no mistake. Nuremberg was an experience flawed by its punitive focus, by its "victors' justice," and, above all, by its failure to look into the Allied side of war crimes (especially, mass bombing of civilian populations in Germany and Japan). The edifice of international law and morality is fragile in conception and sporadic in application. At the same time, what was done at Nuremberg (and Tokyo) embodied certain impulses that might serve us well at this present time of deepening internal crisis. First of all, statesmen had agreed over centuries that certain modes of warfare were intolerable, especially those inflicting excessive suffering and those which failed to discriminate between military and nonmilitary targets and between combatant and noncombatant personnel. Second, Nuremberg stands above all for the prosposition that the planning and waging of aggressive war against a foreign society is a criminal act of great seriousness. Third, Nuremberg—and the Genocide Convention which was drawn up afterwards—condemned as criminal war policies that were cruelly directed at civilian populations as a whole.

The international community, in response to American initiatives, expressed its approval of the Nuremberg experience, most pointedly by unanimously endorsing the Nuremberg Judgment in Resolution 95 (I) of the UN General Assembly in 1946. The Nuremberg Principles were formulated in an authoritative form in 1950 by a group of international law specialists serving in the International Law Commission of the United Nations. This background of legal experience provides the country with decisive criteria for appraisal and judgment. Our leaders were on notice. The evidence now clearly demonstrates that the American conduct of the Indochina war involves a direct challenge to these principles of minimum restraint in world affairs. Any fair-minded reader of these Oslo Reports can hardly question the need for action. Their vividness and comprehensiveness makes evasion of the challenge very difficult. Of course, refuge can still be taken in the claim that these reports reflect bias and embody propaganda. But let it be understood that this is no longer a credible evasion—the basic contours of criminality have been abundantly demonstrated by many other sources and confirm in all relevant respects the contents of this volume. The special value of getting testimony from the participants is to achieve a sense of concreteness, of victimization, and to have this material set forth in a relevant political context. Can anyone genuinely doubt that, if the North Vietnamese were in the kind of ascendant international position that the United States found itself in after World War II, world public opinion would applaud bringing those Americans responsible for napalmings and B-52 carpet bombings to some bar of justice convened on the Nuremberg model? Since the United States has not been defeated in this sense, the government will either persist in its criminal ways (the policies and tactics remain operative U.S. policy throughout the Third World), or it will be repudiated by a domestic movement that grasps the issues clearly and sees through, at last, "the whole apparatus of mystification." It is in this spirit of urgent concern that Americans are urged to confront the material in this volume. These materials give us the closest thing to the proceedings of an international board of review that is likely to be available for some time; indeed, one could draft a "Nuremberg Judgment" for the Indochina war on the basis of the evidence and analyses made available in this volume.

The time is now ripe to organize a comparable set of commission hearings in the United States as a further way of bringing the truth about the war home to America and expanding the awareness of Americans about the criminal character of the basic war policies. Even at this stage, establishment media will probably not deal fairly or significantly with such proceedings, but the creation of a full record by concerned citizens may bring a new measure of coherence to antiwar thinking and a renewed sense of urgency to antiwar activities.

In the meantime, we should ponder, I fear, with the shame and humiliation that only an American can feel, the aptness of the anonymous author of a South Vietnamese committee report to the Commission in Oslo:

No mountain can match in height the towering crimes piled up by the U.S. aggressors and their henchmen in South Vietnam, no ocean can beat them in depth, earth and heaven are angry, vegetation too resents them, entire mankind indignantly condemns them.

Princeton, N.J.
August 1971

America in Indochina:
A Crime against Humanity

At least one of the functions which the International Commission of Enquiry has performed is the gathering of independent scholarly and journalistic material about the social effects of the war in Indochina. Some of the most striking revelations to date have come from those journalists and scholars who have taken time away from their normal pursuits to investigate war crimes committed by the U.S. The following six articles not only contribute important new information from people who have spent many years studying Southeast Asia, but also offer important professional corroboration of the findings of the Indochinese researchers. All of the following articles were delivered at the Oslo hearings except for the Napalm Survey by Professor Neilands, which was specially prepared for this volume.

A Decade of Atrocity: Don Luce

The U.S. Military Command in Indochina is flagrantly violating the various international conventions relating to the conduct of war and bragging about it. Encouragement for such violations is coming from the highest echelons of the United States government. As you know, Article Nineteen of the Geneva Conventions on Sick and Wounded says that "fixed establishments and mobile medical units of the medical service may in no circumstances be attacked, but shall at all times be respected and protected, by the parties to the conflict." I would like to point out that violations of this provision have been condoned and encouraged by the Vice President of the United States, Spiro Agnew. On May 3, 1970, Vice President Agnew said (on the television commentary program *Face the Nation*): "The purpose of the strikes into the sanctuaries is not to go into Cambodia, but to take and reduce the supply depots, the hospital complexes, and so on." And just in case the people did not get the point, he repeated again, "But they"—referring to the NLF and North Vietnamese—"but they cannot move these facilities, such as hospitals. . . ." I would continue to point out that after the invasion of Cambodia, the President of the United States went on to brag about the amount of medical equipment and supplies U.S. troops had captured. He said on June 3 that as of 4 P.M. that day the U.S. had captured 50,800 pounds of medical supplies, and then on June 30, 1970, he gave a list of "significant enemy losses" that included 110,800 pounds of medical supplies. The reason I bring this out is to point out that when the President and Vice President of a country are condoning and encouraging the violations of the various conventions this encourages the soldiers who are operating in that country to commit the violations.

Now let me cite two short quotes from U.S. military newspapers within South Vietnam. The first: *Typhoon*, an authorized publication of the Fifth Public Information Detachment of the Department of Army. In its July–August 1970 issue, it states that after the Cambodian operation "there would be no training centers left in which to indoctrinate troops, no medical facilities left to treat the wounded." Next: the *Observer*, published by the Command Information Division, Office of Information, Military Assistance Command, Vietnam. It described an operation in the Que Son Mountain area around Quang Nam: "According to one Seventh Marine spokesman the two hospital finds could seriously hurt the NVA Units and VC operating in the Que Son area by almost eliminating any chance of intensive medical care." And, ironically, the same front page of the *Observer* has an article saying that the "VC" soldier "has never heard of the Geneva Convention concerning the treatment of the Prisoners of War." Then, distributed by JUSPAO, which is the Joint United States Public Affairs Office of Saigon, they list pictures showing the captured medical supplies. One picture is captioned: "Medical supplies by the ton captured in Cambodia include penicillin, bandages, vitamins, and anti-malaria pills." All of these things, it appears to me, are very obvious violations of Article Nineteen of the Geneva Conventions on Treatment of the Wounded and Care of the Sick.

I would like to go on now to Principle Six of the Charter of the Nuremburg Tribunal which lists the wanton destruction of cities, towns or villages, or devastation not justified by military necessity as a war crime. One of the largest orphanages in Vietnam is the Long Thang orphanage, located about two miles from the large U.S. military base at Long Binh. Now, the last time I visited the Long Thang orphanage—only about three or four months ago—two or three things struck me about it. First, as you enter the orphanage, there is a sign in English which says: "Please Don't Shoot At The Orphans Village." The reason for this sign is that we have been shooting at the orphans' village. Inside the orphans' village on display are seven unexploded shells—and you can imagine the number of normal shells that have hit this village. There are about fifteen hundred orphans in this compound. Thirteen of the orphans as well as four monks have been wounded.

While I was the director of International Voluntary Services, from 1961 to 1967, several of the villages in which IVS members were working were bombed, strafed, and/or hit by artillery shells—either the 105 or 155 howitzers or from naval bombardment. On two occasions, villages in which IVS members were living were hit. One was a village in Laos which was bombed twice, one was a hamlet in South Vietnam which was strafed by helicopters. And I would point out that both of these IVS members were Americans. I talked with these people. They said there were no NLF or North Vietnamese or any other kind of soldiers in the villages at the time. And one of the frustrations which we, as IVS members, had is that as we worked in villages every once in a while we would find that the villages would be bombed or strafed, hit by U.S. military fire. Now, Article Fifty of Hague Convention Number Four states, "No general penalty, pecuniary or otherwise, shall be inflicted upon the population on accounts of the acts of individuals for which they cannot be regarded as jointly and severally responsible."

I would like to add to my testimony parts of a letter from

the Council of Voluntary Agencies in Saigon. The Council of Voluntary Agencies is made up of the various foreign voluntary agencies such as CARE, Catholic Relief Services, Asian Christian Service, Vietnam Christian Service, and so on. They wrote regarding a special program of Colonel Lay Whee Luin, who was Military Regent to Assistant Commander. He had sent a memo to the voluntary agencies; its subject was "request for social support for the implementation of gathering people for hamlet establishment plans from Pleiju, Phu Bon and Darlac provinces." The Council of Voluntary Agencies became very disturbed about this request because of what is being done over the years to that Montagnard people.

The Montagnard people are Vietnamese who live in the highlands. There are about one million who live primarily by slash-and-burn agriculture, hunting, fishing, etc. On March 10, 1971, they wrote: "Since July 31, 1970, about 150 Montagnard hamlets have been relocated. Prior to that, 722 of the total of 1,407 Montagnard hamlets had been relocated. Some hamlets, such as Tam Bo, in Lang Dun province, have been relocated twice. Secondly, Vietnamese government troops—i.e., Saigon government troops—burned the hamlets of Buon Kai, Buon-Y-Yung, Buon Wing A, Buon Wing B, and others in the Darlac province. In Pleiwok hamlet, Phe Bon province, the inhabitants' gardening tools were burned along with their houses. In another hamlet in Darlac the rice crops were destroyed with herbicides at the time of relocation. Third, in most cases the people have not been allowed to carry many of their posessions with them. They have had to leave behind their livestock, poultry, and large personal possessions such as gongs and ceremonial jars. In Buon Kli hamlet, Darlac province, it was reported that the Vietnamese soldiers stole their cattle and other possessions left behind by the Montagnard people. Fourth, in many hamlets the Montagnard were given only corn meal and bulgur wheat, neither of which they knew how to prepare. They were living only on the rice they were able to bring with them. Fifth, in Pleiju Tu village, Fleiju province, it has been estimated since December 1970, about 100 persons have died from treatable diseases including pneumonia. . . ." (As a footnote I should say that when I left in May, over 300 people of the 450 families there had died.) Sixth, most of the hamlets have inadequate water and sanitation facilities. Seventh, the social welfare officials in Pleiju, Phu Bon, and Darlac were not prepared by the military authorities for the relocations. Eighth, where the Montagnard were forced to leave behind certain traditional lands, there are often now Vietnamese tilling the soil. This situation exists in Buon T'Suk, Quang Duc province, Buon Gram, Darlac province, and Dang Gia, Lam Dong province. The primary reason the Saigon government forcefully moved these Montagnard hamlets was to improve what the American Government calls its HES (Hamlet Evaluation System) rating—a figure, which, if you are familiar with American politics, is useful to Nguyen Van Thieu and Richard Nixon when month after month after month they must report that 96 percent, and so on, of the population is under our control. So these hamlets were moved for strictly political reasons to increase this percentage of control.

I want to talk more about the question of forcefully moving people. As I mentioned at the beginning of my testimony, I'm an agriculturalist. I have both a B.S. and an M.S. from the University of Vermont and Cornell University in Agriculture. The major agricultural problem which I faced, particularly during my last years with IVS, was the problem of herbicides or defoliation: in hamlet after hamlet where we worked the people complained about the medicine from the sky, or defoliation, that was destroying their crops.

We were working in the Delta, on a little island in the

Mekong River. It was ideal for introducing a new variety of watermelons because you wouldn't get cross-pollination. You could experiment very easily. Well, one day this whole island was defoliated and all the farmers' full source of income was destroyed. It was defoliated by an American plane. We went to the American authorities and asked that the farmers be paid ten thousand dollars, or the equivalent in piasters, which was a very conservative estimate of the watermelons' value. We were told, "The whole damned country is not worth ten thousand dollars," a response which reflects both an attitude and the fact that the farm people were not repaid for the damage done by the defoliation. When the farmland was defoliated, the people had to move into the cities and around the air bases. There was also forced movement because of the search and destroy missions, because of the bombing, and so on.

I would like to make a special comment on what this relocation does to the people. Basically, what happened is that the old people, the women, and the children are moved into these refugee camps or around the air bases on city slums. Before they are moved, the family has worked together. Each person has his own role. The little children watch the buffalo; later they begin to help their fathers to plow. The girls and the women plant the rice, and all work together. As they move into the city slums and around the air bases, the only work that's available is for the old women to wash the military uniforms of the foreign soldiers, the young women to work in the bars and brothels, and the children to sell peanuts, shine shoes, pimp for the foreign soldiers: you get a tearing apart of the whole family structure. This is one of the greatest dangers to the Vietnamese people. Little children earn more money than their mothers. Girls who work in the bars and brothels are often ashamed to go back to their homes. As a person studying postwar reconstruction, I was faced over and over with the problem of a girl who, for example, worked on a farm and then became a prostitute earning perhaps ten times as much money as she had made on the farm. When the war is over she will be without a job. How do you get this person rehabilitated back into life?

Two other problems generated by this overcrowding and discouragement are the use of drugs and the incidence of venereal diseases. On the corner of the street where I lived, as on many of the streets in Saigon, large numbers of people have begun to use drugs, particularly morphine. Among the bar girls the incident of venereal disease has increased over 50 percent, according to the National Venereal Disease Center in Saigon; this is going to be a tremendous medical problem for the country to face when the war is over. The United States, which is the major spreader of the venereal disease, has refused to admit it is a problem because to admit it would indicate that American soldiers were not behaving themselves and were sleeping with the Vietnamese. So there have been no efforts on the part of the United States to help try to control the spread of the disease or to treat the women who have been infected with venereal disease by U.S. soldiers.

The Geneva Conventions on the Law of War prohibit outrages upon personal dignity—in particular, humiliating and degrading treatment against persons taking no active part in the hostilities. For the past ten years in Vietnam, and particularly for the last six or seven, almost every day I have heard the same kinds of stories which you have heard yesterday and today. It doesn't make it any easier to hear them again today, but I would point out that day after day the same kinds of things were brought to my attention in South Vietnam. I have visited and talked with many of the people released from the prisons. For example, in April of last year several university and high school students were released from the

Saigon police station prisons, and I saw the blackened finger-
nails where slivers had been inserted, the black and blue
spots and welts. One of the boys, for example, who could not
hear out of one ear, said that water had been put in his ear
and then forced in with a cupped hand. Most of these people
could not walk because their knees had been pounded with
billy-clubs. The girls told about having beer or coke bottles
forced up the vagina. All of them talked about cigarettes
being extinguished in sensitive parts of the body, and some
showed me the little round burns which they claimed were
where cigarettes had been extinguished into the body.

Last July [1970] I was given a map of Con Son prison by
a former prisoner showing exactly where the tiger cages
were. I asked for a group of American Congressmen to go to
this island to see what was happening. Congressmen agreed
to go and look. When we got there—myself and Congressman William Anderson and Congressman Augustus Hawkins
—after a great deal of trouble, we finally found the door that
led to the tiger cages and pounded on it. Finally someone
opened it: we walked in and saw the. tiger cages. On the
men's side were three men per cell, or per cage; on the
women's side there were five in each of these tiny, little—
well, they're more like *pits*. As we walked down the aisle and
looked down into the pits upon the prisoners below us, at first
no one said anything and then someone said something to me
. . . and I explained in Vietnamese that I could not speak
French. Then they started speaking to me in Vietnamese,
asking for water and then for food. They began to tell us
about what happened to them. None of the men and few of
the women could walk. To get around in the bottom of this
pit-like cage, cell, they had to crawl on their hands. They
showed me the marks where they had been shackled. They
were not shackled at the time we were there, but they had
the marks on their ankles, so I think that the paralysis was

probably a result both of having been shackled and of a lack of adequate diet.

Article Thirteen of the Geneva Convention relative to the Treatment of Prisoners of War states: "Prisoners of war must at all times be protected, particularly against the acts of violence or intimidation, and against insults and public curiosity." First I want to point out that in Saigon at least once a month, as I traveled through the countryside, I saw the dead bodies of Liberation Soldiers displayed in the marketplace, along the roadsides. The dead bodies were put out for people to see. Given the particular importance of burying the dead in Vietnamese culture, this is an insult. It is certainly putting them forth for "public curiosity." Pictures of the dead bodies are passed out and distributed by the U.S. government through JUSPAO. Another picture I have here shows Saigon troops posing with a wounded NLF Battalion Commander. For example, they write: "Vietnamese Rangers proudly pose with slightly wounded Viet Cong Battalion Commander." This is very obviously a violation of Article Thirteen of the Geneva Convention.

I'd like to go on to another thing which is illegal according to the Conventions of War as I understand them: the parading of captured soldiers, prisoners of war, through villages. I have here photographs of Liberation soldiers being paraded through the city of Quang Ngai. Again they are photographs passed out by the U.S. government. I would like to read the caption on a picture I have here distributed by JUSPAO. It says: "Viet Cong, one a woman, captured during the Communist Tet Offensive in Quang Ngai, are paraded in among the people, who refuse to support them in their so-called 'liberation offensive.'"

In April 1971 I visited a Joint American-Vietnamese Interrogation Center. (I knew its location because a former South Vietnamese prisoner told me he had met two North Vietnamese medical technicians whose hands were twisted up from having been beaten on a table, and they gave him the location of this Joint Interrogation Center.) I went there and did not see the cells. But in the process I was able to make arrangements with an American interrogater at the center. I took very careful notes, and he saw the notes after I took them. I would like to read what he told me. He said about this Joint Interrogation Center: "There are 65 cells for the prisoners. Each cell contains one prisoner. The cells measure one and a half by two and a half meters. The only lighting is from a narrow slit at the top. The mosquitoes are terrible in the cells. No exercise or recreation is allowed. Sometimes the prisoners go three weeks without leaving the cell. Sometimes they are really glad to be interrogated just to be let out of the cells and set under a fan. The prisoners are fed twice a day. They are given rice and some vegetables. The ARVN (meaning the Army of Vietnam, the Saigon troops) soldiers won't eat the stuff. 'It's disgusting,' they say." And he went on: "At mealtime someone goes around with water. Each prisoner is allowed to drink a couple of swallows out of the dipper. Then the guard goes to the next cell and allows the prisoner there to drink from the dipper." The interrogator went on to explain that, time after time, as he interviewed these prisoners in the Interrogation Center—officially prisoners of war—he was begged, they begged him for water. The system he used, and which the American interrogators there used, to get information was what he called a "good guy, bad guy" approach. That is: when the prisoners came in to him he would be, in his words "very kind, give them cigarettes, coffee, water, talk very pleasantly with them," but if they did not give the information he would say to them: "You know, it's really too bad. We're going to have to send you back to the South Vietnamese authorities." And he pointed out that just about every prisoner he had interviewed or interrogated had been tortured at least one time by the Saigon government authorities.

Finally, I want to make just one or two more comments about the question of political prisoners. There are at least— *at least*—100,000 political prisoners of the Saigon regime in South Vietnam. Some estimates go as high as 400,000. The American aid system to the Saigon police has increased drastically over the years. The number of Saigon government police has increased from 16,000 in 1963 to over 100,000 police today. In 1970, we, the U.S.—and I say "we" because I am an American and therefore have to accept part of the responsibility for this—the U.S. government spent $20.9 million for the police system in Saigon; the budgeted amount for 1971 is $30 million. So we have increased our aid to the police system by 50 percent in just one year. I would also point out that in other areas, such as education and public health, U.S. aid has *decreased.* For example, in education the aid in 1970 was $6.1 million. In 1971 it's $4.5 million. So right now the U.S. government is spending more than six times as much money on repression as it is on the whole education system. I'd like to read a quote from a director of the United States Agency for International Development, the American economic aid program. John Mosler, in his 1970 report to Ambassador Ellsworth Bunker: "During 1970 the police continued to improve their capability in traditional police functions. Their timely and positive action effectively contained civil disturbances involving the war veterans, students, and religious groups, thereby preventing the spread of violence." And I think that the U.S. government really must ask itself who is causing the spread of violence when we have put so much emphasis on our aid to the police and our own involvement in the violence.

The final question which may come up in the minds of many people—and certainly one of the excuses which the

U.S. government is using as well—is that the torture of the prisoners and the conditions at Con Son in the tiger cages are Saigon government affairs for which we are not responsible. Well, I would point out that in the budget we are supporting these things. We are paying for them. For example, after Con Son when the tiger cages were found, the government did away with the old tiger cages but then immediately began to build new tiger cages which are smaller than the former ones. They began to do this as a "self-help" project; that is, the prisoners were to build their own tiger cages. Well, the prisoners refused to build their own tiger cages and the U.S. government gave a $400,000 contract to the construction company RMK to build them with one of the specific, stated reasons being that the prisoners would not build their own.

I'd like to end my testimony here, before questions, by reading the text of a letter to President Nixon by 117 Vietnamese with relatives in the South Vietnamese prisons. And I would point out that these are people who are living in Saigon, Da Nang, Cantho, all over South Vietnam. They are certainly not to be considered enemies of the Saigon government—at least they are part of this number that the Saigon government says is under its control. They wrote to President Richard Milhous Nixon, and this is dated April 12, 1971:

"Mr. President,

"Knowing that you share the responsibility for the severity of the prison regime in South Vietnam, knowing that you are paying special attention to all people deprived of liberty, since, many times in the past, you have asked for liberty of the Americans imprisoned by the North Vietnamese, we, the relatives of the Vietnamese arrested and incarcerated in the detention camps and prisons throughout South Vietnam, are sending this letter in order to present to you the painful realties of the prison regime in South Vietnam, and ask you to take urgent action.

"1. Through South Vietnam U.S. Intelligence agencies have been participating in the incarceration of the Vietnamese, and are using systematically, all the refined and scientific methods of torture in order to extract forcefully declarations of guilt and thus encroach upon human dignity and oppose the declaration of human rights. As a result many Vietnamese have become sick or disabled, died, or secretly killed. The facts are hidden from the public by a curtain of secrecy. The Interrogation Centers belonging to the security system of the Republic of Vietnam are now incarcerating the suspects arrested without any proof of guilt or with the only proof of guilt being for 'loving their country and fighting for peace in Vietnam.' These people are tortured in an utterly savage manner in order to obtain their declaration and constituting their file or false proofs of guilt are devised against them and sent to the tribunal. The prisoners are ill treated, repressed, and brutally beaten throughout South Vietnam. The South Vietnamese Administration is using the means provided by the U.S. aid, such as tear gas, tear gas rockets, acid, and so on, in order to repress the prisoners. Many prisoners have died or become sick or disabled because of these repressions. Prisons are too narrow, dirty, and too crowded. There is not enough air for breath. In many prisons, typical of which are the tiger cages in Con Son, the prisoners are shackled day and night so that some of them have become paralyzed. Presently your Government is helping with money and other means in the construction of new tiger cages in Con Son. This has disturbed and angered us as well as the people of Vietnam. The communication between us and our relatives in prison has been limited to a minimum or forbidden completely. Many of us have been denied permission to visit our relatives, or receive letters from them. Our demands are ignored by the Government. Sometimes we have been repressed. For example, the repression that occurred on March 19, 1970 in front of the Lower House. The food in prisons is too poor. It is composed mainly of rotten rice and bitter, dry fish. Medicines are lacking, as a consequence the majority of prisoners have lung disease, mental disease, paralysis, or beriberi. Many people have been arrested or incarcerated for months or for years with [out] trial or sentence, or continue to be imprisoned under the regime of detention without any valid reason. They may be imprisoned or deported, although they are under probation. There are people who are tortured or repressed to death.

". . . and people who die of sickness in prison without their family being notified. We have been presenting to you the real happenings in the prisons throughout South Vietnam. From this presentation you may refer to the prison regime in your country as well as in the other civilized countries of the world. You will see what your aid in human and material resources has contributed to the people of Vietnam. Presently most prisons in South Vietnam have advisors from your country. Most have received physical aid from the U.S. If the material aid serves a useful purpose, we will never forget your kindness and humanitarianism in helping us against poverty and backwardness. On the contrary—the prisons in South Vietnam being considered as inhuman, we wonder whether your effect, and the effect of your administration provoke in us gratefulness or resentment. Thus, we, the suffering Vietnamese, appeal to your sense of fairness and your sense of responsibility and request you to meet the following demands: (1) Order the employees of your government to end their participation with the Government of the Republic of Vietnam in maintaining a prison regime contrary to the conscience and humanitarianism of men and women in the world. (2) Intervene with the Government of the Republic of Vietnam in satisfying our following demands: (a) free all people detained illegally or without evidence for the purpose of

terrorizing and repressing the Vietnamese peace-loving patriots. Free the people who are detained without sentence or
with expired sentences, the people who are on probation, the
people who are old, and small children. (b) Follow a policy
of treating the prisoners with humanitarianism. Change completely the present erroneous policy regarding food, living
facilities, clothes, medical and spiritual activities—the methods of repressing, terrorizing, and brutalizing the prisoners.

"Anxious to safeguard the rights to live of our relatives,
with the conviction that the right and the humanitarianism
will be accomplished, we wish [you] to accept our sincere
thanks."

If I could make another footnote here I would point out
that in South Vietnam, under the Saigon regime, there is a
law which states that people may be held in prison for up to
two years without trial, and then the term is renewable. So
people can be held year after year after year on an indefinite
basis without having any trial. When I talked with the people
in Con Son prison there were men who had been there since
1955, 1956, without ever having had a trial and without even
knowing why they were in Con Son. Furthermore at Con Son
the only criminal prisoners were two. We only met two
criminal prisoners that I can remember, and these two were
the trustee guards—the people who were to watch over the
other prisoners. One of the things prisoners in Vietnam oppose is the use of criminal prisoners to look over, or to super-
vise, political prisoners. These two that we met were both
murderers.

*Commission: You said that there are reported to be how
many refugees? Three million?*

Mr. Luce: Oh, much more. If you take the released figures
and add them up, they will come to at least five million. For
example, in the city of Siagon officially there are no refugees
and yet the population of Vietnam has grown from one mil-

lion in 1958, when I arrived in Vietnam, to three million today. When I say that officially there are no refugees there, it means that no one there has ever received any refugee allotments, which were six piasters a day the last I knew, or about four or five cents a day. But at least a third of the population of South Vietnam has been moved at least once. Today Saigon is the most crowded city in the world. It has a population density twice that of its nearest competitor, which is Tokyo.

Commission: You said that there are at least 100,000 political prisoners.

Mr. Luce: Yes.

Can you only tell us: what do you base this estimation on?

Mr. Luce: Yes. There are several ways. By using the official figures released by the Saigon government on January 5, 1970, in the Owi T'en newspaper, the Vietnamese Senate, Judiciary, and Interior Committees released a report saying that there were 50,000 detainees held in the temporary detention camps alone. So you have 50,000 in the detention camps. At about the same time one of the directors of the correctional institutes—there are 41 correctional prisons, of which Con Son is one—announced that 35,000 people were being held in the 41 correctional centers, and that 70 percent of these were political prisoners. He used the term "communist criminals" in a lot of cases, but these are not Prisoners of War. That's a completely separate issue. They are held at Phu Kwuc. These are people who are picked up in the Phung Whun, the Phoenix Operation; they are people whose crime, really, is to disagree with the government. It has nothing to do with procommunism or anticommunism; they just disagree with the government. So this adds another 25,000. At the same time the American advisor to the interrogation centers stated in late 1969, early 1970, that there were 10,-000 people held in the interrogation centers. I made my own estimate that about half of these would generally be considered POWs, Prisoners of War, and half of them political prisoners, which adds another 5,000. This gives a figure of 80,000 and does not include some of the major prisons. For example, one of the largest systems of prisons are the military prisons in which they put people who are dodging the draft. Many of the Buddhists, for example, refuse to fight in the army. These are people who just refuse to go. Many of the people who are caught, in a sense, trying to get away from the Saigon government are, again, the political opponents of the Saigon government. So, for example, in the prison just near the American golf course—I can't remember the name of it —on the outskirts of Saigon, they have 2,500. In a second prison in Saigon they have another 2,500. Throughout the country you have these military prisons. I don't know the number of political prisoners in these. Another system is the police headquarters prisons where probably the worst torture in the country goes on. Every police station has its own little prison, and I don't know the number of prisoners in these. Every district—almost every district—in Vietnam has its own separate prison which adds about 200 more prisons. So I have here an 80,000 that I can identify by released government figures, and I think that probably it's much much more than 100,000 because the major systems aren't even included in this figure. Mrs. Ngo Ba Thanh, who is with the Women's Right to Live, an international lawyer and one of the officers of the International Association of International Law. She estimates 200,000 prisoners. Other estimates go up to 400,000 political prisoners.

Mr. Luce, will you tell me please whether there is a legal ground for sending people into prison without sentence being pronounced and without any trial?

Mr. Luce: Most of the people who are sent are sent under the so-called law which is called Ahn Tre. This is Decree Law

Number 19—Decree Law Number 004/66 dated February 15, 1966, signed by Major General, now President, Nguyen Van Thieu. The law states: "Those persons considered dangerous to the national defense, public security, may be interred in a prison or designated area, or banished from designated areas, for a maximum of periods of two years, which is renewable. The interrment and banishment shall be ordered by authority of the Prime Minister issued upon recommendation of the Ministry of Interior," which in fact means that these people, according to Article 19 of this law, are not brought to any court, do not receive a trial, and can stay in prison for an indefinite length of time.

You have mentioned the political prisoners. Can you tell us about how many people in South Vietnam are living in strategic hamlets or in camps?

Mr. Luce: Yes. The term strategic hamlet is no longer used. After strategic hamlets there were Ap Tan Sinh, which is new life hamlets, Ap Tan Moi, which is, translated, new life hamlets or new, new life hamlets, something like this, and then there are the refugee hamlets. All these get involved in the general area of definitions. I would say that about a third of the population has been refugeed in one form or another. Many of these people are living in the slums and others live around the air bases and some live in guarded enclosures. Like one which bore the sign: "Refugees from Communism Cannot Leave the Camp." This is about a third of the population which has been forced to leave their homes.

How many prisons did you see or did you visit in South Vietnam?

Mr. Luce: I have visited, in Saigon, Chi Hoa, and Chanh Hung Children's Prison too. I visited Cantho Prison, Con Son Prison, the detention center in Quang Ngai, the prison halfway into the POW camp in Can Tho, into the interrogation center in Saigon, so—ten, fifteen.

The U.S. Food Destruction Program in South Vietnam: Arthur H. Westing

Our nation's food destruction program in South Vietnam, although not secret, has received only scant publicity. It demands wider attention and careful consideration.

The U.S. has been destroying growing crops in South Vietnam (SVN) since at least November 1961 as part of its "resource denial" program. This is accomplished largely by the aerial application of an aqueous solution of sodium dimethyl arsenate (sodium cacodylate; "Agent Blue"; Ansul Co. "Phytar-560G"), applied at the rate of 9.3 pounds of active ingredients per acre. This is a highly persistent (and potentially hazardous) chemical not domestically registered for use on or near crops. Based on released Department of Defense (DoD) data, some 6,397,000 pounds of active ingredients were expended between the beginning of 1962 and the end of 1969. Figures for 1970 or 1971 are not available, although the program continues. Annual area treated, according to the DoD, follows:

YEAR	AGRICULTURAL ACRES SPRAYED
1961	?
1962	1,000
1963	–
1964	10,000
1965	66,000
1966	104,000
1967	221,000
1968	170,000
1969	115,000
1970	?
Total 1962–69	688,000

The 688,000 acres sprayed during the eight years for which data are available represent nine percent of SVN's 7.6 million acres of agricultural lands. Actually, most crop destruction occurs in the Central Highlands so that the percentage of destruction is regionally much higher. These regions have been traditionally food poor; their population consists largely of primitive hill tribes (Montagnards). Spraying is usually carried out near harvest time, destroying the standing crop and rendering the land useless until at least the next growing season.

Additional foods are purposely destroyed by various other ground techniques. Foods are also destroyed incidentally in the large-scale forest destruction program in which, according to the DoD, some 5,517,000 acres or 13 percent of SVN have been aerially sprayed through the end of 1969. No data are available to me on how much food has been destroyed in these ways.

Some estimates can be made for the amount of food destruction via herbicides aerially applied for that purpose. A conservative yield estimate for upland rice fields (the major target) is 500 pounds of milled rice per acre per year. (Crops other than rice are also destroyed, but we can assume for our purposes that their food yield is equivalent to that of upland rice.) One Vietnamese apparently can live on 1.1 pounds of milled rice per day, or 400 pounds per year. Using the above listed areas, one arrives at the following figures of destruction:

YEAR	POUNDS OF MILLED RICE DESTROYED	TOTAL NUMBER OF ANNUAL DIETS DENIED
1961	?	?
1962	500,000	1,250
1963	–	–
1964	5,000,000	12,500
1965	33,000,000	82,500
1966	52,000,000	130,000
1967	110,500,000	276,250
1968	85,000,000	212,500
1969	57,500,000	143,750
1970	?	?
Total 1962–69	344,000,000	860,000

The main avowed purpose of the food destruction program is to deny food to the enemy soldier. Since the Viet Cong (VC) number only about 260,000 out of 17.5 million (or 1.5 percent) but control perhaps 80 or 90 percent of the rural economy of SVN, enormous amounts of food must be destroyed in order to create a hardship for the VC. In fact, studies performed for and by the U.S. in 1967 and 1968 revealed that food destruction has had no significant impact on the enemy soldier. Civilians, in contrast, did and do suffer. Estimates in these studies varied between ten and 100 for how many civilians have to be denied food in order to deny it to one VC. In other words, of the 860,000 total annual diets destroyed during 1962–69, between 774,000 and 851,000 were destined for civilian stomachs. Moreover, it is not unreasonable to assume that the brunt of this civilian burden is borne by infants, aged, fetuses, pregnant women, lactating women, and the sick.

By way of more specific example I single out Quang Ngai province, a particularly war-torn northern province of SVN. During a visit there this past August I learned that 15 crop destruction missions had been approved for 1970, totalling 182,000 acres. (An additional 13 forest destruction missions were scheduled for 1970, totalling another 107,000 acres.) A study done for DoD in 1969 states that 215,000 acres in the province (out of a total of 1,418,000 acres) were then being used agriculturally. Thus approximately 85 percent of the crop lands of Quang Ngai were scheduled for aerial destruction in 1970, presumably virtually all not under physical U.S. control. One hundred eighty-two thousand acres would produce 91 million pounds of milled rice in a year, sufficient to feed 227,500 people for that period. The 1967 population of Quang Ngai province was estimated at 688,200 (of which by crude guess about 110,000 live in Quang Ngai City, three-quarters war refugees). I must add that I have no knowledge of how many acres were actually sprayed in Quang Ngai in 1970 (or in previous years), only the number of acres officially approved for that year.

Finally, another specific example will suggest the extent of incidental food deprivation brought about by the widespread forest spray missions. In December 1969 I visited Kompong Cham province in southeastern Cambodia, where 173,000 acres had been treated by the U.S. during the previous spring. Although rural and largely wooded, the sprayed area supported some 30,000 semidestitute inhabitants dependent for their food on subsistence farming. Essentially, their entire crop already planted for that year was wiped out. Equally damaging, tens of thousands of individually owned papaya, jack, manioc, and other fruit trees lost their fruits, and a high proportion of these trees were killed outright. For example, it was estimated that perhaps 45,000 of the locally important jackfruit trees died as a result. For those whose very existence is so closely tied to the land, the resulting hardships are profound.

It is clear that the acceptability of food destruction as a means of warfare requires an immediate and searching revaluation by the United States.

Addendum

I should like to add that the Senate Committee on Foreign Relations has just released previously unavailable data for 1970–1971 supplied to it by the Department of Defense. A total of 32,600 acres of crop land were reported to have been chemically decimated from the air during the year 1970, but reportedly none so far during 1971—i.e., during the first four months. (The Provisional Revolutionary Government of South Vietnam recently reported a number of aerial crop destruction missions for January and February of this year.)

The additional 32,600 crop acres reported by the Department of Defense were presumably treated with some 303,-200 pounds of sodium dimethyl arsenate, so-called Agent Blue. Thus it can be calculated that an additional 16,300,000 pounds or more of milled rice have been destroyed by this means, thereby denying total annual diets to yet another 40,750 humans, of whom between 36,700 and 40,300 are likely to have been civilians.

Whether or not the U.S. program of food destruction has in fact now ended in South Vietnam is open to question, since food has been intentionally destroyed there by us for years through a variety of other means as well.

Finally, I wonder whether the Republic of [South] Vietnam will acquire a chemical warfare spray capability as a part of our "Vietnamization" program.

Napalm Survey: J. B. Neilands

"Napalm is probably the most inhumane anti-personnel weapon ever invented. The point of a weapon in war is to put an enemy out of action, and that is most readily and permanently accomplished by killing him; but civilized nations have tried not to induce more suffering than is necessary to achieve this end. Napalm maximizes the suffering. It is meant not only to maim permanently, and to kill slowly, but to inspire horror. That its use in Vietnam has involved many civilians, peasant families in undefended villages, has magnified its horror." [1]

BACKGROUND: With the publication of the Pentagon Papers in mid-1971, the American public has come to know more of the political events in Indochina and in Washington which set the stage for the longest war in our history. A great *untold story* of the war, so far as the average United States citizen is concerned, is the intensity and cruelty of the particular weapons employed. We need to begin a dialogue about this aspect of the war, and we especially need to evaluate the status of certain weapons—herbicides, tear gas, napalm, white phosphorus—in terms of both the laws of war and the human rights of civilians who are inadvertently drawn into the conflict.

1. George Wald, "Corporate Responsibility for War Crimes," *New York Review of Books*, July 2, 1970.

26

Napalm was developed in the latter stages of World War II and saw extensive use in Japan; it appears not to have been deployed to the same extent in the European theatre.[2] It was a principal bomb in the Korean war, an estimated 32,215 tons having been dropped in the three years of that engagement. Napalm was used at the outset of American military presence in Vietnam, the annual drop running to over several thousand tons in the first years of the war.[3]

Yet, as already indicated, the American public has remained largely ignorant about the properties and uses of this atrocious weapon. Napalm might be outlawed if the conscience of the public could be aroused sufficiently to bring the requisite pressure to bear on Congress. Accordingly, the two purposes of this survey will be to trace the evolution of napalm as a weapon and to outline the legal basis for its prohibition.

INVENTION: The invention of napalm is documented in a fascinating book titled *The Scientific Method: a Personal Account of Unusual Projects in War and in Peace*, by Louis F. Fieser.[4] The author, a professor of organic chemistry at Harvard University, was one of a group of American scientists involved in research on bombs, fuels, poison gas, and related problems during World War II. As explained by Fieser, the scientific talents of the group were not requisitioned by official edict but were offered to the Government by a "few key leaders" who foresaw a crucial role for scientists in the war.

Initially assigned to work on explosives, Fieser was later switched to research on vesicant chemicals (blistering

2. cf. however: ". . . napalm . . . scored a high record of success in the bombing of Germany . . ." See footnote 4 below.

3. *San Francisco Chronicle*, March 19, 1968.

4. L. F. Fieser, *The Scientific Method: A Personal Account of Unusual Projects in War and in Peace* (New York: Reinhold Publishing Corp., 1964).

agents). Subsequently he welcomed the opportunity for a second transfer, this time to work on incendiaries, since the development of poison gas seemed to him "inhumane."

The practical requirements for the new incendiary to be perfected by the Fieser team were that it consume the maximum amount of combustible material and that it extend the fire over a considerable area. Once the concept of a sticky gel had been adopted, it was necessary to assure that the gel would not thin out at tropical temperatures or solidify at $-40°$ C (the temperature of a bomb bay). Other specifications were that the gel should withstand the violent blast of the detonation and that it should remain stable during long periods of shipment and storage.

By early 1942 Fieser and his coworkers had prepared a suitable gel by mixing a soap powder (labeled "aluminum palmitate"), aluminum naphthenate, and gasoline. On February 14 of that year he christened one preparation *napalm,* the name derived from the ingredients *na*phthenate and *palm*itate. Subsequently it was discovered that the product marked "aluminum palmitate" was in reality the mixed aluminum soaps of whole coconut oil. Since coconut oil is almost 50 percent lauric acid and contains, in fact, less than 10 percent palmitic acid, the word napalm is obviously a misnomer for the type of product compounded by Fieser. However, the name has been adopted as a generic term for all types of gelled incendiary bombs.

Napalm production is a simple procedure which can be performed by mixing the ingredients in the field. The components are cheap and readily available, the naphthenic acid being a by-product of the refining of petroleum. On stirring the aluminum salts into gasoline, gelation occurs in about a quarter of an hour. The product is a greyish, tough jelly which meets all of the military requirements for handling. On ignition it burns with a temperature which may reach

2,000° C. The flaming gel becomes sticky and adheres well to both materials and human flesh.

White phosphorus, which ignites spontaneously in air, and hence does not occur in nature, has been the classical ignition substance for napalm. The molten white phosphorus is contained in a burster core inside the napalm bomb; when detonated by a fuse and explosive charge, the chunks of gel are imbedded with particles of white phosphorus. In this manner the fire is carried to the maximum distance traversed by the pieces of gel.

Napalm burns with an orange flame and generates a large amount of black smoke. One bomb can plaster burning gobs of gel over an area the size of a football field.

Chemical and Engineering News, organ of the American Chemical Society and spokesman for the chemical industry, reported in early 1966 on the development of a superior type of napalm, designated napalm B.[5] The new product was produced in response to a demand from combat forces in Vietnam for a gel incendiary with improved "adhesion." The new formulation was discovered by scientists at Eglin Air Force Base working with polystyrene from the Dow Chemical Company. The polystyrene substitutes for the aluminum soaps of the earlier formulations and serves to concentrate the burning gasoline and benzene so that the effectiveness of the fuel is not dissipated in a flash fire. Like its predecessor, napalm B is compounded of cheap materials and is composed of 50 percent polystyrene and 25 percent each gasoline and benzene. Table 1 records the approximate chemical composition of the two types of napalm.

In 1966 I directed a request to Professor Fieser in which I asked him to comment on the use of napalm against civilian targets in Vietnam. He replied that the entire thinking and

5. *Chemical and Engineering News,* March 14, 1966.

Chemical Composition of Napalm Types

Napalm
(as used in World War II and Korea)

$\sim$ 5%

$$\left[\text{CH}_3(\text{CH}_2)_{10}\text{COO}^- \right]_3 \text{Al}^{+++}$$

aluminum laurate

$\sim$ 5%

$$\left[\text{cyclopentyl-}(\text{CH}_2)_n\text{-COO}^- \right]_3 \text{Al}^{+++}$$

aluminum naphthenate*

$\sim$ 90%   Complex mixture of hydrocarbons   gasoline

Napalm B
(as used in Indochina war)

50%

$$\left[\text{CH}_2 - \text{Ch} \right]_x$$

polystyrene

25%

benzene

25%   Complex mixture hydrocarbons   gasoline

*Naphthenic acids are carboxylic derivatives of alkylated cyclohydrocarbons expectation of his group was that napalm would be employed for burning down enemy factories, munition dumps, etc.[6] However, chapter 13 of his book[7] is devoted to the "bat bomb," a mini-bomb filled with napalm. The incendiary was to be attached to bats which were then to be released from bombers flying over Japan. According to Fieser, the hope was that the bats would fly "into highly combustible Japanese houses at sites very favorable for starting fires." The project never came to fruition and was scrapped without explanation. Fieser speculates on the reason: the U.S. would be accused of introducing biological weapons.

Fieser's role in napalm invention came to the fore in 1967 during a demonstration against a Dow Chemical Company recruiter at Harvard University. At that time he is reported in the press as saying: "It's not my business to deal with the political or moral questions."[8]

MANUFACTURERS: Napalm manufacture can be segregated into three eras, namely pre-1965, 1965–69 (when Dow Chemical was the prime contractor), and post-1969.

In 1965 the noted economist Victor Perlo listed a number of chemical companies believed to be engaged in napalm production; Dow Chemical was not mentioned.[9] However, with the appearance of the new polystyrene-based napalm it was inevitable that Dow should seek a portion of this lucrative market.

Dow Chemical Company, with head offices in Midland, Michigan, is the fourth largest company of its kind in the United States. It is the second largest manufacturer of plastics and ranks in the top 50 U.S. corporations of all types. It

6. Letter from L.F. Fieser to J.B. Neilands, dated September 29, 1966.
7. Fieser, *Scientific Method*.
8. *San Francisco Chronicle*, December 26, 1967.
9. *Worker*, December 19, 1965.

went into the napalm business in 1965 with two contracts awarded to its Torrance, California plant.[10]

Virtually all styrene is made by the following reactions, a

sequence of transformations which U.S. chemical industry is well equipped to perform.[11] Although the total capacity is in excess of several billion pounds annually, the demand for napalm forced up the price of styrene and caused a shortage of certain consumer items made of the plastic. It was predicted that napalm would consume about 25 million pounds of polystyrene per month, almost half of the total U.S. production.[12]

Officials of Dow Chemical are reported to have accepted the contract for napalm "... because we feel that simple good citizenship requires that we supply our government and our military with those goods they need when we have the technology and the capability and have been chosen by the government as a supplier."[13] The company thus made a hard-nosed defense of its decision to make napalm, claiming patriotism as the main motivation. However, at the 1966 price of 14 and one-half cents per pound, Dow would receive $43 million for the 300 million pounds of polystyrene converted to napalm.[14]

Dow continued to supply napalm until late 1969, at which time the company announced it had lost the contract to

10. *Chemical and Engineering News*, March 14, 1966.
11. Ibid., July 17, 1967; September 22, 1969.
12. Ibid., March 14, 1966.
13. Statement attributed to officials of the Dow Chemical Company and quoted in a pamphlet published by Citizens Campaign Against Napalm.
14. Letter to *The Daily Californian from Robert A Harris et al.*, November 6, 1967.

American Electric Company in Los Angeles.[15] During most of this period Dow appears to have been the sole producer of napalm, although the United Technology Center filled at least one contract for 100 million pounds before its plant at Sunnyvale, California, was closed down in 1967.[16]

Prior to receiving the direct contract for napalm, American Electric had made bomb canisters which were filled with material supplied by the Torrance, California, plant of Dow. The company is based at La Mirada, California, and operates a plant at Long Beach. The parent company is City Investing of New York City. The same source of information reports that a subsidiary of American Electric, Diamond Plastics, furnishes the polystyrene component of napalm.[17]

According to the Pentagon, prime contractors for napalm in 1971 were American Electric and Sargeant Fletcher.[18]

EFFECTS: Reich and Sidel, writing in the *New England Journal of Medicine*, claim that napalm casualties are caused primarily by thermal injury and by carbon monoxide poisoning.[19] In the vicinity of a napalm explosion the available oxygen will be rapidly consumed and asphyxiation may result. The lack of sufficient oxygen to combust the carbonaceous material of napalm completely to carbon dioxide leaves a substantial residue of carbon monoxide, the latter a respiratory poison.

Obviously, napalm can be considered in many respects to be a chemical rather than an incendiary weapon.

15. *New York Times*, November 16, 1969.
16. *Chemical and Engineering News*, March 14, 1966, and *Berkeley Barb*, April 21, 1967.
17. *New York Times*, December 2, 1969.
18. Letter from Lt. Col. Vincent R. Tocci, Office of the Assistant Secretary of Defense, to J.B. Neilands, dated August 18, 1971.
19. Peter Reich and Victor Sidel, *New England Journal of Medicine*, July 13, 1967.

The burns inflicted by napalm are apt to be severe. This is because of the stickiness of the material and its prolonged burning time at a high temperature. It may give rise to keloid scars which ultimately become cancerous. Napalm burns may be complicated by the presence of phosphorus particles which continue to smolder and irritate the tissue. Further details of the medical aspects of napalm burns are contained in the specialized literature of the Indochina war.[20]

INDOCHINA USE: In March, 1968, the Pentagon released figures on the volume of napalm deployed in Vietnam.[21] The Air Force is said to have dropped 2,181 tons in 1963 and in the following three years 1,777, 17,659, and 54,620 tons, respectively. The report acknowledged that in excess of "100,000 tons" had been used through early 1968, but no precise information was given on the actual amount deployed.

An inquiry to the Pentagon on August 2, 1971, brought the response that in the period January 1969 through June 1971 an estimated 125,000 tons of napalm was employed by U.S. forces in Indochina.[22] President Nixon is thus seen to be a more active purveyor of napalm than his predecessor. A reading of the *New York Times* reveals that the weapon has been thoroughly institutionalized in the weaponry of the Indochina war. The incident surrounding the 7,500-ton ship Columbia Eagle is instructive in this regard. In early 1970 the ship took on cargo in San Francisco and Long Beach and headed for Thailand. En route two youthful hijackers took

20. John Takman, ed., *Napalm, An International Symposium* (Stockholm: Raben & Sjogren, 1967); John Duffett, ed., *Against the Crime of Silence: Proceedings of the Russell International War Crimes Tribunal* (New York: Simon and Schuster, 1971).
21. *San Francisco Chronicle,* March 19, 1968.
22. *New York Times,* November 16, 1969.

over the Columbia Eagle and diverted the freighter to Ream, Cambodia, where she lay at anchor from March 15 to April 8, 1970. When the ship was released on the latter date by the Government of Cambodia, it was revealed that the cargo consisted entirely of 1,753 long tons of napalm in 500- and 717-pound bombs.[23] The shipment was sent on to U.S. bases in Thailand for use by the U.S. Air Force.

Further evidence of the increased use of napalm under the Nixon administration comes from North Vietnamese sources, which charged that more than 2.25 million acres in the South were destroyed by "toxic chemicals, gases, napalm and phosphorus bombs."[24] Reports in the U.S. confirm that napalm has been adopted as a routine antipersonnel weapon.[25] Napalm spilled over into Cambodia and was used for the same purpose in that part of Indochina.[26]

INTERNATIONAL USE: The American product, napalm, has appeared in the arsenals of other nations. In South Africa, Defense Minister Pieter Botha told his Parliament that scientists had developed a napalm bomb from local raw materials.[27] Press references to napalm in foreign wars prompted this letter from a Mr. Donald Gardner to the *New York Times:*

In the *New York Times* for February 13 there is a short column mentioning that the Portugese Government has been using napalm against rebels in Angola. In your issue for March 29 there is a column mentioning that the Government of Bolivia is using the same weapon against the guerrilla movement in that country. Whose napalm?[28]

23. Ibid., March 16, March 26, and April 9, 1970.
24. Ibid., January 21, 1970.
25. Ibid., April 13, 1970.
26. Ibid., August 5, August 6, 1970; January 17, 1971.
27. Ibid., March 14, 1968.
28. Ibid., April 10, 1967.

Napalm has seen active use in the Middle East, especially in the hands of the Israeli air force. Syria and Egypt both complained about use of the weapon,[29] and President Gamal Abdel Nasser formed a citizen's committee to combat "prohibited means of warfare," an apparent reference to napalm.[30] Finally, in response to a question in the Knesset, Israeli Defense Minister Moshe Dayan acknowledged that napalm was used against Egyptian military targets.[31]

LEGAL ASPECTS: As both an incendiary and a chemical weapon, napalm could be banned under the following instruments of international law:

• 1907 Hague Convention which specifies that belligerents are not unlimited in regard to the means used to cause harm to the enemy.

• 1925 Geneva Protocol on Chemical and Biological Warfare. This treaty has been ratified by 95 nations, although not by the United States. This aberration is a consequence of the use of tear gas and herbicides in the Indochina war.[32]

• Nuremberg Principles covering both war crimes and crimes against humanity. Under war crimes proper, the "wanton destruction of cities, towns or villages" is expressly forbidden under the Principles. "Inhuman acts done against any civilian population" constitutes, in the terminology of Nuremberg, a crime against humanity.

• 1949 Geneva Conventions on the protection of war victims.

Sidel is of the opinion that incendiary and chemical weap-

29. Ibid., February 3, February 13, 1970.
30. Ibid., February 5, 1970.
31. Ibid., March 5, 1970.
32. J.B. Neilands et al., *Chemical Warfare in Indochina* (New York: Free Press, 1971).

ons should be separately controlled, implying that napalm *per se* is not presently illegal.[33] Wald, on the other hand, wants "business orders" given equal status with "military orders" under Nuremberg, and, with others, he initiated a civil action in the District Court in Washington, D.C. against manufacturers of napalm.[34]

Recently, a meeting sponsored by the International Committee of the Red Cross considered means for increased protection of war victims. Experts from five countries proposed that conventions be tightened to bar, among other things, the use of napalm against civilians. The suggestion was received coldly by the U.S. representative, and the meeting ended inconclusively.[35]

The experience thus far suggests the need for a specific law prohibiting the use of napalm and all similar weapons which employ the principle of concentrated combustion on the target area. This is the approach of H. Bruce Stewart, who has proposed a "Napalm Prohibition Act," a Bill which would introduce a *policy declaration* against the use or possession by U.S. Armed Forces of incendiary weapons, the latter defined as "a napalm weapon, or any weapon which contains, discharges, or ignites jelled gasoline or a flaming or flame-inducing agent, or any other incendiary weapon or analogous substance, material, or device, or any part thereof."[36]

33. V. Sidel, in *CBW: Chemical and Biological Warfare*, edited by S. Rose (London: Harrap, 1968).

34. *New York Times*, February 3, 1970.

35. Ibid., June 14, 1971.

36. Draft bill submitted by H. Bruce Stewart to Congressman Ronald V. Dellums (D-Cal.).

CS—Gas an Imperialist Technology:
Hilary Rose and Steven Rose

Ortho-cloro-benzal-malonitrile—or CS as it came to be called —was initially synthesized by two American chemists, Corson and Stoughton, in the 1920s. The report they published drew attention to certain physiological effects of the compound—that is, that it acted as a lacrimator.[1]

There the matter lay, a finding of basic research with no particular social implications, until 1956, when the British War Office issued a research directive to find a more effective agent than the traditional tear gas CN. 1956 was not a year without political significance for a declining imperial power. It was the year of Suez and also a time when direct action was beginning to be used at home in Britain as a method of political protest.

CN had been used extensively as "an effective lacrimatory agent, of comparatively low cost, and simplicity in use from pyrotechnic distributors." Its major deficits, however, seen in the technical paper from the British Chemical Defense Establishment at Porton, dwelt on its technical limitations in the context of the struggle for colonial freedom. It was expressed not in the language of politics but in the language of "technique." CN had three weaknesses: a) it melts in tropical temperatures; b) it is not sufficiently stable in storage; and c)

1. *Journal of the American Chemical Society,* vol. 50, p. 2825.

its effectiveness is short-term; though tolerance builds up; it is not in fact "adequate for incapacitating or even seriously discouraging fanatical or highly motivated rioters."[2] The brief to Porton was therefore to find a compound of greater effectiveness and no greater toxicity. Some 91 compounds were screened, including DM, which was ruled out as too toxic—a point which has not troubled the U.S. government either in Vietnam or in its own cities—and ortho-chloroben-zal-malonitrile—now codenamed CS in honour of its synthe-sizers—was selected.

CS suffered from none of the disadvantages of CN; it was stable, affected several physiological systems at once—nose, throat, eyes and stomach; hence tolerance to its effects seemed less likely. In the words of the Porton technical report:

Men exposed to 1 part per million experienced within 15 seconds acute stinging of the eyes—spasms of the eyelids, along with an acutely burning sensation in the whole of the upper airway—within 20 seconds all the subjects (soldiers of 18–30) were quite incapable of any hostility whatsoever . . ."

Furthermore CS was no more toxic. CS production began at Nancekuke in the early 1960s, though only four to six tons a year were produced, transported to a firm called Schermu-leys in Dorking, and there packed into the Porton-patented grenades. Production actually picked up after use in North-ern Ireland, but it was also used against liberation move-ments in Aden, Hong Kong and Singapore. Information regarding CS manufacture resulted not only from its export to many countries; it made its way to the U.S. through the Quadripartite agreement, an information sharing system be-tween Britain, the U.S., Australia, and Canada.

2. D. Crichton et al., "Agents for Riot Control, Chemical Defense Experi-mental Establishment," *Porton Technical Paper*, no. 651 (1958).

This information-sharing system is of considerable importance, since, unlike most major powers, the U.S. has never
signed the Geneva Protocol of 1925 limiting the use of
chemical weapons—despite several declarations over the in-
tervening 26 years that she is about to sign. The significance
here is that while Britain is limited by her status as signatory
to "defensive" research, America as a nonsignatory can and
does conduct "offensive" chemical weapon research. The
sharing arrangement in effect means that there is no distinction between "offensive" and "defensive research"; they are,
both in the laboratory and in the Quadripartite agreement,
complementary activities.

The 1925 Protocol itself is of such major importance to
chemical welfare that it is worth quoting in some detail:

> . . . the undersigned Plenipotentiaries, in the name of their re-
> spective Governments,
> Whereas the use in war of asphyxiating, poisonous or other gases,
> and all analogous liquids, materials or devices, has been justly con-
> demned by the general opinion of the civilised world:
> and
> Whereas the prohibition of such use has been declared in Treaties
> to which the majority of the Powers of the World are Parties; and
> To the end that this prohibition shall be universally accepted as a
> part of International Law, binding alike the conscience and the
> practice of nations;
> Declare;
> That the High Contracting Parties, so far as they are not already
> Parties to Treaties prohibiting such use, accept this prohibition,
> agree to extend this prohibition to the use of bacteriological meth-
> ods of warfare and agree to be bound as between themselves ac-
> cording to the terms of this declaration.

The developments subsequent to 1925 were slow: chemicals were used by Mussolini against Abyssinia, to a chorus of
protest. There were wide fears that they would be used in
the Second World War, and research and development in

belligerent countries was stepped up. But, excluding the concentration camps, little happened, except for a major breakthrough in research in Germany when a new class of agent outdoing all previous types in toxicity—the nerve gases—was developed. These can kill by absorption through the skin in low concentration: a gas mask will not protect. Nerve gases were stockpiled in quantity by the Germans under the names Sarin, Soman, and Tabun. The captured stocks were renamed G-agents and removed after the war to the USA, USSR, and the UK, and a new era of research and development commenced.

The next breakthrough in highly toxic agents, which came in the early 1950s, was British, and it was based on a discovery at I.C.I. (a firm with a close relationship to the defense establishments) of a highly toxic class of substances related to the G-agents. The good news was relayed to Porton and the V-agents—some 30 times more toxic than the G-agents—were developed. When the U.S. received the information, missiles with V-agent warheads were added to the stockpile; they remain there potentially available for use in Vietnam. Since defense against them requires individual plastic suits which have to be changed every 12 hours, their potential threat against an economically poor agricultural people is great. Thus, the Quadripartite agreement has already facilitated the release of offensive chemical weapons into Vietnam and, with them, the breach of the Protocol; because CS was presented as a "nonlethal harassing agent," its use in Vietnam provides a case book study of how to use the thin end of the wedge strategy to breach international law.

Initially CS was one of three agents in use in Vietnam, but gradually DM and CN have been largely phased out since 1965. Indeed CS appears so popular that it has itself been Vietnamized, and is now in production at Da Nang base, supplementing the imports from the U.S. In 1968, a new form of CS was introduced, and by 1969 it constituted more than half the total of all agents used in Vietnam. This new form is a more sophisticated variant of CS, dispersed in microparticles on a siliconized base. Its military advantages are that the particles remain in suspension for greater duration than in the earlier form, and we understand that there are chemical data suggesting that its specific effects—as between lachrymation, irritation, vomiting, etc.—vary with differing particle size.

The U.S. Army Field Training Manual describes no fewer than 18 different dispensing methods for CS, varying from pocket grenades of the Porton type, through the "Mighty Mite" which dispenses up to 80 pounds (and is specifically designed for use in tunnel systems), to 130-pound cluster bombs which are designed to be dropped from helicopters or low-flying planes. The scale of CS use has increased sixteen-fold since 1964; total Army supplies since that date amount to 7000 tons (compared with 12,000 tons of mustard gas used by both sides in World War I). Some 6,063,000 pounds were procured in 1969, and the total is enough to spray the whole area of Vietnam 1.3 times.[3]

Although it was initially described as useful in controlling situations where mixed NLF and civilian groups were present—a classical "riot" situation, reports since 1965 have referred to its use in tunnels and caves for "flushing out" purposes, or to be dropped by helicopter and plane prior to use of conventional weapons such as high explosives and napalm. Official U.S. Army pictures have confirmed this usage, which is manifestly *not* a nonlethal one. However, we have here concerned ourselves only with the toxicity of CS as such, not its use as an adjunct to conventional weapons.

3. *Washington Post,* July 24, 1969.

TOXIC EFFECTS: From the time of its first use, statements have appeared from the North Vietnamese and NLF sources claiming that CS use in caves and tunnels has resulted in severe injury or death. Thus between January 1965 and July 1966, according to the NLF, some 300 deaths resulted from gases used in caves and tunnel systems. The full list can be found in Kahn's work.[4] The scale of reported deaths has increased in the subsequent years with increased use of the agent. Thus an NLF communique of November 19, 1969, claims that in Tay Ninh Province in the last ten days of September 1969:

. . .Helicopters and other kinds of airplanes were used over 200 times to drop thousands of pounds of CS and other chemicals on the two communes (on a surface of 10 square miles). They even used cannons to fire 5000 bullets containing toxic mixtures. More than 1000 people belonging to the Cao Dai sect were affected; 15 babies were killed . . . (in) Thang Binh district in a raid in Feb 12, 1969. They caught 10 elderly men between 64 and 77 years of age and one woman pregnant near her time, forced them into a trench and sprayed them with toxic gas, killing them all . . . during the ten months (of 1969) . . . 500 people were killed, most of them women, children and old people. . . .

However, it is often argued that data of this sort is unverifiable because it comes from non-Western sources and the nature of the agent used is not always identified. If we ignore the racist implication that only Western journalists tell the truth, the first report from a Western journalist concerning the lethal effects of CS in Vietnam was the now famous Bowtell case, worth quoting in full:

Non-toxic gas and smoke being used against Vietcong guerillas in tunnels north-west of Saigon have killed one Australian soldier, sent

4. M. F. Kahn in *C.B.W. Chemical and Biological Warfare*, edited by S. Rose (London: Harrap, 1968).

six others to hospital. Officials said today Cpt. Robert Bowtell, 21, of Sydney, died of asphyxiation although he was wearing a gas mask.[5]

It has been argued that Bowtell's death was due not to CS but to CO intoxication. As CO is one of the products of combustion of CS grenades in enclosed spaces, the argument that CS has not "caused" the death seems metaphysical, and only emphasizes the point made above that it is necessary to examine the effects of the use of CS under real and not simulated conditions. This point is explicitly accepted by the U.S. Army Field Training Circular for 1969: *"When burning-type grenades (HC Smoke or CS) are used in a tunnel or other enclosed space, they may cause asphyxiation to personnel in the tunnel because of oxygen depletion and carbon monoxide built up. A field protective mask will not protect against this condition."*

There have been a series of other subsequent eyewitness reports of the effect of the agent, by journalists and GIs, e.g.:

I have seen unconscious women and children dragged out of tunnels and bunkers into which tear gas bombs had been thrown. The effect on the peasants was frightful. Several times peasants who had been brought under control in this way tried to fell [sic] screaming. They believed the troops wanted to gas them to death."[6]

Similar reports can be multiplied, but it is perhaps of more value to quote here the letter written by Dr. Alje Vennema, Director of the Candian Medical Service in Vietnam, working at the civilian tuberculosis hospital at Quang Ngai, to Professor E.W. Pfeiffer of the Department of Zoology, University of Montana, dated November 23, 1967.

During the last three years I have examined and treated a number of patients, men, women and children, who had been exposed to a

5. *New York Times*, March 25, 1965.
6. *Victor Charlie*, Kuno Knoebl, 1967, pp. 256–67.

type of war gas, the name of which I do not know; the type of gas used makes one quite sick when one touches the patient, or inhales the breath from their lungs. After contact with them for more than three minutes one has to leave the room in order not to get ill.

The patient usually gives a history of having been hiding in a cave or tunnel or bunker or shelter into which a canister of gas was thrown in order to force them to leave their hiding place. Those patients that have come to my attention were very ill with signs and symptoms of gas poisoning similar to those that I have seen in veterans from the First World War treated at Queen Mary Veterans Hospital in Montreal. The only difference between the cases was that these Vietnamese patients were more acutely ill and when getting over their acute stage presented a similar picture to that of the war veterans.

Patients are feverish, semi-comatose, severely short of breath, vomit, are restless and irritable. Most of their physical signs are in the respiratory and circulatory systems. Both lungs exhibit rales throughout, severe bronchial spasm, heart rate is usually very high and all of the patients had pulmonary edema. In most cases active treatment for pulmonary edema and complicating pneumonia was helpful and they survived. Those that survived developed a chronic bronchitic type of picture complicated by infections.

The mortality rate in adults is about ten percent, while the mortality rate in children is about ninety percent. I have only kept accurate records of the number of such cases that I have seen since last June. Since then I have seen seven cases of which:

> there was one child of six years of age who died;
> there was one child of 15 years of age who survived;
> there was one lady of approximately 40 years of age who died;
> there were four other adults who survived.

Although Dr. Vennema did not at the time know the gas used, we have since been able to speak directly with him and give him some samples of gas to smell. He identified the smell from a CS grenade as "one that he recognized on the breath of his Vietnamese patients." The symptoms described for the patients are comparable with the known clinical effects of CS.

In public debate, the Director of CDEE has stated that Dr.

Vennema's patients were all suffering from pneumonia or other chest infection *before* the CS attack. Once again, in personal discussion with us, of which we have a transcript, Dr. Vennema has denied this. However, even if it had been the case, it in no way exonerates CS, the use of which, here or elsewhere, is bound to affect the noncombatant ill and elderly most severely. Finally, the fact that CS has caused deaths in Vietnam is explicitly stated in a paper given at a recent U.S. symposium by Professor M. Meselson of Harvard University (substituting for Dr. I. Bennett, the U.S. government's official adviser on CBW), as follows: "The third agent is CS. . . . it is not lethal when used in the open in police-type operations. Heavy exposures as in confined spaces or after massive application can kill."[7] There is no question that CS as used in Vietnam kills. It kills because it is applied at high concentrations and in confined areas, and because it is used as an adjunct to "conventional" weapons for flushing people out of caves or shelters, for instance, and into the range of explosives, fragmentation bombs and napalm.

This multiplicity of weaponry is of particular significance and one which we feel has not been sufficiently stressed in the context of chemicals agents used in Vietnam. Our own understanding of it comes almost accidentally when we were in Hanoi early this year piloting a social survey questionnaire with people from the South who had lived in defoliated areas. Because we sought very definite concrete descriptions of the agents these peasants had been exposed to, it was relatively straightforward to identify the agents involved. Thus, herbicide orange was used in conjunction with herbicide white, or blue with white, or, as on one occasion, orange herbicide was simultaneously used with CS and napalm. The

7. In Proceedings of the Conference on CBW of the American Academy of Arts, Science and the Salk Institute, July 25, 1969, p. 4.

interaction of these agents has not been considered in any of the laboratory or field trials which we have seen reported. Thus not only is the type of military research phony in the sense that it is not properly extrapolated to the actual community where it is used (controlled laboratory or field trials are simply not like the actual usage of the weaponry in the paddy fields of Vietnam or the streets of Paris, Berkeley, or Londonderry), but, more importantly, chemical warfare weapons must *not* be considered in chemical isolation but in *combination.*

It is beyond our competence to go into detail on existing research regarding toxicity of the isolated agent. However, the work of Roussel reporting tissue lesions in mice exposed to the agent,[8] the clinical studies of Kahn[9] and Vennema, the inadequacies of published military studies, together with the June 1971 report in the *New Scientist* by Jones of cyanide concentrations possibly causing brain damage, raise more disquieting questions than they answer concerning the toxicity of CS.

No animal data appears to be available concerning the chronic toxicity of the gas. Many Vietnamese are exposed to CS gas (and as our pilot enquiry showed in the case of herbicides, peasants were able to describe as many as eight separate occasions when they had been exposed to the agents); in this situation knowledge of the potential *chronic* toxicity is therefore vitally important. Neither is there any evidence concerning its possibly carcinogenic role nor of its effects on pregnancy.

The Porton animal studies suggested that sensitivity to CS may be influenced by sex, but whether women are more

8. Roussel cited by M. F. Kahn, *C.B.W.*.
9. See for example S. P. R. Rose and R. L. Smith, "CS, a Case for Concern," *New Scientist,* September 4, 1969.

sensitive than men or vice versa has not been established. Other factors may also be involved. Thus the population of South Vietnam—generally of low income and with poor nutrition and a high incidence of chest infections—may be more susceptible to CS intoxication. Similarly, racial groups may differ in their reaction to CS (as indeed proved to be the case in the Edgwood Arsenal studies showing differential skin burning between skin color groups.[10]) What happens to CS in the body? If absorbed from the lungs and skin, is it retained in the body; or if metabolized, are the products nontoxic?

In 1969 public awareness of the hazards of CS had sufficiently developed for a British Member of Parliament to have secured from the Home Secretary a promise that the gas would only be used in extreme situations, to flush out an insane armed man, for example. Not long afterwards we were to see the uncontrolled use of CS in the Bogside in Derry, where the police used it as a means of punishing an entire oppressed community.[11] This caused a storm of protest, and the significance of an agent which had hitherto been felt to be acceptable for use against colonial peoples was suddenly realized. The shared experience of a technology of oppression became one of the links in the international struggle for socialist liberation.

On the international scene at this time, Britain made a significant contribution to devaluing the Geneva Protocol. Labor Foreign Minister Michael Stewart declared that CS was not a "gas" but a "smoke" and therefore did not come within the terms of the Protocol—a view which was explicitly in conflict with the British official position during the 1930s.

10. A. Hellrich et al., "Effects of Thermally Generated CS Aerosols on Human Skin," Edgwood Arsenal Technical Report 4075 (1969).
11. The social implications of the use of CS are discussed in a survey report, "What Gas Did in Derry," New Society, September 25, 1969.

However, while the British made life easier for the U.S. government,[12] even if both had accepted UN Secretary General U Thant's view that CS and the defoliants are banned by the Protocol, nothing would have altered the essence of the war in Vietnam. Science and technology are not the source of repression in Vietnam, nor of repression in American ghettos; the technology is different in form but not in essence from the more traditional ways of massacring civilian populations or burning rice crops.

Neither the traditional nor the scientific modes of atrocity are mindless, even though the actual men—the bomber pilots, the GI infantrymen—may impress us by their apparent mindlessness. Instead we have to see both as the concrete expression of a ruthless imperialist power determined to stop the movement of liberation of whole Indochinese people. The real enemy is neither CS, the fragmentation bombs, nor even Lt. William Calley, but the social order which breeds them. What we can do by exposing the criminal nature of science in the service of the ruling classes is, yes, to play some small part in the struggle of the Indochinese people, but also, as an integral part of this struggle, to help our own people to perceive the nature of our own capitalist and imperialist societies and to enter the struggle. In the West, in the face of tolerant and not-so-tolerant repression, there is a growing movement of antiscience. But this is to settle for the pseudo-enemy. Instead what we have to do is to wrest science from its present owners and their criminal abuse of it, and restore it to the service of the people. In this, as in so many ways, the Indochinese peoples are in the vanguard of the struggle.

12. M. Meselson and J. Perry Robinson "Escalation of Chemical Warfare," *New Scientist*, August 14, 1969.

Canada—The Butcher's Helper:
Claire Culhane

I am a Canadian citizen of the country bordering on the United States. Many of us realize that Canada is playing the role of the "Butcher's Helper." I propose to present the basis for this hateful designation.

I was sent by the Canadian Government in October 1967 as an advisor to work as Administrative Assistant in the Canadian Antituberculosis Hospital in Quang Ngai, South Vietnam, located six miles from My Lai.

Every day that I was there I was horrified at the inhuman destruction of life and land about me. I can never forget the baby I had to lift out of a pool of its own blood. I heard the sounds of aerial bombing every night which left behind each morning a devastation beyond belief. In the midst of this agonizing carnage I recognized the Canadian-made planes flying above our Canadian-funded hospital. I knew that the bombs were filled with Canadian-made explosives. I knew that classified research into chemical and biological warfare was being carried out jointly with the United States in my country. I knew that hundreds of millions of dollars worth of weaponry were being delivered annually from Canada, some of which were to find their final destination in the corpses of tiny infants in the village where I worked.

In December 1946 the General Assembly of the United

Nations unanimously passed a resolution (No. 95–1) affirming the principles of international laws. It recognized the Charter of the Nuremberg Tribunal which includes a Code of Offences against the peace and security of mankind. Principle VII of Section VIII of this Code states, in part:

> . . . complicity in the commission of a crime against peace, a war crime or a crime against humanity . . . is a crime under International Law.

In April 1968, when I subsequently filed my report with the Canadian Department of External Aid documenting my findings during my period of service, I recommended an immediate parliamentary investigation in Canada's role in Vietnam. I stated, in part:

> . . . the mere fact of my being in South Vietnam (within the given terms of reference) deprived me of my right to stand aside from some measure of responsibility for all the brutality and horror being inflicted upon innocent human beings . . . however, when I found myself being required to associate with those elements which were not only impeding the solution but employing the most cruel and savage methods to do so, I was left with no other choice but to detach myself from them.

I felt that my efforts should instead supplement the demands being made by church and peace groups across the country for an embargo on all arms sales to the USA. I also recommended that the only meaningful aid we could offer the Vietnamese people would be to send massive supplies of medical and surgical equipment directly through channels already utilized for these purposes. I also wished to be relieved of my deep sense of criminality for having worked within the infrastructure of a highly suspect US-AID program. This has since been confirmed in the report filed by A. D. Horne of the *Washington Post* (July 7, 1970), who asked Dr. John Hannah, Director of US-AID program: "How do you respond to complaints that the aid program is being used as a cover for CIA operations in Laos?" The doctor replied, "Well, I just have to admit that that is true."

While making rounds in the wards of many hospitals in South Vietnam, I gradually began to realize that there were some wounds and conditions which did not correspond to the usual categories of bomb splinters, artillery, cannon fire, napalm, grenades, mines; but had to be explained some other way. Such examples as included: a peppering of the skin which did not always penetrate deeply into the organs and therefore could not have resulted from gunfire and which was later explained to be from antipersonnel bombs calculated to penetrate only flesh but not metal or wood; or a girl with her breasts closely sliced off; or a baby with a hole in its back the size of a small orange; or a buffalo boy castrated; or the pattern of tracer bullets across a two-year-old's face extending from the lobe of one ear across the cheeks, under the nostrils and across to the lobe of the other ear; an old man with literally no distinguishable features on his face, only the sockets where the eyes, nose and mouth once were; or a young girl with clear evidence of vaginal passage destruction by sharp and jagged objects; and of course the numerous crushed bodies run over by Armored Patrol Cars. (During my first week in Quang Ngai two sisters brought in the remains of the body of their little brother just destroyed by such an accident). The shrill hysteria of very young babies when approached by a non-Vietnamese person whether in hospital or in the countryside became a consistent pattern.

In presenting my testimony to this International Commission of Enquiry, I wish to underscore the fact that when I filed my report with the Canadian government, I specifically urged an immediate investigation be undertaken by a responsible Parliamentary Committee. Due to the very nature of the charges laid and the relative elements of time and distance in a country at war, it was clearly apparent that any delay could then be used to try and destroy the accuracy and urgency of my report. It is therefore my considered opinion that the Canadian and American governments will have to jointly answer before the next international bar of justice for the crimes related herein.

My material is divided as follows:

1. Conditions at the hospitals in South Vietnam
    a) Canadian Antituberculosis Hospital
    b) Quang Ngai Provincial Hospital
    c) Da Nang Provincial Hospital
    d) U.S. Military hospitals
    e) Canadian Rehabilitation Hospital in Qui Nhon
2. Miscellaneous observations

Canadian Antituberculosis Hospital

There was a three-month delay in opening this hospital following my arrival, mainly due to the lack of supplies and equipment, some of which had been declared "lost on arrival" but had been disposed of on the black market, and due to faulty and irresponsible construction and wiring which caused a section of the ceiling to cave in, narrowly missing bedridden patients.

On three occasions, in my presence, Dr. Michel Jutras, director, refused treatment to local people seeking minor surgery (e.g., superficial bullet wounds). On another occasion when the uncle of our hospital electrician was brought in, gravely burned and having just lost his wife and ten children (who were all found dead in the tunnel behind him, as they hid from a bombing raid), the same Dr. Jutras ordered the patient removed from the half-empty ward in our hospital to the overcrowded, poorly equipped Provincial Hospital down the road.

The Canadian Hospital was occupied by the ARVN troops

during the Tet offensive of February 1968, and used as a military base. It became necessary to evacuate all 43 patients and send them home with ten days' supply of antibiotics while the bombs were falling, since Dr. James Connolly (MILPHAP head at the Provincial Hospital) refused us permission to transfer them back to the old tuberculosis ward there, which was still empty.

When I protested later to the Canadian Ambassador in Saigon that we were not operating as a 100 percent independent Canadian humanitarian team (as we were officially known) and should therefore be withdrawn officially under protest, the reply was made that I should be satisfied with a ratio of 50 percent humanitarianism and 50 percent political work as that was what we were really there for. Our presence was evidently required to provide another facade for the so-called pacification program.

Also within this context is the construction of the $570,000 housing unit in Ming Manh suburb of Saigon under the publicly hailed "aid to refugees program." Only government and military officials could afford the rents, while on the grounds adjoining the Canadian hospital in Quang Ngai, 2,000 refugees continue to crowd around a single mud hole for their water supply.

Quang Ngai Provincial Hospital

Located in a compound, approximately 700 patients filled about 400 beds, averaging two patients to a bed. Each patient usually was cared for by a member of the family. Plumbing, water, and electricity services were totally inadequate, as were medical and nursing care. Under the Saigon administration there are only about 100 Vietnamese doctors caring for the entire population. The government food allotment was 30 piasters per patient per day (less than 20 cents value in 1967), which was also the amount intended to feed the tuberculosis patients in the Canadian hospital. The standards fell far below those considered humane in the treatment and care of human beings.

Following are examples from the various wards:

In the Burns Ward I have seen patients so disfigured from napalm as to make it impossible to verify whether they were men or women. I have seen skin and bone sizzling on a child's hand from phosphorous burns for 24 hours resisting any treatment. I have heard Dr. Van der Houf (MILPHAP Director) assure visiting journalists and doctors that the victims in the Burns Ward were mostly the result of gasoline explosions, as he was sure they [the patients] would confirm through the aid of the interpreter. However, on many occasions, when a second question was placed asking "Where did the gasoline come from?" the patient would point to the sky. It must also be noted at this point that the black market indiscriminately sold kerosene and gasoline in similar unmarked cannisters, so it was another cause for unnecessary, painful, and serious burns.

There were seldom enough daily supplies of vaseline and gauze to wind around the limbs and bodies of these patients. Dressings were left unchanged indefinitely. One soon realized, with great bitterness and frustration, that this type of nursing care was totally futile. We once nursed a small boy through three months, after which he was discharged although not totally healed. He had been brought into hospital originally by an American helicopter from his village several hundred miles away. This was a common practice since U.S. transport dropped off wounded civilians wherever convenient to their own schedule. Since they were sometimes picked up after a military operation had destroyed their village, they were further victimized by being deposited many miles from their hamlets, unattended by a member of their family (an absolute essential to provide nursing care, food and the irreplaceable psychological sustenance). In this case, this particular child only partially healed of the excessive napalm burns, was sent home (to a home which possibly no longer existed) to live and to play in unsanitary conditions which could only result in reinfection of his open wounds. He was fatally infected within a short period of time.

It must then be concluded that even while trying to lavish the best possible care upon him during this three month stay in the hospital, it had to be carried out with the full knowledge that, unless the patient could be maintained in clean sterile conditions until the healing process was entirely completed, one was nursing a doomed child with little or no hope of surviving upon discharge. Even though this was the considered fate of every civilian in South Vietnam, the farce of caring for the sick under such circumstances could only be labeled as a futile exercise of macabre proportions.

In the Surgery Ward I have seen patients lifted off a soiled litter which had carried them many miles and many days, with the same caked blood and mud and splintered bone and protruding organs and entrails, and in this same condition placed on an operating table for surgery, without even the benefit of washing the operative site. The shortage of water was not solved by the water tower constructed within sight and sound of the Surgery Ward. This tower had been constructed immediately prior to the 1966 tour of Senator Edward Kennedy when he came to investigate where US-AID funds were being spent. However, he left before the water tower was connected to the surgery ward, and so it was never completed and the lack of water continued. It obviously was not a matter of funds, as that same season $4,000 had been allotted to redecorate a villa where four doctors lived and for which they spent $400 monthly rental. (By comparison, the rental for the Canadian house across the road was $75.00.)

The Soft Tissue Ward, which Dr. Vennema (former Director of Canadian Medical Services in South Vietnam) had volunteered to take charge of, contained an assortment of injuries. It was in this ward where one of the young Canadian male nurses used to perform grafting operations. The first one I witnessed was that of a young girl who was transferred from her bed to the end of the ward where there were less mosquitos, dirt, and dogs. The donor area in the thigh was slightly anaesthetized, and the recipient area where three toes had been blown off was washed with hydrogen peroxide. The small islands of skin removed from the donor area were then transferred to the recipient area. The wound was bandaged and the girl returned to her bed. Supervision and further care were then just left to chance visits. The prognosis was entirely irrelevant.

It was in this ward as well where we saw gas victims who demonstrated much difficulty in breathing and exuded an overpowering stench from their very pores.

The Children's Ward was the saddest and had the highest mortality rate. Amoebic dysentery, typhoid, pneumonia and malaria, took a nightly toll as the children went into convulsions and died.

During the Tet offensive of February 1968, three refugees families moved into the Maternity Ward. They could not be removed during the labor and delivery period. When a Quaker friend, Margaret, and I requested that the American Red Cross people start providing shelter and food for the refugees who were camping on the hospital grounds in large numbers, we were told it was impossible since it could not be done without the permission of the Vietnamese medical director, who had already left for Saigon for an indefinite period. In the Medical Wards Dr. Paul Schmidt of the "Vietnam Project"[1] reported that one of his patients, an 11-year-old boy suffering from severe malnutrition and decreased blood count (hemoglobin 4 gms., approximately 30 percent normal blood count), disappeared every weekend. It was finally discovered that he was walking fifteen kilometers every Friday to care for a baby sister left with neighbors after their parents had been killed, and then he returned every Monday to quietly get back into his bed.

Two small prison cells on the hospital grounds were inspected by the Quaker friend, Margaret, and myself on the fourth of February 1968. The French-speaking guard, who had held the same job since the days of the French occupation, revealed in the one cell a radiant young mother, proudly showing us her newborn baby as if the world was all aglow with the wonder of it all, and hardly an indication of her circumstances.

In the adjoining cell was a girl whom the guard called "une folle." She was approximately 16 years old with her hands manacled, her hair all disheveled, her face scratched, her blouse torn at both shoulders; having just flung the small bowl of rice crashing against the wall, she turned on us shrieking "Meeeee" (meaning American). When I asked the

---

1. A two-month volunteer service sponsored by the American Medical Association whereby doctors volunteered to go to Vietnam for two months. This was a self-defeating program in the sense that the few doctors who did manage to sustain a sincere motivation became deeply frustrated because of their inability to accomplish anything worth their efforts. The others just didn't care because even if they did, in order to perform their duties with any measure of ethical concern they would have been obliged to get to the basic causes, namely, lack of clean water, supplies, electricity, sewerage, and equipment; and, of course, the war.

Doctors trained in modern American methods were entirely dependent upon lab and X-ray reports before they could formulate their diagnosis. On one occasion an infant died of severe constipation which required only rectal stimulation to increase the peristalsis. The death certificate read: "Massive abdominal tumor cause of death."

guard how long it was since she had been violated, he shrugged, turned away, and answered that he did not know.

Da Nang Provincial Hospital

During the period of evacuation after the Tet Offensive of the American civilian personnel from Quang Ngai, I assisted Dr. Patra Mosely (of the Vietnam Project). We removed the sutures from the shaved scalp of a woman which were bursting from the purulent pressure at the tension points. The flaps of the scalp were laid back while the infected areas were washed with hydrogen peroxide. Instead of resuturing the flaps of the scalp, they were just held firmly at the meeting edges while a fresh circular head bandage was applied.

Dr. Mosely, anxiously watching the time in order to meet an officer to play tennis at 12:30, was preparing to leave as I proceeded to straighten the bed clothes. At that point the condition of the patient's body beneath the bed covers was revealed, displaying an evident perforated intestinal wound, shattered upper femur, portion of foot severed and bleeding profusely—an altogether desperate sight! Upon being called back and shown the woman's condition, Dr. Mosely laughingly replied: "Don't be silly, she won't live till morning anyway; she'll just smell a little sweeter when she dies."

American Military Hospital

On November 8, 1967, a Dr. Early, neurosurgeon and medical director of the Naval Military Hospital at Da Nang, learned that I was working with Dr. Vennema in a Tuberculosis Hospital and asked what Dr. Vennema thought of his experiments. Dr. Early had been injecting tuberculi bacilli into simians (monkeys) and found that they died within 24 hours and therefore had absolutely no resistance to the injection. He wondered if there was any correlation between the monkeys and the Vietnamese, who have a very low resistance to tuberculosis. (One in seven has tuberculosis in Vietnam.) He was serious.

Canadian Rehabilitation Hospital—Qui Nhon

Upon my return to Canada I was contacted by Dr. Lotta Hitchmanova of the Unitarian Services, for background material on Vietnam as she was planning to go to Saigon to set up a children's home. I advised her that this was not the time, since she would have to work within the Saigon structure which cared nothing about 95 percent of the population . . . that we did not go to Hitler's Germany to set up hospitals but that we worked to end the war first and then helped survivors.

Apparently she went ahead anyway, and later I received an enquiry from her office about a reply they had received from the Canadian team in Qui Nhon when asked to refer war-wounded children. In the reply the writer stated they were having a difficult chore in finding war casualty disabled children, much to his joy but not surprise! Such an observation reflects an ignorance and unconcern of the conditions in Qui Nhon as could be expected from a casual observer, but hardly from a dedicated worker. But such was the nature of the project. The proportion of amputees, injured, and sickly children could not possibly vary in Qui Nhon from the rest of South Vietnam.

Further on Qui Nhon: In December 1970, it was reported

that the American forces were attacked and vehicles burned by angered civilians following the indiscriminate killing of several local students. This had happened on three occasions, and finally the area was declared to be out of bounds for all American forces. When I enquired of the Canadian government what was the status of the Canadian medical team in an area where it was entirely dependent upon American logistics under such circumstances, I received no answer to my question.

Upon filing my report with the Canadian government as a former advisor, it has been my contention that the medical aid project which we have been funding directly to the Saigon administration over the years, neither has been intended nor has effectually served the alleged purposes of "meeting the needs of the Vietnamese people." It has been, on the contrary, serving the needs of the Pentagon policy to systematically and deliberately commit biocide in the whole of Indochina under the pretense of offering medical assistance.

In spite of the three-year protest and exposé which I had been carrying out, trying to persuade the Canadian government to withdraw its involvement in South Vietnam, in February 1971, the Toronto *Globe and Mail* newspaper announced the construction of nine new medical centers in An Giang, province of Long Xuyen. This happens to be located right on the Cambodian border. Within the context of my report, I submit that this project can only be intended to facilitate the collection of information and the movement of troops and/or agents both during the present conflict and (more insidiously) for the period following the withdrawal of American forces.

Two exposés, published in the *New York Times* this very week, bear out the role which the Canadians in the I.C.C. have been playing. It revealed that the Canadian delegate to the I.C.C. officially, but secretly, carried messages from for-

mer President Johnson to Hanoi, containing threats of further escalation. The shocking part is that the substance of
these messages was kept from the public since the terms
offered Hanoi were so inherently unfair. And so, in effect,
Lester Pearson, then Prime Minister of Canada, with some
knowledge of the strategic plans, facilitated diplomatically
the American escalation. It is within this context that the
Canadian medical aid policy in South Vietnam obviously
functioned.

It is now undeniably corroborated that Canada has been
providing an umbrella under which the most savage brutality has been carried out. Depending upon the sympathy of
good people everywhere to support the channels established
for alleged medical aid, the real program to destroy the land
and its peoples was able to proceed. It has been said that "the
world is bleeding to death in Vietnam." To the extent that
we have done even the smallest thing to prolong this agony,
we are guilty. In my professional opinion and based upon the
above facts, the larger issue of war crimes constitutes the
total sum of this report. It indicates that the basis was deliberately laid to prolong the war by creating an entirely false
atmosphere of aiding and developing the Vietnamese people.

Bombing in Laos—A Crime against Humanity: Fred Branfman

My name is Fred Branfman. I spent nearly four years in Laos, from March 1967 until February 1971. For the first two years I was an educational advisor with International Voluntary Services, a private voluntary group under contract to the United States Agency for International Development in Laos. I spent the last two years as a freelance researcher, writer, interpretor, and journalist. As a volunteer, I learned to speak the Laotian language.

I have devoted most of the past year and a half to researching American bombing in Laos.

Most of this bombing has occurred in the two-thirds of Laos controlled by the Pathet Lao. This is a mountainous, forested region of some 50,000 square miles. It is inhabited, according to an estimate of an American Embassy official in March, 1970, by over 900,000 people in some 3,500 villages.

From September 1969 until February 1970, some 30,000 refugees were taken out of Pathet Lao zones by CIA-directed irregular forces and settled in the Mekong Valley. This gave outside observers their first opportunity to learn of conditions of life in Pathet Lao zones.

I have subsequently interviewed several thousand refugees and several hundred defectors from Pathet Lao portions of Sam Neua, Xieng Khouang, Saravane, Sedone and

Attopeu provinces. In addition, I have spoken with M. Jacques Decornoy, Southeast Asian desk editor of *Le Monde*, who visited Sam Neua province in the spring of 1968; a Belgian television crew who visited Phong Saly province in the spring of 1970; and American and Lao officials working with refugees from Pathet Lao zones in Houa Khong, Luang Prabang, and Khammouane provinces.

All of these sources have reported widespread American bombing of villages in the areas with which they are familiar. *Each one of well over one thousand refugees interviewed —without exception—has said that his town or village was damaged by American bombing while he still resided there.* Each one has also said that all other towns and villages with the general area with which he is familiar has been leveled as well.

Refugees sketch four main phases of bombing. The first ran from May 1964 until about October 1966. Bombing during this period was rather sporadic, carried out mostly by prop-driven T-28s, and directed largely against troop concentrations out in the forest. From October 1966 until the beginning of 1968, bombing first began to be directed against villages and towns. American jets became more prominent, people began evacuating their homes in certain areas, and civilian casualties became more frequent.

A third escalation came in 1968. American jets outnumbered T-28s. Bombing was directed primarily against villages and towns, and began to be carried out on a regular basis. Most of the villages and towns were evacuated during this period, and the people moved to the outskirts. They began spending much of their time in holes dug in the ground or into the bases of mountains and hills. A number of villages were razed. Bombing in forested areas was relatively light.

But it is as of 1969, after the bombing halt in North Vietnam and the subsequent diversion of jets into Laos, that refugees speak most.

They say that during this period the jets came over daily, bombing both day and night. They say that they dropped 500-pound bombs, napalm, phosphorous and antipersonnel bombs, fragmentation and delayed-action bombs. They also report frequent strafing. They say that American jets—including F-4s and F-100s—far outnumbered T-28s, which became an insignificant factor. They say that the jets bombed both villages and forests, that the people spent most of their time in holes or caves, and they suffered numerous civilian casualties. They say that everything was repeatedly fired on, even after villages had been evacuated. Buffalos, cows, rice fields, schools, temples, tiny shelters erected outside the village—in addition to all the people—were struck at by the aircraft.

Civilian casualties were heavy. Most were caused by antipersonnel bombs dropped in and around the villages. In addition, case histories have been recorded of death or injury due to being burned by napalm or phosphorus, burned by 500-pound bombs, slashed by fragmentation bombs, and strafed with machine-gun fire from the air.

A high percentage of the casualties were children and old people. The children, refugees say, lacked discipline, would often be playing, and tended to get confused when caught in the open. Children would also be more likely to tamper with delayed-action bombs. Old people, many of whom could not hear the planes coming simply "could not run fast enough" to make it to the holes.

In some cases, whole family lines were obliterated. Since civilians tended to hide together in family groups, when a 500-pound bomb scored a direct hit on a hole or cave, three generations—grandparents, parents and children—would be killed.

A number of massacres from the bombing have been reported to me. These include the death of some 300 civilians killed in a cave west of Ban Ban in a bombing raid in the

summer of 1968; 63 prisoners killed in a bombing raid on
a prison five miles east of Xieng Khouang in the winter of
1969; well over one hundred patients and medical personnel killed in a bombing raid on a hospital in a cave near
Muong Kham in May 1968. Deaths have also been reported due to normal illness which could not be treated as
a result of the bombing.

Refugees say the soldiers were broken up into small units
and spent most of their time moving around in the forest
under cover of the night. Little ammunition was stored in
their villages, and porterage lines did not pass through the
villages. Neither were antiaircraft positions located in the
villages. But, they say, civilians, tied down by their possessions and families, were not mobile like the soldiers and thus
suffered the brunt of the bombing.

Dozens of American pilots bombing Laos from Da Nang
Air Force Base in South Vietnam, and a half-dozen American
officials intimately concerned with targeting bombing strikes
in Laos corroborate the refugees' stories. For example, an
official who did the staff work on approving targets from both
Ambassadors Sullivan and Godley, told me, "The U.S.? What
can we do? Nothing . . . just keep on killing, destroying,
bombing, devastating. . . . But how much longer can we keep
it up? Pretty soon the Pathet Lao will have the whole country
except for the cities and land corridors between them. What
will we do then? Bomb Savannakhet, Pakse? The problem is
we have no policy."

And a pilot told me in Saigon on November 14, 1970, that:

I'm as liberal, as much for peace as anyone else. But war is not a
pretty thing. In a guerrilla war, the civilians are going to pay a price.
War has now progressed to a point where you're going to bomb
civilian targets and that's it. I'll be frank. I'm trained to kill people.
I don't like it particularly, but when the time comes I'm prepared
to do it.

All Americans interviewed have stated that antipersonnel bombs are useless against nonhuman targets such as structures, ammunition stores, or bridges. They have confirmed refugee reports of the use of antipersonnel bombs in Laos, as well as napalm, white phosphorous, fragmentation, and delayed-action bombs. In addition, they have stated that laser-guided and teleguided missiles of several different types, as well as acoustic and seismic sensors, are in daily use in Laos.

Conversations with these men have indicated two basic reasons why villages are bombed. First, *difficulties in locating and striking "military" targets have inevitably led to villages being bombed.* Pilots sent into Laos are in general prohibited from returning to base with bombs in place. At the same time, they are discouraged from dropping their ordnance in the sea or in uninhabited "dump zones." Thus they will drop their bombs somewhere in Laos. Pilots frequently have great difficulty finding "military" targets to bomb. Even when military targets have been located, in the process of trying hit them planes have hit villages. The one set of military targets most frequently bombed are roads. Yet it is near the roads that many of Laos's villages are located. Much of the bombing in Laos is done by instrument, either at night or because of cloudy weather conditions. Instrument bombing, pilots say, can be quite imprecise. Even if a pilot is trying his best to hit a road or truck with instrument bombing, the bombs he drops are as likely as not to strike populated areas.

In addition, American personnel interviewed say that pilots tend to be rather indifferent about where they bomb in Laos. They take relatively little antiaircraft fire; there are few textbook strategic targets, such as factories, large bridges, major military camps, or missile sites; bomb damage assessment is not carried out after each strike, so that pilots do not have a chance to measure their results. As a result, they do not regard bombing in Laos as much of a challenge and tend to "strew their bombs all over the countryside," as one targeting officer puts it.

Second, *villages have been bombed as a matter of policy* primarily because of the weakness of American-supported Asian soldiers vis-à-vis their adversaries.

Highly reliable American targeting sources have said that the CIA has since 1967 attempted to place inhabited villages on the approved target listing. One example was their insistence that the village of Sap Nao be bombed in September 1967. Although the Ambassador refused, the CIA went ahead and had the village bombed anyway by planes of the 56th Special Operations Wing at Nakhon Phanom, Thailand.

CIA insistence that villages be bombed appears primarily to result from its direction of the Armée Clandestine of hill-tribe irregulars on the ground. Once the tide of battle turned against the Armée Clandestine in 1967, the CIA apparently decided that it was necessary to weaken the Pathet Lao army by destroying its civilian infrastructure.

The American Embassy in Vientiane, which bears the legal responsibility for controlling all American air strikes in Laos, initially resisted CIA pressure to bomb villages. But during 1968, sources say, it gradually changed its policy. This first became apparent in the winter of 1968, when American Ambassador Sullivan approved bombing strikes in retaliation for Pathet Lao capture of Nam Bac on January 10, 1968.

By 1969, the bombing of villages had become policy. It appears that the decision was made to bomb civilian targets in an attempt to demoralize the civilian population, deprive the Pathet Lao of indigenous food supplies, force them to employ civilians to do porterage, kill off potential recruits and porters, and cause a population to flow away from their homes.

It has become, in the words of Robert Shaplen (writing in *Foreign Affairs* in April 1970 after a CIA-sponsored trip to northern Laos), an attempt to "destroy the social and economic fabric in Pathet Lao areas."

I would like at this point to place before you a document entitled "Documentation of American Bombing of Civilian Targets in Laos." This compendium, totaling nearly one thousand pages, includes all known evidence—from western sources and refugees themselves—of the bombing of populated areas in Laos.

• It includes dozens of articles that have appeared in newspapers, magazines, and books, each of which indicates that civilian targets have been bombed in Laos. It includes eyewitness reports of the bombing and destruction of Sam Neua town by M. Jacques Decornoy.

• It includes excerpts from a staff report of the Kennedy subcommittee on refugees stating that "the bombing has taken a heavy toll among civilians."

• It includes an excerpt from an in-depth study by UN expert Georges Chapelier who interviewed some fifty refugees from the Plain of Jars. This report states that "all of the interlocutors, without any exception, had his village completely destroyed. In the last phase, bombings were aimed at the systematic destruction of the material basis of civilian society."

• It includes an excerpt from the now-famous United States Information Service report, which recorded interviews with people from 96 separate villages from the Plain of Jars. This study reported that "75 percent of 190 respondents said their homes had been damaged by the bombing," "68 percent of 168 responses tabulated indicated that the respondents had seen someone injured by bombing, and 61 percent had seen a person killed." It concludes that "the bombing is clearly the most compelling reason for moving."

• It includes photos from the files of the Lao Ministry of Information which show extensive bombing damage to the towns of Xieng Khouang and Khang Khay.

• It includes copies of letters written by American field personnel who have had direct experience with American bombing of civilian targets in Laos.

• It includes a report by a United States Congressman who, after a visit to Laotian refugee camps and Thai air bases, concluded that "the significant and incontestible conclusion is that 76 percent of 96 small villages in Northern Laos were destroyed by bombing in 1969. Cluster bombs and white phosphorous were used against the civilian population of a country against whom the United States is not at war."

• It includes written transcripts of tape-recorded conversations with refugees. These have been made by a United States Congressman, CBS television, and myself. Tapes are available for inspection by anyone interested. They confirm the personal report given of conversations with refugees offered in the first section of this report. In particular, they confirm that they observed soldiers, arms, stores, and antiaircraft fires in villages being bombed.

In addition, this documentation includes direct testimony gathered from refugees from Pathet Lao areas, and recorded on paper, film, and tape.

While I was in Laos I spoke with hundreds of refugees from Pathet Lao areas, victims of American bombing on the Plain of Jars, who are presently refugees in camps around the capital city of Vientiane.

These people came from the Plain of Jars, in the province of Xieng Khouang. It was a thriving, vibrant society of 50,000 people back in 1964 when American bombing began. With its cool climate, rich, well-watered soil, thousands of head of livestock, it was Laos's most prosperous region.

In subsequent years American planes bombed virtually

every village on the Plain. In September 1969, the people were taken off.

The Plain of Jars is today a deserted wasteland—an entire society wiped off the face of the map by American bombing. Following are interviews with the refugees from a film to be released.

Thao Siphan, 6 years old, is from Ban Ngoui. His father explained: "In July 1969, we were all sitting in our small shelter out in the forest, when planes bombed around 11 A.M. My son's hand was hit and his fingers flew up, embedding themselves in the roof." From our experience with him Thao Siphan has suffered trauma from this event. In some ways, he was lucky though. On that same day a sixty-year-old man, and a little girl aged seven were killed in his shelter.

Sao Doumma's mother is holding forward a wedding photograph of Sao Doumma, her youngest child, who was killed in a bombing raid on Ban Tham about 11 A.M. in August 1969. When the planes came over, Sao Doumma was nursing her three-month-old baby. At the sound of the planes she jumped up and ran to the door, before her mother's eyes, and fell to the ground, crushing her baby beneath her. Two children, aged three and seven, were killed during the same bombing raid.

Thao Somdii is from Ban Theun, and is about 10 years old. The village chief explains: "On August 13, 1968, planes came over suddenly. Everyone was taken by surprise. Somdii began running for a trench, but he didn't make it. He was burned in his leg from the explosion of the bombs." The village chief later explained that his wife, named Me Bou Tii, two of his children, and a nephew were all killed in the same raid, along with a seventy-year-old man named Ong Ngieng.

Drawings and essays done by the refugees further describe their experience under the bombs. (Spoken in accompaniment to display of drawings.)

a. This drawing was done by a thirty-two-year old man. His written description explains: "In the earlier times of my village we had good fortune and there was nothing to cause us fear or danger. . . . Our region was like other regions. But in 1965, the airplanes began to come and drop bombs on the people of Xieng. They caused death and injuries to the people. There were people who died in the holes, as in this drawing. There were many people who couldn't get out. All that could be seen were heads and legs and hands only. . . . there was one man who went to dig out his child and wife who were buried inside."

b. This drawing was done by a 27-year-old man, who wrote: "In the region of Xieng Khouang there was a war which caused death for the population and made it impossible to work, to grow rice, and earn a livelihood. . . . As in this picture, there were people working in the ricefields, the gardens, the village, who were hit by the airplanes. The earth was struck and many, many cows, buffalo, horses and chickens died."

c. This drawing was done by another man, aged 22 years, who wrote: "The blood coloring the ground where the people died like animals. The airplanes came destroying causing the deaths of so many people that it was impossible to count how many. Like in this picture all these people died until all you could see was blood. There was a young child who came and saw this and was so sorry that he cried. So afraid of that. The planes came to bomb everyday, everyday."

d. One drawing by a thirty-seven-year-old person is titled "Confusion and Change in the Life of the Laotian Rice Farmer." He describes it: "In the region of Xieng Khouang, there came to be a lake of blood and destruction. Most pitiful for friends and children and old people. Before my life was most enjoyable, and we worked in the ricefield and in the garden. Our progress was great. But then the changes in the manner of the war, which caused us to lose our land, our upland, and lowland ricefields, our cows and our buffalo. For there airplanes and the sound of bombs throughout the sky and the hills. All we had were the holes. One day I saw a person who had been hit and injured just near the mouth of the holes. But he couldn't get up so I went to help him. I took him to the hospital. He was hit in the side in a spot so that he lost a lot of blood."

And another by a woman, aged 33:

"The life which had only the value of dying. Like I saw in the region of the village of my birth. Every day and every night the planes went to drop bombs on us. We lived in holes in order to protect our lives. There were bombs of many kinds. . . . Like in this picture which I have drawn. It is not beautiful, but it shows the shooting and the death from the planes, and the destruction of the bombs. This kind of bomb would explode in the air and was much more dangerous than just one. . . . I saw my cousin die in the field of death. My heart was most disturbed and my voice called out loudly and I ran to the houses. Thusly, I saw the life of the population and the dead people on account of the war with many airplanes in the region of Xieng Khouang. Until there were no houses at all. And the cows and buffalo were dead, until it was leveled and you could see only the red, red ground. . . . I think of this time and still I am afraid."

The following was written by a 21-year-old man: "Before my village had prosperity as I have drawn. And good homes for Laotian rice farmers. This led to much progress for our wide land. Then came the present time, hit by the planes and burned ricefields, hit and burned by the bombs of napalm. And the houses were hit and burned and belongings were completely lost. I think back and in my face tears want to fall, but there are not enough for I have fled from the village of my birth."

In an essay describing his people's life from 1964–1969 a teenager writes: "In 1964 we knew another danger: the bombs falling from the sky. In fact, from this year on, Xieng Khouang began to be bombarded. The population underwent another war, the air war. They learned another form of civilization, the trenches.

"My family and I had dug our trench in our garden in the middle of a shower of bombs. Such difficulty! But we fought to save our skin. We dug day and night. Between times the planes bombed day and night. I thought that I would surely be killed.

"Finally, my village was bombed and reduced to ruins. Our granaries of rice were set on fire. . . . Finally, the planes bombed the bamboo forest where we hid in our tunnels, wounding two children who did not have time to seek refuge. Our village was filled with bomb craters, the land made barren. Nothing would grow on it.

"I grieved very much to see my village in ruins, my animals disappeared, my crops destroyed . . . each day, news came about such and such a village being bombed, more and more deaths and wounded."

Legal controversy has swirled over Laos ever since the 1962 Geneva Accords, guaranteed by its 14 signatories, provided for the neutralization of Laos. The major issues raised have centered on American charges that the North Vietnamese have violated the accords, and corresponding accusations by the socialist bloc that the United States has broken them.

But to determine whether American bombing in Laos has resulted in crimes of war, it is not necessary to make reference to the 1962 accords. The bombing is subject to international agreements which long antedate the 1962 provisions. Under international law, the United States is forbidden to bomb nonmilitary targets under any circumstances. Whether or not the North Vietnamese have also violated the 1962 Geneva Accords is totally irrelevant to this question.

The community of nations, including the United States, recognizes the 1907 Hague Conventions. Article 25 of this agreement stipulates that "the attack or bombardment, by whatever means, of towns, villages, dwellings, or buildings which are undefended is prohibited."

The membership of the United Nations, including the United States, recognize the 1946 Nuremberg Principles. These principles are regarded as an authoritative summary of the Nuremberg judgment, by which the United States and other allied powers condemned a number of German and Japanese leaders to death and imprisonment.

Principle VI of the 1946 Nuremberg Principles states in part that the following acts "are punishable as crimes under international law." (b) War Crimes, which are defined in part as "murder, ill-treatment . . . of civilian population of or in occupied territory . . . (and) wanton destruction of cities, towns or villages, or devastation not justified by military necessity. (c) and Crimes against humanity, where are defined partially as "murder . . . and other inhuman acts done against any civilian population on political . . . grounds . . . when such acts are done . . . in execution of or in connection with any . . . war crime."

And the nations of the world, including the United States, recognize the 1949 Geneva Conventions on the Law of War. Article 3 of these conventions states in part that "persons taking no active part in the hostilities . . . shall in all circumstances be treated humanely. . . ." and that "to this end the following acts are and shall remain prohibited at any time and in any place whatsoever with respect to the above mentioned persons: (a) violence to life and person, in particular murder of all kinds, mutilation, cruel treatment. . . ."

The United States has not repudiated the 1907 Hague Convention, 1946 Nuremberg Principles, or 1949 Geneva Conventions on the Law of War. It is therefore clearly responsible to the international community to conduct bombing in Laos in accordance with these international agreements.

The United States has specifically recognized its legal responsibility with regard to bombing civilian targets in Laos. When the United States began bombing in Laos in 1964, the American Embassy drew up what it called Rules of Engagement and Operations Authorities which prohibited the bombing of civilian targets. Assistant Secretary of Defense Dennis Doolin testified before a Congressional committee on May 7, 1970, that ". . . in Laos . . . our air activities are governed by strict rules of Engagement and Operations Authorities designed to minimize civilian casualties."

At a press conference on April 25, 1971, Mr. Doolin stated that these Rules of Engagement held that no air strikes could be made against an "active village" even if it is inhabited by enemy soldiers or is being used as a supply storage area. An "active village," he stated, is one "with one structure or more with signs of habitation." He said that villages could only be attacked when fire has been received from the village and then only under the guidance of an aerial observer with specific permission from the American Embassy in Vientiane. And he added that the Rules of Engagement prohibited the use of napalm or white phosphorous against civilians or noncombatant camps.

American leaders, therefore, freely acknowledge that they are legally bound to refrain from bombing civilian targets in Laos.

Claims that the bombing they have done was due to military necessity, or because villages were defended, would seem to be controverted by the evidence. As we have seen, all refugees state that neither soldiers nor antiaircraft positions were located in the villages. Even if they were, however, this would not seem to justify American bombing of villages. For the United States has no legal basis for waging aerial warfare in Laos. To date, however, American leaders have not offered "military necessity" as grounds for their bombing of civilian targets in Laos. In fact, they have simply categorically denied that the United States has bombed inhabited villages in Laos. They cite only four exceptions to this in the last two years, all of which have been laid to pilot error or to confusion in the orders given to pilots.

On October 21, 1969, former American Ambassador to Laos William H. Sullivan testified—under oath—to a Congressional committee that "the United States Air Force contribution was limited to striking at the logistic routes, what were allied choke points on those routes, or at points of concentration which fed into the area where the actual ground battling was taking place . . . it was the policy not to attack populated areas." On April 24, 1971, Mr. Sullivan testified, again under oath, to a Congressional committee that "the policy of the U.S. is deliberately to avoid hitting inhabited villages . . . I know of no villages that have been bombed."

At this hearing, Mr. Sullivan did name—in the first and

only public admission to date—a town which had been bombed: Phonesavan on the Plain of Jars. He stated, however, that it was uninhabited at the time it was bombed, the villagers having evacuated it. Only North Vietnamese soldiers were present when it was bombed, he said.

Firsthand documentation of American bombing of civilian targets in Laos clearly indicates that such statements by these officials are a monstrous lie:

• The burns suffered by a thirteen-year-old novice, Thao Ampha, Thao Somdii, are clear testimony that napalm and white phosphorous have been dropped on inhabited areas of Laos.

• The tape transcript of an interview with refugees from Phonesavan clearly indicates that Phonesavan was bombed frequently for years while civilians still inhabited it, and that it had not been occupied by the North Vietnamese. (This tape has not been disputed by the United States State Department, which one year ago sent an official to listen to it.)

• The photographs, reports, essays, drawings, and news articles detailing the wanton destruction of towns and undefended villages clearly indicate that Nuremberg Principle VI; Clause b, American Rules of Engagement; and Article 25 of the 1907 Hague Conventions have been violated.

• The murder of Sao Doumma and Sieng Vong and dozens of others is witness of violations of the 1949 Geneva Conventions and Land War and the Nuremberg Principle VI, Clause b.

• The mutilation of Thao Diphan and Thao Vong and Nang Khamphong and dozens of others are evidence of ill-treatment and inhuman acts equally prohibited by these agreements.

• The murder and other inhuman acts committed against the civilian population of the Plain of Jars, culminating in the evacuation of the survivors from their ancestral homes, is proof of violation of Clause c of Nuremberg Principle VI.

In sum, American bombing in Laos has resulted in the frequent commission of Crimes of War as established in the 1907 Hague Conventions on Laws of War, the Nuremberg Principles, and the 1949 Geneva Convention on Land War.

And American aerial destruction of whole societies in Laos, in particular that of the region of Xieng Khouang, constitutes a Crime Against Humanity as defined by the sixth of the Nuremberg Principles, Clause c.

The war waged by American leaders in Laos is unprecedented in the annals of man.

The United States, as an industrialized giant of some 200 million people, has a per capita income of over $1,000; its Gross National Product is over one trillion dollars, its annual budget well over $100 billion. Its officials are spending well over $2 billion annually on waging an air war, ground war, and maintaining civil administration in Laos.

They are using their most sophisticated technology short of nuclear weapons daily in a sparsely populated rural land of some three million rice farmers. The per capita income of Laos is estimated at $70 a year, its annual budget at some tens of millions, its GNP at a few hundred million. The military weaponry possessed by its inhabitants consists primarily of automatic machine guns and a limited number of rudimentary antiaircraft guns.

And what American leaders have brought to Laos is the most fully automated war in history—a war waged primarily by machine.

Over 50,000 American airmen at air bases and on aircraft carriers outside of Laos's borders, and thousands of aerial machines of war, have been involved in the air campaign against it, at a cost approaching $2 billion a year. The American ground war in Laos has involved a few thousand Americans directing and leading Asian troops in battle, with an expenditure of several hundred million dollars annually. By conservative estimate, over two million tons of bombs have been dropped on the one million people of Pathet Lao zones. This is as much American bombing as was absorbed by several hundred million people throughout Europe and the entire Pacific theatre during World War II (2,057,244 tons).

This saga of suffering, however, has remained almost unknown to the outside world. For American leaders have waged this war far from the consciousness of the American people. It has been a war, to paraphrase the prophetic words of George Orwell in *1984*, "fought on the vague frontiers . . . whose whereabout the average man can only guess at."

It is a feature of such an automated war that those waging it can also manage much of the news that seeps out about it. Unlike the bombing of North Vietnam, American leaders have largely succeeded in keeping their bombing of Laos secret. They have not permitted newsmen to go out on bombing raids over Laos, as they have in South Vietnam; they have refused to allow newsmen to interview the American air attaché in Vientiane or American pilots bombing Laos from Thailand; they have consistently denied to both Congress and the American public that they are bombing any villages in Laos; they have made few public references of any sort to bombing in Laos, unlike their daily announcements a few years ago of strikes in North Vietnam.

As a result, the Laotian people have been forced to bear their burden almost alone, without the worldwide support their struggle demands.

All mankind has incurred a debt to these good and kindly people that it can never repay. These good-natured and patient people, so bereft of physical resources, have not merely *withstood* an onslaught of fire and steel to which few men anywhere have been subjected; they have begun the task of constructing a new society, even under the bombs. They have demonstrated conclusively, as few have before them, the strength of the human spirit face to face with a superior technology bent on their destruction. They have not countered mechanized war with technology of their own. Rather, they have drawn upon such perseverance, intelligence, and a near-mystical faith in their human right and ability to live as they will.

In so doing, they have not only provided a model and inspiration for the powerless and disinherited throughout the world; they have made a direct contribution to the struggle of all those, both within the United States and without, who would refuse to submit to the will of a tiny group of American leaders; to all those who struggle to control their own destiny, free from fear and domination by American technological might.

Task Force Report

Following is an edited version of the official Task Force Report of the International Commission of Enquiry into U.S. Crimes in Indochina. The report was compiled by five investigators who went to North Vietnam in May 1971. They included Sven Ekberg, a Swedish microbiologist and journalist; Martin Rossdale, a British doctor; Jostein Nyhammar, publisher of the Norwegian *Aktuel*; Victor Maievskij, a Soviet journalist; and Dorothy Forman, an American and member of Women Strike for Peace. As the report makes clear, the team not only collected their own data, but also were careful to evaluate the methodology used by the Vietnamese to collect and analyze data.

Introduction

On behalf of the International Commission of Enquiry into U.S. Crimes in Indochina, a team of investigation visited the Democratic Republic of Vietnam, [DRV] on May 14–29, 1971.

Purpose and Scope

The team was assigned to investigate and clarify data and evidence relating to warfare in Indochina. The objective of the visit was the preparation of data and evidence for the second session of the International Commission to be held in Oslo, June 20–25, 1971. The following subjects were considered to be of particular interest:

1. Intensification, prolongation, and extension of the war in Indochina, as measured by acts of aggression and methods of warfare;

2. The Vietnamization policy and the means by which this policy is implemented, i.e., the "pacification" program;

3. Conditions in refugee camps, "strategic hamlets," and city slums in South Vietnam, Laos, and Cambodia;

4. Extent and effects of chemical warfare in Indochina.

Situation and Difficulties

Due to the war situation—the devastating bombing of Laos and the situation in South Vietnam and Cambodia—and the limited time at our disposal, we were not able to perform on-the-spot investigations in these areas. Further, the war seriously hampers the collection of relevant data and material evidence from these areas. Because of this, reports and material cannot be obtained which would meet all requirements or scientific standards, as defined in any narrow sense.

However, we do not interpret this to mean that reports and additional materials received should be dismissed; rather every effort should be undertaken to clarify reports focusing on both future aspects and consequences of the war. Much of the material presented during our stay met the most rigid scientific standards.

As a result we can only give a preliminary report on the overall situation. Together with reports from South Vietnam, Laos, and Cambodia, we believe this might contribute to a deeper understanding of the character of warfare waged by the U.S. in Indochina.

Methods

With these difficulties in mind, we tried to establish methods adapted to the situation at hand. We soon found, however, that our methods could not be applied in every instance or in every field of investigation because much of the data is still preliminary and some areas have not been covered.

We therefore had to develop a method of evaluation. In a rather crude way we tried, in each field of investigation, to establish the following to our satisfaction:

1. What we regarded as being beyond reasonable doubt;
2. What we could not find as fully confirmed, but which we thought merited further serious study;
3. What we were unable to confirm, but which might merit further study.

It should be clearly understood that we use this method of categorizing within limits set by our professional ability, knowledge, and intellectual capacity. Some of our assessments can thus be seen as preliminary ones.

Chemical Warfare and Implications for the Future

Serious concern has been expressed in relation to chemical warfare in Indochina—the use of gas and herbicides against the people and the land on which they live today, and on which they must rely for their future existence.

A number of preliminary observations have been performed in the areas controlled by the U.S. Army and the Saigon government.[1] The Provisional Revolutionary Government (PRG) of South Vietnam and the Democratic Republic of Vietnam have published data on areas affected by herbicides in South Vietnam and on the effects on people and environment. The discrepancy between U.S. Department of

1. F.H. Shirley. "An Assessment of Ecological Consequences of Defoliation Program in Vietnam," U.S. Department of Agriculture, April 1968; E.H. Orians and Egbert, Pfeiffer, "Ecological Effects of the Vietnam War," *Science*, vol. 168, May 1, 1970; M. Meselson et al. "Preliminary Report of AAAS Assessment Commission on Herbicides. *Science*, vol. 171, January 8, 1971.

Defense data, U.S. Air Force data, and those of the PRG and DRV is substantial. We therefore tried to evaluate the methods of information-gathering used by the PRG-DRV. In order to be able to make distinctions between the different chemicals used, we applied the following questions in relation to data on chemical warfare:

1. Effects on people and environment
2. Means of delivery
3. Situation in which chemicals were used
4. Date and location
5. Breakdown of statistics on forest areas, rice fields, along canals, etc.
6. Analysis performed on soil samples, leaves, etc.

The answers to these questions would provide an estimate of the effects of chemical war on the people, land, and wildlife, and its implications for the future. Given the present state of knowledge, however, only a preliminary evaluation can be made.

Inspection in Laboratories and Hospitals

There is generally a bias, explicit or implicit, against data and reports given by the one party involved [PRG-DRV] while the other party is given credit for its data as being correct in all its essentials. In order to evaluate data we considered important, we therefore believed it would be valuable to visit facilities where such data were produced and summarized.

In chemical and biological experiments and tests of some complexity, minor changes in methodology might cause substantial alterations of results. In order to establish whether such faults in methodology existed, we observed different methods used in the laboratories and hospitals in great detail.

We also had long conversations with scientists at the afore-mentioned facilities and were able to get a general impression of their work and the way in which they solved problems. Generally we found the methods used were satisfactory, i.e., they met the highest requirements of biological analysis.

In one instance of particular interest concerning cytogenetic methods in analyzing chromosomes in leucocytes from mothers and children from chemically treated areas in South Vietnam, we went into minute detail in observing methods of isolating cells, preparation of cells for staining, and final analysis of results. We were able to conclude that methods used were entirely satisfactory.

Material and Evidence Received

During our visit we were given reports relevant to the current situation in Indochina by representatives of the PRG and DRV. We were also able to examine the material evidence, listen to testimony from witnesses from South Vietnam and DRV, question these witnesses ourselves, and have discussions with physicians.

Travel in the DRV

We had the opportunity to travel in the provinces of the Democratic Republic of Vietnam and were able to visit parts in the south. During this trip we were able to view and evaluate some of the damage caused by heavy U.S. bombing.

The U.S. Aggression against the DRV

The extension and escalation of the war to the Democratic Republic of Vietnam (North Vietnam) was initiated by the Gulf of Tonkin incident August 1964, and the subsequent resolution adopted by the U.S. Congress authorized President Johnson to take measures against DRV that he deemed necessary.

The heavy attacks on DRV were initiated in February 1965. The U.S. aggression against DRV has taken three main forms:

1. Bombings

2. Shellings from naval units, in particular the U.S. Seventh Fleet, offshore of DRV

3. Shellings from artillery south of the demilitarized zone, DMZ, on DRV territory across the DMZ

Air War

The air war is by far the most important. A wide variety of aircraft, including B-52s, have been used. The weaponry includes a wide variety of bombs: blast and demolition bombs up to the size of 3,000 pounds; incendiary weapons like phosphorus, thermite, magnesium, and napalm; and various kinds of antipersonnel bombs. Guided missiles have also been delivered from air platforms. According to DRV authorities, more than one million tons of explosives had been delivered on DRV when President Johnson declared the "bomb halt" October 31, 1968—i.e., a quota of 50 kilograms per inhabitant. The planes attacking DRV have taken off from bases in the South and from Japan and Thailand, as well as from aircraft carriers.

ESCALATION OF AIR WAR

The air raids of the U.S. Air Force and U.S. Navy were first directed mainly at coastal provinces near the DMZ. Gradually they were intensified and extended up to the 20th parallel, until the entire country was subjected to heavy air attacks.

From February 7 to May 12, 1965, U.S. aircraft attacked areas from Vinh Linh to Than Hoah province, extending from the 17th to the 20th parallel. From May 18, the U.S. Air Force attacked targets beyond the 20th parallel. Fifteen provinces were subjected to air attacks north of the 20th. On April 12, 1966, B-52 strategic bombers were used for the first time for "carpet bombing" of inhabited areas in western Quang Binh.

On June 29, 1966, a new phase in the air war against the DRV was initiated with the attack on Hanoi. In the following months, both Hanoi and the important harbor and industrial center of Haiphong were repeatedly subjected to attacks. According to the Hanoi Commission for Enquiry into U.S. war crimes, Hanoi was attacked 90 times from 1966 to 1968. 6,260 structures in the capital were destroyed; 21 health centers including nine hospitals were damaged.

On March 31, 1968, President Johnson declared a "limitation" on the bombings of the DRV. This step was taken in the face of mounting domestic opposition to the war, pacifying public opinion within the U.S. and abroad. For the DRV this meant that bombing missions, previously extended to the whole of the DRV, were now concentrated within an area extended from the 17th to the 20th parallel. This area, where 25 percent of the DRV population lives, was subjected to extremely heavy bombing, coordinated with shelling from U.S. naval forces and artillery south of the DMZ. The damage in this area subjected to "limited bombing" was severe. The area from Nghe An to Vinh Linh was practically, if not officially, turned into a "free fire zone."

Seven months later, on October 31, 1968, the U.S. Government declared a halt to the bombing of the DRV although this declaration has been violated several times. Even after October 31, 1968, the U.S. continued to violate DRV territory and air space by great numbers of reconnaissance flights. A monthly average of reconnaissance missions in 1970 was reported at 1,150.

RESULTS OF THE BOMBINGS

From the very beginning, the U.S. air war against the DRV was directed against population centers—cities, villages, and hamlets—in addition to military targets such as bridges, railways, roads, and communication centers.

Every single city in the DRV has been attacked by U.S. aircraft. Out of 30 province capitals, 29 have been hit—nine of them (Dong Hoi, Ha Pinh, Than Hoa, Phu Ly, Ninh Binh, Phue Tho, Yen Bari, Bac Giang, and Son La) to such an extent that they were completely demolished. Out of 258 district capitals, 133 were raided; out of 5,778 villages, a total number of 3,275 were attacked.

The destruction has been especially devastating in the provinces of Quang Binh and Ha Tinh and in the Vinh Linh area. In these parts of the DRV, practically 100 percent of the villages were bombed, several of them completely wiped out. A few examples of the intensity of the air war are:

———Vinh (population 72,000), composed of six districts and five suburban villages, was subjected to 4,131 attacks over a four-year period. More than 30,000 bombs from 500 pounds to 3,000 pounds in size were poured on the city. All of Vinh's houses were destroyed; 31 schools, the university, four hospitals, and two churches were demolished.

———Dong Hoi (population 16,280), in the province of Quang Binh, was subjected to 1,143 attacks. Forty thousand demolition bombs, pellet bombs, and napalm bombs were delivered and hundreds of people were killed in the town, which covers an area of three square kilometers.

———Nahn Trach village (population 3,051, mostly fishermen and families) was completely destroyed by 1,000 demolition bombs, 192 napalm bombs and phosphorus bombs, and 200 CBUs. In this case the air raids were coordinated with artillery shelling. In all, 3,000 shells hit the village, and all the houses—716—were destroyed; 107 fishing vessels were sunk.

The U.S. bombing has not been restricted to urban areas. Farms and cooperatives have been subjected to attacks on a systematic basis. Out of 743 agricultural cooperatives in the province of Ha Tinh, 703 have been bombed. In Nghe An, 1,800 cooperatives were attacked; in Quang Binh and Vinh Linh not a single cooperative was spared.

Out of the 68 state farms established in the DRV, 66 were subjected to U.S. air attacks. The Ben Hai State Farm in Vinh Linh was attacked 1,450 times, the Viet Tring State Farm 4,000 times. These attacks not only destroyed all kinds of dwellings but also inflicted considerable damage to plants.

The dikes and water conservation network in the DRV, so absolutely necessary to an agrarian society, have been heavily bombed. The dikes in the 17 provinces were attacked at 661 different locations with both demolition bombs and blast bombs; 1,627 water conservation works in 20 provinces were bombed. Sea dikes as well as river dikes have been attacked. The dikes of Ho Giang in Quang Ninh province were partly destroyed during raids in 1966. Sea water flooded 1,200 hectares of fields.

A number of hospitals and schools are among the structures destroyed in the DRV. One hundred hospitals and 533 health centers have been attacked. In all, 1,589 schools—from universities to primary schools—have been targets for U.S. aircraft. In Hanoi 87 schools were damaged, in Thanh Hoa 154. Four hundred seventy-five churches and convents have been damaged or destroyed. Pagodas and Buddhist temples have been targets: 420 were subjected to attacks. Of particular interest is the fact that attacks on churches and pagodas occured at times of worship; that is, they were attacked when the maximum number of people would supposedly be there.

"Carpet bombing" has been used to a great extent, particularly in the Vinh Linh area and the Quang Binh province. One hundred forty-eight such bombings were recorded during 1968.

SHELLINGS FROM NAVAL PLATFORMS

U.S. naval forces have played a considerable part in the war against the DRV. Since 1965, when the U.S. escalated the war across the DMZ, the whole U.S. Seventh Fleet, part of the U.S. Sixth Fleet, including 15 aircraft carriers, has at some time or another been engaged in operations against the DRV. Naval units took part in the shelling of many coastal villages and sank or captured thousands of fishing vessels.

Shelling across the DMZ

U.S. artillery, based south of the 17th parallel, has caused heavy damage on the area close to the DMZ. More than 750,000 shells of different calibres, including the shells from naval units, were centered on the DRV.

Violation of the "Bomb Halt"

The bombing halt declared by the U.S. government on October 31, 1968, has been violated on several occasions, and severe attacks have been launched against targets between the 17th and 20th parallels.

Coordinated with the invasion of Cambodia in 1970, U.S. aircrafts of various types conducted massive bombings against Nghe An, Quang Binh, and Vinh Linh provinces. In 1971 the U.S. Air Force systematically attacked targets south of the 20th parallel.

The investigation team was able to visit areas currently under attack by U.S. aircraft. A small hamlet ten kilometers east of Vinh was attacked on April 22, 1971. We had the opportunity to investigate the area hit. We were told that a mother and her child were killed in the attack, and that a 16-year-old girl was injured. She was still in the hospital being treated when we were there. We were able to investigate the missile launched. We were also shown the remnants of another missile which had been launched against a village in the western part of the province, on the same day (April 22).

Evaluation

Most of the information given in this part on air raids, shellings, damage, etc., has been supplied by the DRV authorities. For obvious reasons our team has not been in the position to visit all the cities, villages, and hamlets subjected to attacks. We are, therefore, not able to provide definite proof of all the attacks mentioned. We can, however, offer an assessment on the allegations made by the DRV authorities, and we find that there is a substantial amount of evidence to support them.

The DRV has organized a network of investigation committees under its own National Commission for Enquiry into U.S. War Crimes. Such commissions have been established in all provinces, districts, and cities—even at the village level. We met several representatives of these commissions. Our impression is that they were careful to register the attacks and collect facts on what actually took place, what damage had been caused, what kind of weaponry was used, how many people were killed or injured, etc. When these commissions cannot judge complicated technical questions like weaponry, experts are sent from Hanoi to investigate.

For five days our team visited the provinces of the DRV and went as far south as the city of Vinh. We saw the results of the bombings in many places, not only in important industrial cities such as Haiphong, but also in a great number of villages and hamlets. Practically every bridge south of Hanoi had been destroyed or severely damaged, as were the railroads and roads at several places. We also saw towns and hamlets practically wiped out and bomb craters in the strangest places.

In two of the heavily bombed cities we have mentioned, Thanh Hoa and Vinh, the team was in a position to verify allegations by the DRV authorities. The city of Vinh had been completely wiped out; most houses were in ruins and not one house in the city remained undamaged. The waterworks had been destroyed and the adjacent area was covered with bomb craters.

On the basis of what we were able to see, we have no doubt that the bombing had been totally indiscriminate and that part of the bombing was aimed at terrorizing the people by destroying their villages and DRV as a viable society in a military as well as economic capacity. The cultural unit, social fabric, health, education, religious systems, etc., are also thus destroyed. The people of DRV designate the U.S. aggression as a "war of destruction." The investigation team finds this an appropriate and adequate description based on reality in the DRV.

Weapons Used by U.S. Air Force and U.S. Navy against the DRV

There are two major elements to the U.S. aggression against the Democratic Republic of Vietnam:

1. The attack on what would be legitimate military and economic targets if: a) the U.S. had declared war on the DRV —which it has not; b) the DRV had attacked comparable U.S. targets—which it has never done and is not even in a position to threaten.

Such targets include means of transportation: roads, railways and canals, coal mines, quarries, cement works and power stations, and all sorts of factories producing goods whose use is, primarily or secondarily, applicable to the defense of the DRV. Much of this is covered in the section on the U.S. aggression against the DRV. It should be noted, however, that it is not possible to make a sharp distinction between goods which might be of use to the war and those which are not.

2. The attack on the population itself of the DRV. Since this country is still, in international terms, at a low level of eco-

nomic development, its most important resource is its population and their willingness to struggle for "peace, independence, and neutrality" so as to be able to build their society and fulfill their desires within that society. The attack on the population, therefore, has two purposes: a) actual destruction of the population; b) a war of terror against them.

Since the greater part of the population of the DRV is agrarian, their grouping in sufficient density to justify risking U.S. pilots' lives and U.S. material to deliver weapons by air is not feasible. Attacks on them are, therefore, carried out wherever and whenever they gather. This means there may be ruthless attacks on hospitals at any time; on factories, mines, quarries, and so forth during hours of work; on schools during classes; on religious buildings during hours of worship. Primary weapons of aggression may be high explosive shells or bombs; or, secondarily, attacks may be launched on those who may come to help others who have already been attacked. In addition to this form of attack against the population, it is also possible to attack the rural population working in or moving through the country.

WEAPONS CLASSIFICATION

As we were confronted with the results of weapons used, we found it useful to classify these weapons in relation to their effects. A crude classification of effects follows:

1. Injuries due to metallic pellets or splinters
2. Injuries due to blast
3. Injuries due to burn

A metallic pellet or splinter of about $\frac{1}{4}'' \times \frac{1}{4}''$ causes the greatest degree of injury to a person whom it penetrates. We saw numerous such cases, as have other visitors to the DRV. We were also shown victims, postmortem materials, and X-rays, and had the opportunity to talk to the doctors and the victims.

A considerable degree of surgical skill is required to remove metallic pellets or splinters. We visited the Hanoi University School of Postgraduate Surgery in the Vietnam-Deutschland Hospital in Hanoi. According to Professor Tung That Tien, all the surgeons trained in the DRV must spend a part of their training period there. There are 20 surgical teams training in all the major branches of modern surgery; general and abdominal surgery, urological surgery, orthopedics, arterial and vascular surgery, neurosurgery, etc.

Not all pellets or fragments of shrapnel need to be removed from a wounded person. The decision depends on their clinical consequences and is an index of the difficulty of removing them, so many may be left *in situ*. If they remain in tissues, they may cause discomfort and pain and even some loss of function. We received reports of such effects from several witnesses.

We divided those weapons which produced metallic splinters or pellets into three categories:

1. Those which seemed to have been designed for and directed specifically against the civilian population;

2. Those which could be directed against the military, but which we found, typically in this country, were widely used against the civilian population;

3. Those which seemed to be designed for the defense of, or attack against fixed military positions, but which could be used to wound or kill a civilian in such an area;

4. Those which are used against the population of DRV and could be construed as being in violation of international military usage.

CATEGORY 1

1. Cloth Wrapped Mine XM 12; 2½″ × 2½″, weight 50–80g. This mine contains no metal parts, so that it is not possible to detect it with a conventional mine detector. Two

different forms were shown to us: one wrapped in jungle green cloth and the other in sand-colored cloth. Inside the wrapping is a mixture of black powder, glass powder, and potassium chlorate. It is detonated by pressure, and it causes severely penetrated flesh and tendon wounds to the bare feet. A sandal gives protection from it. We noted that in the countryside, the great part of the peasantry works barefoot. Also, full protection from the effects of the mine requires a fairly robust sandal, not commonly worn by civilians in the country.

2. Bats-wing bomb (so-called by the Vietnamese because of its shape). (It is referred to as Leaf Mine in the Congressional Records, Extension of Remarks, page 2844, April 6, 1971.) Seven thousand six hundred eighty of these are scattered over large areas at a time. The core contains a detonator which is set off by shock. These mines, too, cause severe penetrating wounds.

CATEGORY 2

In this category belong most of the other splinter and fragment producing antipersonnel weapons which we were shown, namely:

Butterfly bomb, M 83

Pineapple bomb, an "improvement" of the above mentioned

Teleguided "Strike" missile ACM 45 A

Guava bomb M 83

40 mm High Explosive Fragmentation Grenade XM 561 576

Steel Pellet High Explosive Shell which is released from a parent cannister and causes antipersonnel effects over an area of 150 square meters

Grenades XM 405, XM 406, 40 mm HEFG M 79, 40 mm HEFG M 26,

Orange bomb OLU 24

Spider bomb

OLU 24/another model with internal and external stria-
tions cut in different directions to insure more "satisfactory" fragmentation

(For the effects of these weapons, see Appendix I.)

CATEGORY 3

Mine M 18. Bottle Bomb BLU P/B MA 18. This high explosive device is designed for use against pill boxes, but can be
used against shelters and their inhabitants as well. In addition
to its directed explosive charge, it also produces splinters.

CATEGORY 4

We were also shown two other types of weaponry whose
use by the U.S. could be construed as a violation of international military usage.

A soft-headed bullet of the "dum-dum" type which was
fired from a 20-mm machine gun. X-rays of injured tissues
were shown to us.

Flechettes: metal arrows, 2–3 inches long. Their use and
form is described in *Military Medicine* by N. M. Rich (January 1968, p. 9). They are also described by J. S. Wood in
Infantry, September-October 1969. We were shown an X-
ray of one of these in the maxillary sinus.

INCENDIARY WEAPONS

The U.S. armed forces have used three main types of incendiary weapons against the people of Vietnam: napalm, white
phosphorus, and thermite. We were also shown cannisters of
these which suggested that they are used in *combination*.

International military usage of *white phosphorus* is that

this substance should be used for making smoke. Phosphorus grenades and shells are fitted with a small detonator which exposes the phosphorus to the air, in which it burns vigorously. In contact with tissue, phosphorus causes deep penetration with necrosis and subsequent hepatic toxicity. One witness from South Vietnam was presented who suffered these consequences. Some reports indicate that U.S. troops use white phosphorus to ignite jungles. Delivery of white phosphorus on targets of different kinds is usually referred to as shelling "Willie Peters." It seems to be quite obvious that those targets in some instances are civilians.

Napalm, "a purely American invention," was compounded by Louis Fieser during World War II. The mixture of substances have since been "improved." Napalm B consists of 50 percent polystyrene mixed with equal quantities of gasoline and benzene (25 percent of each). The function of the polystyrene is to make the mixture adherent so that, once ignited, it may not be easily brushed off. While burning it produces extremely high temperatures and large quantities of carbon monoxide and carbon dioxide. Although it could be argued that napalm may be used against military targets such as tanks or pill boxes, it should be emphasized that modern tanks are designed so as to protect the occupants, and that fixed military installations, of which pill boxes form a part, were little used by guerrilla troops. The principal use of napalm in Indochina is against the civilian population. It is an effective means of driving the population from their shelters. We heard accounts of this during our visit.

The use of napalm against civilians and their homes in South Vietnam is recorded in testimonies published in the Congressional Records of February 11 and March 1, 1971. In one instance, a U.S. soldier was killed, whereupon the village was napalmed. When the troops got in afterwards they found numbers of corpses, among them 30 children. It is also described that the population is driven from shelter and then fired upon from helicopters.

Another case is described where C-130 cargo planes released gasoline over an area, whereupon another aircraft dropped napalm, setting the whole area on fire.

We had the opportunity to examine victims of napalm and were also shown postmortem material from napalm-killed people.

The DRV commission also demonstrated cannisters which they stated contained napalm, thermite, and phosphorus. The amounts of napalm used, according to the Department of Defense, were:

1963.	2,181	tons
1964.	1,777	tons
1965.	17,659	tons
1966.	54,670	tons

By March 1968 it was estimated that the Air Force had used in excess of 100,000 tons of napalm in Vietnam. This figure does not include use by U.S. Navy and Army.

Although we were shown weapons which had been used against the population of the DRV, there is no reason in our opinion to believe that there were any restrictions on the use of similar weapons elsewhere in Indochina. Reports from testimony by returning soldiers of the U.S. Army confirm such a conclusion, as did testimony by witnesses from South Vietnam whom we were able to question.

NOTE ON LEGALITY OF NAPALM USE

The report of the Secretary General of the United Nations on the question of chemical and biological weapons and their effects (chapter I) should be closely studied.[1] In this chapter

1. Report of the Secretary General of the United Nations on Chemical and Bacteriological (Biological) Weapons and the Effects of their Possible Use (1969) A7575, 59292, pp. 90–91.

the basic characteristics are given for weapons to be included in the category of chemical or bacteriological/biological. Apart from the loopholes for the continued use of gas and herbicides in this section, it also contains the following in relation to incendiary weapons:

We also recognize there is a dividing line between chemical agents of warfare in the sense we use the terms, and incendiary substances such as napalm and smoke, which exercise their effects through fire, *temporary* deprivation of air, or reduced visibility. We regard these latter as weapons which are better classified with high explosives. . . . They are therefore not dealt with further in this report (our italics).

The first chapter of this report appears to be written for the purpose of legalizing a number of weapons employed by the U.S. Armed Forces in Indochina. In a report by the organization NARMIC (National Action/Research on the Military Industrial Complex), included in Congressional hearings of November 18–December 19, 1969, the following explanation is given:

It was discovered that the first chapter of the UN report . . . was written by a team headed by Dr. Ivan Bennet, Director of the New York University Medical Center, Research Contract Director of the U.S. Army Chemical Corps and advisor to the Army on epidemiology and pathology. His staff includes three Pentagon officials, and the first draft of Bennet's chapter was written by the Army's CBW experts, according to representative Richard D. McCarthy.[2]

EVALUATION

In a time of war it is difficult to use weapons whose nature

2. "Chemical-Biological Warfare: U.S. Policies and International Effects," Hearings; Subcommittee on National Security Policy and Scientific Development, House of Representatives. November 18–20, December 2, 9, 18, and 19, 1969.

is to cause damage to objects without doing damage to people as well. Colonel Ha Van Lau's team, which was responsible for the presentation of evidence to us, seemed aware of this and, while presenting the entire U.S. war against the people of Vietnam as a war crime, did not specifically present high explosive bombs and shells as evidence of crimes.

Customarily, too, even the aggressor is held innocent until proven guilty. We have, therefore, when assessing whether the use of the weapons cited was criminal or not, always tried to assess whether the weapons were used near a target which might—within the generous limits the Americans have set themselves—be construed as being of military or economic importance. We have applied this method so that where there are no such mitigating circumstances, the importance of our judgment might be so much the clearer.

In these terms the team established to its satisfaction as being beyond reasonable doubt that *weapons have been specifically designed and employed against an innocent civilian population which was not engaged in acts of war against the U.S. or any other country.*

Vietnamization Policy and Pacification Programs

Present U.S. policy in Indochina is referred to as "Vietnamization" by the United States government and other agencies responsible for the formulation and execution of U.S. foreign policy. The political and military leadership of the U.S., for various reasons, claims that this is a new policy, a new formula for United States' relations with countries in Southeast Asia. Implicit in such an interpretation is that the administration of the U.S. is prepared to abandon or modify some of its economic, political, and military interests in this part of the world.

Explicitly, the objectives of the policy have been declared to be:

- reduction of U.S. military presence and commitment in Southeast Asia;
- an end to the war in Indochina;
- unification of the U.S. society-priority given domestic economic, political, and social problems.

We find that both the interpretation of goals and the explicit declared policy neither is found in facts, nor reflects in the realities of Indochina or in the U.S. Thus, in fact, it is misleading for the following reasons:

1. So far the "Vietnamization" program has not contributed to ending the war; rather, the results have been:

- *escalation in intensity* (as measured by amounts of explosives delivered in Indochina and the forced evacuation of civilians);
- *extension* of the war into Cambodia;
- *continued aggression* against the Democratic Republic of Vietnam (as measured by systematic attacks on air defense facilities and explicit threats by the present U.S. administration);
- *intensified aggression* against Laos (as measured by increased delivery of explosives on that area, and the recent large-scale invasion in the southern part of the country).

2. We have seen no indication suggesting that basic U.S. foreign policy objectives in Southeast Asia have changed. "Vietnamization" appears to be a tactical move within the framework of those objectives.

3. The U.S. political and military leadership appears to try to keep options open for continuation of the war and eventual further escalation in the future, the nature of which cannot be predicted at this time.

Why Vietnamization?

To understand the present situation in Indochina and the specific character of the warfare employed by the U.S., we believe it is essential to give some background on the major causes that forced the administration to adopt its present policy.

This policy can be seen as the logical consequence of the failure of the U.S. Armed Forces and their allied troops, with the methods of warfare employed, to attain anything resembling military victory during the 1964–68 period. Further,

the war had a number of consequences that seriously threatened to disrupt U.S. society and affect U.S. economic interests abroad. These can be listed as follows:

1. The *cost* of war was, and is, considerable. As no
measures were taken to cope with economic consequences of these costs in the early years of escalation, the
U.S. economy was, and is, seriously affected.

2. The cost of the war is, in all its essentials, an *outflow*
of dollars not invested so as to give profitable returns.
The U.S. international payments deficit increased. In the
long run this is a threat to the U.S. dollar as reserve
currency in the international monetary system. Such
nonproductive outflow is also contradictory to continued
U.S. finance investment abroad.

3. As U.S. *casualties* increased, large groups within the
U.S. regarded the war at best as meaningless, at worst,
as morally repugnant. Consequently, resistance against
the war, and against the forces that initiated it and kept
it going, mounted. The war also served to illustrate con-
tradictions within the framework of U.S. economic, political, and social structure. This in turn made the busi-
ness-political-military leadership rely increasingly on
totalitarian methods in the attempt to maintain *status
quo ante.*

The explosive political situation within the U.S. and
the long-term economic consequences of a continued
outflow of nonproductive dollars forced those responsible for the formulation and execution of U.S. foreign
policy to introduce the concept of Vietnamization. Economic and political costs of the war were calculated to
decrease in relation to reduced casualties and dollar outflow. The only way of achieving this goal within a reasonable time was the withdrawal of U.S. troops from Vietnam. This policy was explicitly delcared by Nixon in
1969.

Means of warfare

If basic U.S. strategic objectives were to be maintained in this part of the world, a number of conditions had to be met. These requirements can be listed as follows:

1. Support of a government in South Vietnam friendly to and cooperating with the U.S. government in pursuit of these goals.

2. Financial and military aid to that government to enable it to maintain *status quo ante* within the country.

3. This, in turn, calls for the reliance on mercenary troops in fighting the war—the "Asian kill Asian" concept, on U.S. air support, and on the presence of U.S. "advisers."

4. The special character of guerilla warfare in turn called for the elimination of the guerilla forces' material support and of the political intrastructure of the liberation movement.

5. As guerilla warfare is based on covert ond overt support from the rural population, this meant the *forced evacuation* of that population from the countryside to the cities and into fortified villages under strict governmental control.

6. This in turn required reliance on increased firepower, increased terror, and the use of starvation as a weapon in order to secure mass migration of people.

MILITARY AND PARAMILITARY FORCES

The South Vietnamese armed forces had increased from about 500,000 men to one million in January 1971. In addition there are about 1.5 million men in the "civil guards." By mid-1970 it was reported that there were 11,000 men in the South Vietnamese Navy and around 1,200 pilots in the Air Force. The army had been supplied with 200 aircrafts, 700 river patrol boats, 200 tanks, 1,000 armored cars, 600 artillery pieces, 800,000 M-16 rifles, 10,000 machine guns, and 10,000 grenades and mortar launchers.

The invasion of Cambodia, it was explicitly declared, served among other purposes to strengthen the fighting capacity of the ARVN forces, to delay attack on these forces before they had the capacity to defend the Saigon government objectives, and to destroy "sanctuaries" within the territory of Cambodia.

We find this action, and the stated objectives, contrary to ending the war in Indochina.

ESCALATION OF THE AIR WAR

During the 1969–70 period the amount of explosives delivered on South Vietnam was reported at a yearly average of 1,377,000 tons. The U.S. Department of Defense reported an amount of 2.1 million tons for the period early 1969 to August 1970. In addition 2.3 million tons of shells and other explosives were delivered during the same period. Documents from the Provisional Revolutionary Government of South Vietnam report around 1,000 sorties of tactical aircraft per month, and an increase of B-52 attacks from 1,600 to 1,800 per month.

The massive bombing with conventional explosives and the creation of "free fire zones" forced the people from the countryside toward the cities and refugee camps. The same tactics are employed in northern Laos, where the devastating pounding of bombs turned the formerly inhabited areas into "chaotic seas of explosion, fire, ash and devastation."

In mid-May 1971, U.S. officials admitted that B-52s were

used over Laos on a regular basis. The result of the heavy
bombings in Laos is an ever increasing number of refugees.
Reports on the conditions among these refugees in South
Vietnam, Laos, and Cambodia have been presented to the
U.S. Senate.[1]

The French newspaper *Le Monde* reported a total tonnage dropped over northern Laos during the period mid-
October to early December 1970 at 50,000. We have been
fed figures and facts for a long time relating to bomb tonnage, numbers of grenades, etc. The team would like to
emphasize that 50,000 tons of explosives, were it TNT
equivalents, would correspond to *3.5 nuclear devices of the
size dropped on Hiroshima.* We use the figure of 14 kiloton
TNT as equivalent to one Hiroshima-size bomb.

"MOP-UP" OPERATIONS

Since the massacre at Son My, March 16, 1968, became
known to the press and the public in the western world, a
number of similar operations have been reported. It should
be pointed out, we believe, that the Son My case was reported by the NLF within a matter of days after the massacre. This does not mean that all data given by NLF sources
should be taken at face value. But it does mean that such
documentation should be given the most careful consideration.

The United States government and its related agencies
would have us believe that the case of Son My was an isolated
incident, primarily sparked off by a number of individuals. A
study over the years, however, reveals a fairly clear pattern:

First, these operations must be viewed as an integrated

1. "Civilian Casualty and Refugee Problems in South Vietnam," staff report: Foreign Relations Committee, U.S. Senate, May 9, 1968.

part of U.S. tactics as a whole in South Vietnam. The basic aim of the operations seems to be the forced removal of the agrarian population from the countryside.

Second, scientific advisers close to the U.S. government and the U.S. Department of Defense have argued that the "solution in Vietnam" is to remove the material and political base of the guerilla forces. Since this base is the rural population, the only means to achieve this must be the "removal" of this huge number of people into cities or camps under government control. We have no direct proof of any statement that this is a policy adopted by the U.S. government. But *when we observe and measure the end results* and the actual reality in South Vietnam, *there can be no doubt that this policy has indeed been implemented in Indochina*, explicitly expressed or not.

The representatives of the Provisional Revolutionary Government of South Vietnam provided us with a number of documents, among which one dealt exclusively with the "mop-up" operations.

Since Nixon took office, around 40,000 "sweeps" had been performed by forces of battalion size and upward. In the Ben Tre province, only about 6,000 such incidents had occurred. Four thousand were reported killed, 3,500 wounded, 4,000 arrested, and houses had been leveled. The total number of hamlets destroyed in South Vietnam was 3,000, out of which 1,600 were completely demolished.

Reading these documents leaves one with the strong impression that "Son My" massacres are common indeed; that as a general policy cattle are slaughtered; that rice and crops are destroyed; and that the people remaining alive are transferred to refugee camps and strategic hamlets. A minor part of these actions correspond to reports given by U.S. sources and especially to testimonies given by U.S. sources and especially to testimonies given in the recent informal hearings in the U.S. Congress. We had the opportunity to listen to people who had experienced such operations. The tapes of these testimonies and our questions to the witnesses are filed with the commission.

As we did not have the opportunity to visit any places in South Vietnam, we are not in a position to verify all these reports. The close correspondence of the reports we received with what is known from other sources, however, strongly suggests that they are in all their essentials correct.

CONCENTRATION CAMPS

The term concentration camps is used by the Vietnamese sources to describe what the U.S. call "refugee camps" *and* so-called strategic villages—i.e., fortified villages under strict government control, where the inhabitants work outside the village in agricultural occupations.

The information we received concerning the locations of and conditions in these camps seemed to correspond fairly closely to information about conditions given in hearings before the U.S. Senate. We had the opportunity to listen to witnesses who had been living in what we would term "strategic villages." It is quite clear that conditions in these places strip the occupants of all human dignity and deprive them of all democratic rights, that numbers of people are forcibly enlisted into the Saigon armed forces, and that inhabitants are frequently executed.

PRISONS

As the number of people drastically increases in the cities in Indochina, "control" of the population requires an increased police force trained and equipped to suppress protests and actions directed at the Saigon government. The facilities to detain people must also be increased, or the number of prisoners per unit area in those facilities must increase. The U.S. government actively supports the Saigon government in building new facilities and in training and equipping police forces.

At present the number of prisoners in South Vietnam is estimated at a total of about 200,000. Among these are at least one thousand children between 12 and 16 years of age, sentenced to 8–10-year prison terms on October 16, 1970.

The largest prisons in South Vietnam are:

Chi Hoa, Saigon, with 6,–8,000 prisoners;

Thu Duc, Gia Dinh province, with 3,–4,000 prisoners;

Tan Hiep, near Bien Hoa air base, with 3,–4,000 prisoners;

Phu Quoc, Phu Quoc province, with 30,000 prisoners;

Con Doc, Con Son province, with 12,–15,000 prisoners.

We were informed that in one prison a room of 54 square meters contained 150 prisoners. At another prison the same number of people were forced to live in a space of 50 square meters. The symptoms reported among the prisoners in these places include anemia, oedemia, and pulmonary diseases. Torture is reported to be very common. Food and water rations are scarce.

The investigation team got the strong impression that the conditions reported from the Con Son island—the "tiger cages" and torture of prisoners—are not exceptions but appear rather to be a rule. We have, of course, not been able to confirm this.

Effects of "Pacification" Program

Apart from the killing of people and cattle, the destruction of their land and houses, and the atrocities committed against women, children, and elderly persons, the result of pacification is the uprooting of people on a massive scale.

The number of people uprooted from their homes and forced into city slums and camps appears to be around 6 million in South Vietnam only, between 700,000 and 800,000 in Laos, and close to one million in Cambodia. These people are victims of the U.S. Armed Forces' combined efforts—terrorization of civilians, massive bombings, chemical warfare, and, especially, imposed starvation.

When migration occurs on such a massive scale, a number of extremely serious consequences follow, and the social fabric is completely broken down. As this happens, apart from serious psychological effects such as apathy, basic patterns of behavior serving to protect rural populations from disease are also broken down. As people are crowded into cities or camps, where health facilities are inadequate or totally absent and where medically trained personnel is inadequate, disease frequently occurs. The lack of adequate food supply, often bordering on a state of serious starvation, makes the individual even more susceptible to these diseases.

In South Vietnam we have had numerous reports of epidemics of cholera, typhoid, and even plague. We have had reports of plague among children in orphanages and among soldiers returning to the U.S. from Vietnam. The Saigon health authorities, however, do not release any reliable statistics on the health situation.

Another effect of the migration, together with inadequate food intake, is the long-term effect this might have on the children. We know very well that children who do not receive an adequate protein diet during early years suffer from serious damage to the brain. This results in mental retardation and other nutritional damage which cannot be repaired. In this context it must be mentioned that the complete social breakdown may add serious psychological consequences to the organic damage of the brain.

It is our impression that the end result we observed in Indochina is planned and carried out under the "Vietnamization" and "pacification" programs.

Effects of Chemical Warfare in South Vietnam

The United States has embarked upon a tactic never before used in warfare: the concerted destruction of ecosystems— people, plants, trees, animals, the land, the soil, the waters— in particular using antiplant agents that have never before been used for military purposes. Indeed, information is sparse because there is nowhere on earth where the level of application of herbicides and defoliants was comparable to that used in Vietnam. Nowhere on earth have antipersonnel gases been used against civilians to the extent that they have been so employed in Vietnam.

The use of this type of weaponry was outlawed by international agreement. The Hague Gas Declaration (1899) was the first specific prohibition of gases in warfare—banning the use of projectiles with "asphyxiating or deleterious" gases. The United States neither signed nor ratified it, and the treaty did not prevent its signatories from using "cylinders" instead of "projectiles." It is an instructive fact that escalation of gas warfare proceeded once the semantics of the Declaration had been circumvented.[1]

The treaty of Versailles (1919) forbade only the defeated

1. J. Bellin and D. Forman, "Statement of Women Strike for Peace Concerning the Geneva Protocol," Hearings: Committee on Foreign Relations, U.S. Senate, April 1, 1971.

Central Powers to manufacture war gases.

The League of Nations Declaration (1921) condemning the "use in war of asphyxiating, poisonous or *other gases and all analogous liquids and devices*" led the way to the Geneva Protocol of 1925. This protocol was reported favorably out of the U.S. Senate Foreign Relations Committee, but the Senate refused to ratify it. Nonetheless, during the years since the treaty came into force, the United States has insisted she had been an informal party to the treaty and did, in fact, observe its provisions.

Throughout World War II, President Roosevelt refused to allow the use of any chemical or biological weapons, except flame and phosphorus. During the Korean War, the U.S. did not use "riot control" agents or pesticides. It would now seem that the use of these agents in Vietnam by the United States has significantly weakened the internationally accepted, broad interpretation of chemical weapons as defined by the Geneva Protocol.

The United States declaration[2] that there is a distinction between "asphyxiating, poisonous, or other gases" and "harassing agents" should be subjected to scientific scrutiny, as should also the rationalization for the use of herbicides.

The classification of an agent as "lethal" or merely incapacitating is a relative one. A chemical is called incapacitating if the ratio between the incapacitating and lethal dosages is very high. Individuals within the same species vary widely in their sensitivity to *any* chemical. Their reactions are further influenced by general state of health, age, pulmonary status, etc. Maintaining the "ideal" incapacitating dosage under battle conditions is impossible; some individuals are killed and others remain relatively unaffected. The

2. "Chemical and Biological Weapons." Hearings: Committee on Labor and Public Welfare, U.S. Senate, May 1967.

same may be true for civilians in shelters, tunnels, and houses.

When the Geneva Protocol was drawn up, the term "poisonous" still had the simple connotation of immediate lethality; mutagenic, teratological, and carcinogenic action were as yet unsuspected manifestations, to be elicited by branches of sciences as yet unconceived of in 1925. Pesticides had not yet been discovered.

The investigating team tried to gather evidence by the methods cited concerning the use of various chemical agents in Indochina. This included on-site inspections, discussion and evaluation of written reports, and interviews of victims of the warfare.

Herbicides

It is quite clear that the people of South Vietnam and their environment have been seriously affected by the massive use of herbicides. Millions of hectares of cropland and forest have been destroyed—in some areas perhaps permanently. Large numbers of domestic animals have been affected and killed: cattle, water buffalo, pigs; fruits have shown malformations: jackfruit, papaya, banana, custard apple, etc.[3] Professor Pfeiffer, who was able to make on-the-spot investigations in South Vietnam, stated that eight months after aerial spraying of herbicides the custard apple was growing grossly malformed, dessicated, and black. He made similar observations on papaya. It appeared that the herbicidal weapons are ". . . very effective against subsistence farmer populations of the sort that we have in Indochina."

3. E.W. Pfeiffer, "Veterans Testimony on Vietnam," in *Congressional Record*, April 6, 1971.

PRG sources[4] reported that in 1970 alone, intensified spraying was carried out in the South Vietnam plains, including the provinces of Ben Tre, My Tho, Tra Vinh, Bien Hoa, and Cao Mau. These areas were repeatedly sprayed.

On February 13 and 15, 1970, four-hour sprayings were carried out along the Mekong banks. They covered hamlets of four villages in the Cai Lay district and "destroyed over 300 hectares of crops and poisoned many people." In other areas, spraying missions were accomplished by means of helicopter.

Agent "Orange" continues to be used, in spite of the U.S. declaration that this agent would no longer be used in Indochina. An American who worked for three years in Vietnam Christian Service reported seeing barrels of agent "Orange" at Da Nang airport. The duplicity of the U.S. government is revealed when one learns that this is a part of the "Vietnamization" plan. DOW Chemical Company now supplies this material to the South Vietnamese forces. But, due to the fact that the ARVN has no pilots trained to fly the C-123 cargo aircraft, U.S. pilots continue to fly U.S. planes, this time with Vietnamese markings.

A number of preliminary studies have been performed in the U.S.-controlled areas of South Vietnam.[5] The observations in these studies indicate the severe effects of chemical warfare on the ecology of Vietnam, and indicate some of the implications for the future. The observations seem to confirm

4. "Communique on the Employment by U.S. and Puppets of Various Types of Chemical Weapons in South Vietnam in 1970." Document issued by the Provisional Revolutionary Government of South Vietnam.

5. E.H. Orians and E.W. Pfeiffer, "Report," *Science* 168 (1970); E.W. Pfeiffer, "Recent Developments in Indochina and the U.S. Related to the Military Uses of Herbicides," *Etudes Vietnamiennes*, December 12-14, 1970; Meselson et al., Report of the Herbicide Assessment Commission to the annual meeting of the American Association for the Advancement of Science, Chicago, Illinois, December 29, 1970.

the reports given by the PRG and DRV authorities. The effects can be summarized as follows:

EFFECTS OF HERBICIDES ON FORESTS

1. Mangrove forests appear to be especially susceptible. The most optimistic estimates on mangrove forest recovery after agent "Orange" is about 20 years, while other estimates are much longer. Some of the forest is not defoliated, but the trees in the areas appear to be dead. This may have serious consequences on animal and bird life in the area.

2. Effects of defoliation on hardwood forests appear to depend upon the number of sprayings. Recovery appears possible after a *single* spraying, but two or three applications may kill up to 50 percent of the trees. In these areas the invasion of worthless bamboo may pose a problem for future use of the areas. Recovery might take decades.

EFFECTS OF HERBICIDES ON ANIMALS

Under the conditions in South Vietnam this is very difficult to study. Some observations on bird life have been made[6] and it appears clear that defoliated mangrove forests in South Vietnam contain "drastically fewer—if any—birds than are found in such areas elsewhere in the world." Reports from Vietnam indicate that animals have miscarried and that hens have stopped laying eggs.

EFFECTS OF HERBICIDES ON CROPS

The U.S. Army admits spraying about 500,000 acres of cropland in South Vietnam—i.e., 7 percent of the total crop

6. Orians and Pfeiffer, "Report."

area. This figure does not include sprays from helicopters, and it is not clear whether sprays along roads and canals are included in the figure. Further, the area is calculated from the number of flights and may err quite substantially. The chemical used against rice crops is thedimethylform of caco-dylic acid, containing 53 percent arsenic. This may, of course, pose a long-term danger to the population of Vietnam if they are forced to eat food affected by this chemical. Warnings on the cumulative nature of arsenic have been issued. Current U.S. budget plans include an $8 million expense for the purchase of, among other things, 700,000 gallons of this agent.

Agent "Blue" has been extensively applied in the highland region, the "rice bowl" of the NLF. Reports of use in the Mekong Delta area have been forwarded. It is not clear whether this is agent "Blue" or agent "Orange." Data given by the PRG indicate "Orange" used against rice, banana, and papaya.[7]

In order to clarify the areas given by the PRG of South Vietnam in relation to the areas given by the U.S. Air Force (Appendix II), we supplied a number of questions referring to reports as given in Paris December 12–14, 1970 and in documents received in Hanoi.[8] The questions and answers appear below:

1. On December 12, 1970, preliminary data for spraying was given at 1,086,000 hectares for 1969 and 415,000 hectares for the first nine months of 1970. In the report of January 1971, the data for these two years is given at 1,836,950 hectares "rice fields, crops, orchards, and forests" sprayed. Is there any breakdown of this figure for crops and forest? Can this be broken up into province and district?

7. Nguyen Khac Vien, ed., *Chemical Warfare: Documents of the International Committee of Scientists on U.S. Warfare in Vietnam* (Paris: Orsay, 1971).
8. *New York Times*, March 15, 1970.

Answer: The data on damage caused by U.S. chemical sprays in South Vietnam are given by responsible services in the provinces. The Committee . . . sums them up and issues them at intervals of three months, six months, or a year. Under wartime circumstances, split data or more detailed statistics are yet not available. However, public figures are usually lower than actual damage because several districts or villages in the same province fail to report in time. Yet, some more detailed breakdown can be provided. For instance: in 1969, an estimated *1,034,300* hectares of forests and 51,700 hectares of rice fields, crops and orchards were destroyed by toxic chemicals.

For the first nine months of 1969:

Province	Crops and forest destroyed (hectares)	People poisoned
Quang Tri, Thua Thien	15,000	5,000
Quang Nam, Quang Ngai, Binh Dinh, Phu Yen, Khan Hoa, Gia Lai, etc.	100,000	30,000
My Tho, Ben Tre, An Giang, Tra Vinh, Chau Doc, Kien Phong, Vinh Mong, Rach Gia, Ca Mau, Long An, Tay Ninh, Bien Hoa, Ba Ria, Co Cong, Kien Tuong, Bac Lieu	300,000	150,000

Ordinarily in the delta provinces, along communication lines, rivers, and canals, only rice fields and croplands are found. That is the objective of U.S. chemical warfare.

2. The U.S. speaks of a 65 percent kill ratio as expected from herbicide use on crops. Can you give an idea of how much of an area is completely destroyed before it is counted

as destroyed in the statistics? That is: how is the collection of data standardized?

Answer: A week or so after sprays in forests, leaves whither and fall. After repeated sprays, plants perish. In sprayed cropland, vegetation dies within three to seven days.

The standardization of data collecting is usually based upon the sprayed area and the degree of damage inflicted upon forests, rice fields, orchards, and crops.

3. Are there any figures on repeated sprayings in South Vietnam?

Answer: Specific figures on repeatedly sprayed areas in South Vietnam are not yet available.

Other questions relating to soil samples from areas sprayed and further details on means of delivery could not be answered in every case. In some cases, however, we received very detailed information about the technique used by U.S. aircrafts on spray missions along rivers. During talks and reading of reports, the team got the impression that quite a substantial number of spray missions are performed from helicopter or by hand. We are not in a position to give any figures on this, however.

The study established that the first symptoms—irritation of the eyes and nose—appeared within 24 hours to a few days. After this there appeared to be some disturbance in the digestive tract—i.e., vomiting and diarrhea. A direct "hit" may result in irritation of the skin.

Later symptoms seem to include general weakness and ocular complications, as measured by reading tests. Of the 19 adult women being treated in Hanoi, four were pregnant. These women had been in defoliated areas through the sixth to eighth weeks of pregnancy. Of the children born, there were three abnormal births and one normal one. The women testified that there had previously been no abnormalities in their families. Lymphocytes from the mothers and children were cultured and observed for chromosome damage. The report concluded:

1. The above mentioned congenital anomalities result through chromosomal damage in the first steps of the development of the embryo.

2. Defoliants (like 2,4,5-T or dioxine) are inducers of both chromosomal aberrations and congenital abnormalities, and these facts are widely supported by experimental results as well as by our clinical observations.

3. The massive and prolonged use of defoliants apart from permanent ocular lesion can bring about chromosomal damage in an entire population sticking to its ancestral soil.

4. These aberrations may cause congenital malformations, the importance of which remains to be specified. . . .

In our meeting with Professor Tung we received additional information on women from sprayed provinces in South Vietnam under treatment for one reason or another in the hospitals of Hanoi. These figures are reproduced in Appendix III. We were also provided with some statistics on birth of children with pure cleft palate and cleft palate with cleft lip.

Reports from South Vietnam, the results in Hanoi, the studies performed at the Bionetics Laboratory and later at the Food and Drug Administration in the U.S., the finding of the AAAS team (headed by Meselson in the Tai Ninh province) on numbers of miscarriages, and finally the findings in Hanoi all indicate that there might be a relation ship between herbicide use and effects on as-yet-unborn children.

The team realizes that the number of patients is limited and that direct—or indirect—relationships between causative agents and observed effects are extremely difficult to establish especially in human populations, even within the framework of larger experimental programs or observations. We further recognize the lack of adequate background statistics, the effects of starvation, stress, disease, and other factors in a war-torn country on pregnant women.

The gravity of the biological consequence of the combined massive use of chemical agents make it of the utmost importance that serious consideration is paid to the problems arising. It should also be noted that the number of miscarriages reported may well conceal malformations, since *if* such malformations occurred they would probably not show in the statistics. This appears to coincide with reports on miscarriages among domestic animals in South Vietnam.

Further, as among starving people, mental retardation is common among children raised on an inadequate diet. This could well be the case in South Vietnam. The results of such effects, however, cannot be observed today unless they are of extreme character. In this area we have almost no knowledge whatsoever.

The team further wants to emphasize that what we measure and observe on children in Vietnam are *the most obvious end effects there are.* We have no methods measuring damage to the central nervous system or the brain unless that damage is so severe so as to completely transform the child.

Gas Warfare

Gas warfare has been used continuously in Vietnam since 1964. For the years 1964–69 a total amount of 13,736,000 pounds of CS, CS-1, and CS-2 has been used.[12] The following table is given by Kahn:[13]

12. F. Kahn, "Employment of Gas by the U.S. in Vietnam," *New York Times*, March 15, 1970.
13. Ibid.

Amount of CS gas used by U.S. forces in Vietnam
(in thousands lbs)

Fiscal year	1964	1965	1966	1967	1968	1969	Total
CS	225	93	378	437	714	2,018	
CS-1	142	160	1,217	770	3,249	160	
CS-2	0	0	0	0	288	3,885	
	367	253	1,595	1,207	4,251	6,063	13,736

The use of these agents, and the implication for future use indicated by U.S. government efforts to exclude these agents from international agreements on prohibition of chemical warfare, make it important to focus attention on this use.

Therefore, the team attempted to get first hand information regarding their use and the effects on the civilian population, and, if possible, to make distinctions between these agents and herbicides. The DRV Committee did not report on any *direct* use against the people of the DRV. Some drift seemed to have occurred across the DMZ into DRV territory. All the information we could get, however, indicated the spray of herbicides and not gas in these cases.

On August 23, 1970, sprays occurred in the northern parts of the DMZ. The DRV commission reported that although "human contaminants were rather unimportant, crop damage was heavy." They further stated that five villages in the northern part of the DMZ, covering some 160 square kilometers of populated areas, fields and orchards, were sprayed. The aircraft operated south of the Ben Hai river. Reports on crops damaged revealed that corn was broken at the stalk, rice leaves shriveled and dried up, etc. This indicates the use of herbicides and not gas.

Other reports said that "toxic shells" were fired across the DMZ into the Vinh Linh area. The wind brought the chemicals north into populated areas, "slightly affecting people, domestic animals and crops." The nature of the chemical was not specified.

From reports supplied by the PRG of South Vietnam, we got the impression that CS gas is used in very large quantities, released in barrels over populated areas. In some cases they report on a very long-lasting effect, indicating silicone-treated CS.[14]

During our stay we had the opportunity to see films and pictures on chemical warfare and its effects. From previous reports we know that the gas employed by the U.S. forces in Vietnam is a far cry from what we used to term "tear gas" in the past.[15] In one of the pictures shown, we could observe a gassed shelter being emptied of its inhabitants. Several small children were taken out and thrown aside—these children were clearly dead.

Summary

We conclude that the U.S. is engaged in chemical warfare in Indochina. It should be stressed that herbicide sprays of crops are usually performed during seasons of harvest. There can be no doubt, in our opinion, that this aims at using starvation as a weapon against an agrarian population. In addition, the gas is used on a vast scale. Further details on this can be obtained from the U.S. Army training circular on gas warfare in Indochina.[16]

The gases used are assuredly deadly weapons, and the use of more than 7,000 tons by the U.S. forces since 1965 has no

14. Provisional Revolutionary Government of South Vietnam, "Communique on the U.S. Puppets' Crimes in South Vietnam in the First Nine Months of 1970" (filed with the Commission).

15. J.B. Neilands, "Vietnam: Progress of the Chemical War," *Asian Survey*, March 1970; Hearings: Subcommittee on National Security Policy and Scientific Development of the Committee on Foreign Affairs, U.S. House of Representatives, November 18, November 20, December 2, 9, 18, and 19, 1969.

16. Department of the Army, Training Circular TC 3-16. Washington, D.C., April 9, 1969.

parallel since the use of Sarin and Tabun by the Nazis in World War II.

The U.S. has delivered more than six pounds of herbicides per man, woman, and child in South Vietnam. From laboratory experiments we know some of the effects of these chemicals on experimental pregnant animals. The doses used in Vietnam, the danger that the preparations used are contaminated with dioxines—on which we have some indications[17]—and the calculated doses a pregnant woman may get if living in a sprayed area, give cause indeed for alarm. The indications so far received from investigations in Hanoi make the matter even more serious.

The team urges the Commission strongly to emphasize this aspect of the U.S. war in Indochina. We are of the opinion that the use of herbicides in warfare and on this scale may seriously affect the Vietnamese people, their environment, and the society as a cultural unit for decades to come.

Appendix I

On May 17 we met the Commission of Inquiry into U.S. War Crimes in Indochina.

The Investigating team was shown a number of morbid anatomical specimens of Vietnamese who had been subjected to attacks with weapons which produced splinters of pellets, and victims of incendiary weapons. We were also shown specimens illustrating the toxic effects of phosphorus. These were of three kinds: macroscopic, microscopic, and photomicroscopic.

1. Macroscopic: these comprised specimens of brain, spinal cord, stomach, lungs, kidneys, and bone.

Brain: three specimens were shown. The first of these, we

17. Pfeiffer, "Recent Developments."

were told, was a small boy's brain. The passage of fragments through the substance of the brain could be seen. The second specimen was that of a woman, we were told, who had survived about six months after being wounded with metallic splinters. There was a large cortical area (5 × 3 cm., depth undetermined) of necrosis. The last specimen showed a large cyst in the substance of the cerebral hemisphere.

Spine: one specimen was shown. This showed complete transection of the cord just above the enlargment of the cord above the cauda equina. The meninges were torn and the fragment had lodged in the disc space.

Stomach: one specimen was shown. This showed a penetrated ulcer.

Lung: one specimen was shown, which showed bronchopneumonia and emboli.

Kidney: one specimen was shown, which showed a tear through the upper pole.

Bone: two specimens were shown. One showed osteoporosis and the other necrosis.

Skin: areas of burnt skin with necrotic muscle and bone were shown.

2. Photomicroscopic: We were shown photographs of Curling's Ulcer, keloids, hepatic degeneration, renal tubular necrosis, osteoprorsis and osteomyelitis, suprarenal cortical necrosis, pneumonia, and pulmonary emboli.

The original microscopic slides were available to us.

Testimonies and questions with victims presented on May 17 and 18, 1971, Hanoi:

Bui Van Vat, male, age 20, was presented to us. He related that he was working in the fields of Dien An village, Dien Ban district in Quang Da province, not far from the U.S. base at Da Nang. On March 19, 1970, aircraft dropped bombs producing smoke. He was burned all over the body. He screamed for help and was taken by villagers to the hospital near Da Nang. On the way there the villagers were ambushed by GIs and shot. Then the soldiers came over and cut them with their swords. Vat pretended to be dead, even when a soldier cut him on the back and the front of his neck. He was left for dead. He was then discovered by local villagers, taken to a hospital in the liberated zone and later to a hospital in Hanoi. He also stated that the villagers told him that smoke came out of his wounds and that they glowed at night.

Q. What was the "sword" used by the GIs?

A. This was his bayonet.

Q. Was his neck stabbed or cut?

A. It was cut.

Q Did the Americans speak to him or ask any question?

A. I did not understand them.

Q. Did he know of any reason (military) for using phosphorus bombs in his district?

A. There had been no attacks in the U.S. and puppet-controlled area.

Q. What kind of field was he working in?

A. A rice field.

Q. Rice paddy?

A. Yes.

The patient was then asked a number of questions about his illness. He reported that his skin was yellowish (according to the villagers) and that wet bandages were used to treat his burns.

Q. How was the phosphorus delivered?

A. I do not know what kind of aircraft.

Q. Was there any explosion?

A. Many, they were not big.

Cao Thi Ngoc, female, age 44, was walking at ten o'clock in the morning of April 14, 1967, with her child in her arms in the streets of Tanh Hoa in DRV. There was an air raid and she took shelter in an air raid shelter. A napalm bomb fell by the entrance of the shelter and the heat became so intense that she had to abandon the shelter. She was burnt on her feet and her hands caught fire as she tried to remove the burning napalm. She fainted and was taken to hospital. In the hospital she was told that her mother, her uncle, her aunt, and her nephew had been killed in the shelter. From the hospital in Tanh Hoa she was taken to a hospital in Hanoi. She has undergone eight operations and is still under treatment.

X-rays were shown of her feet and hands. They showed R wrist flexion and gross bilateral metacarpo-phanangeal extension and phalangeal flexion.

The joints were subluxed. On the feet there is moderate metatarso-phalangeal extension. Keloids are present on the feet.

Q. Was she at work at the time of the bombing?

A. I was at home.

Her child, who was left at the entrance of the shelter, was dead. She has four other children. She worked in a tannery before to support them. Now she is unable to work.

Vu Thi Chi, female, age 33, related that she is a member of Van Phu cooperative in the Ha Tay province 11 kilometers from Hanoi. On May 22, 1967, there was an air attack on the cooperative in which her cousin was killed. At 8:00 on the morning of December 27, 1967, she was hoeing the fields. Her hoe struck a steel pellet bomb and she fainted. She was told that the members of her cooperative took her to the emergency station where she was given treatment and then she was taken to Hanoi. She recovered consciousness four days later. She had lost her left leg and she was told that 80 cm of her intestines had been removed. There were 11 holes in her abdomen. Her right foot was swollen, and she was told that if she wanted to live some of it had to be removed.

The physician who had treated her reported that she had been shocked and exsanguinated on admission to the hospital. The left leg had been badly wounded and had to be amputated. Because of the 11 abdominal wounds, a laparotomy was necessary which showed serious lesions of the small intestine. The distal half of the right foot had been shattered and required amputation.

Dr. Nguyen Bac, Staff Member, Hanoi Municipal Council. Between June 1966 and March 1968 the U.S. flew 90 air strikes against Hanoi. They used demolition bombs, fragmentation bombs, CBUs and missiles. Total number of casualties was 1,235. Twenty-one medical establishments were damaged, nine of them hospitals.

Q. Were the roofs of the medical establishments marked with a red cross which could be seen from the air?

A. We do not mark the roofs of our hospitals. They have a red cross on the gate and sometimes they fly the red cross flag.

Q. How big is the flag?

A. Not very big, about this size. (He demonstrates about a meter.)

Q. How many were killed or wounded in medical establishments?

A. I will give some examples. In Dong Anh hospital a nurse was wounded, carrying a patient into the shelter, with a steel pellet from a CBU. That took place on April 25, 1967. One doctor was killed in the hospital Hoan Kiem in Hanoi on August 21, 1967. The X-ray department of the hospital of Thanh Tri was destroyed. This attack was no accident; they attacked the hospital twice—on December 2nd and 14th of 1966.

Dr. Phuc, a surgeon in Hanoi, related that he was operating on patients wounded during the attacks on Hanoi. He presented case notes. These consisted of a synopsis of the circumstances under which the injuries had occurred, a brief description of the injuries, surgical findings, photographs, and radiographs of the patients and fragments or pellets, if there were any. He presented a child's PA and lateral chest X-rays which showed a fragment lodged in D4. He said the girl, eight years old, had been paralyzed since her injury.

He presented the case notes of a school boy, age 11, wounded on April 25, 1967. A photograph showed pellet punctures. The surgical findings included tears of the jejenum and duodenum.

He presented a teacher, Vu Thi Hao, female, age 23. She was wounded on May 20, 1967. There were X-rays of a fractured left tibia and fibula and of shrapnel and pellets in her right leg. The sciatic nerve was severed in that leg and resutured. There was paralysis and a small area of hypoaesthesia. Photographs of the patient taken at the time showed multiple puncture wounds.

Q. What were you doing when you were wounded?

A. I was preparing classes in the classroom.

Q. Do you have any difficulty walking now?

A. I can walk well, but when I hear a bang I feel pain in my right leg.

Q. I notice you have difficulty standing up?

A. I can walk and stand well, but when there is a change in the weather I feel pain in the wounded leg.

Q. Which leg is that?

A. The right.

Q. Are you teaching again?

A. Yes.

Nguyen Thi Dang, female, age 18 when wounded.

Q. What were you doing when you were wounded?

A. My family and I were preparing to rest. When we heard the warning that the planes were about 20 kilometers away, we went down to the shelter. I was in front of the shelter when I was wounded.

Q. Where were you wounded?

A. In the belly. I was seven months pregnant at the time.

Q. Are you well now?

A. Yes. But I feel pain in my wounds when the weather changes.

Q. Have you had any children since?

A. Yes, a daughter.

We were shown an uncut film of Hanoi during the air raids. In this film there is a shot from the Thanh Tri Hospital, showing destroyed laboratories. There is also a shot of Dong Anh Hospital showing a destroyed ward. Other shots in the film showed a dead mother and a child, a female, a dead baby, and a wounded boy.

At the Tien exhibition we observed a photograph of the leprasarium at Quynh. On questioning we were told that there were no other buildings nearby. Bomb damage can be seen. There is also a photograph of the Nam Dinh maternity hospital, showing damage.

Appendix II: Effects of Herbicide Usage: South Vietnam 1961–1969

Sources	Total South Vietnam land area /km²/	Total: "Destroyed" "Sprayed" /km²/	Forest Total	Forest "Destroyed" "Sprayed"	Crops Total	Crops "Destroyed" "Sprayed"
US area	172,540	22,336	14×10^6 acres	$4{,}98 \times 10^6$ acres	$7{,}6 \times 10^6$ acres	$0{,}532 \times 10^6$ acres
% (totals)		12	–	13	–	7
Vietnamese area	170,000	38,000	56,000 km²	25,000 km²	30,000 km²	13,000 km²
% (totals)		23	–	44	–	43

/Compiled by M Leitenberg, SIPRI Stockholm, December 1970/

Vietnamese sources give their figures as "Destroyed" and are based on ground observations and compilations of data. US sources give areas as "sprayed" and are based on number of flights and calculations from those.

Chemical Composition, Rates of Applications and Use of Military Herbicides

AGENT	COMPOSITION %	CONCENTRATION /lb/gallon AE/	APPLICATION /lb/acre/		USE
			Vietnam	US	
Orange	n-Buthyl 2,4-D 50	4,2	27	2	Defoliation of forest, brush and broadleaved crop
	n-Buthyl 2,4,5-T 50	3,7			
White	Triisopropanolamine salt, 2,4-D	2.0	6	0	Forest defoliation where long-term control desired
	Triisopropanolamine salt, picloram	0,54			
Blue	Sodium Cacodylate 27,7	3,1	9,3	5-7,5	Rapid defoliation. For grass control, use of rice
	Free acid 4,8				

/ Adapted from U.S. Department of Defense sources. E. H. Orians and E. W. Pfeiffer, *Science*, May 1, 1970. One lb. per gallon AE equals 114 grams per liter. 1 lb per acre = 1.12 kilogram per hectare.

Appendix III

On May 22, 1971, we met with Professor Tung That Tien at the Hanoi University School of Postgraduate Surgery at the Viet-Duc Hospital in Hanoi. We also met Dr. Bach Quoc Tuyen, head of Department of Hematology and Genetics at the Bach Mai Hospital in Hanoi. The latter is the department where leucocytes from women and newborn children from sprayed provinces are cultured and analyzed for chromosomal alterations.

During our talk we discussed at length the preliminary results presented in Paris, December 12–14, 1970, on malformed children and chromosome alterations in children and mothers. We were not able to get any prewar statistics on this. Professor Tung, however, presented the following data on women who had lived in heavily sprayed provinces in South Vietnam and were now under treatment for some reason or another in the hospital in Hanoi:

DATA ON PREGNANCIES AMONG 112 WOMEN IN SPRAYED AREAS
AND ON THE SAME WOMEN AFTER LEAVING THESE AREAS

	During stay in sprayed areas	Some women before and after living in sprayed areas
Number of pregnancies	80	95
Abortion before 3 months of pregnancy	6	6
Miscarriages	12	3
Twin births	3	1
Visible malformations	8	3
	29	13

Most of the women had lived in the provinces of Quang Tri, Thua Thien, and Quang Nan in South Vietnam. The table is based on interviews with the women on their experienced pregnancies and child births. A more detailed breakdown of these figures could not be provided at the time, and they are to be considered preliminary. Further details on the question might be forthcoming. Professor Tung promised us statistics on operations performed on pure cleft palate in Hanoi. This we received on May 27, 1971.

STATISTICS ON FISSURES PALATINES

1942 a/ : No cases of pure cleft palate and one case of cleft palate with cleft lip out of 1,440 patients operated upon.
1949 a/ : One case of cleft palate with cleft lip and nine cases of cleft lip only out of 840 patients.
1968 b/ : *one case of pure cleft palate* and six cases of cleft palate with cleft lip *out of 2,491 newborn babies.*
1968 c/ : 18 cases of pure cleft palate and 30 cases of cleft palate with cleft out of 443 patients operated upon.
1969 b/ : *No case of pure cleft palate* and three cases of cleft palate with cleft lip *out of 3,091 newborn babies.*
1969 c/ : 25 cases of pure cleft palate and 26 cases of cleft palate with cleft lip out of 410 patients operated upon.
1970 c/ : 57 cases of pure cleft palate and 46 cases of cleft palate with cleft lip out of 410 patients operated upon.
a = Department of surgery at the Viet-Duc Hospital in Hanoi.
b = l'Institut de Protecrion de la Mere et des nouveaux-nes, Hanoi.
c = Section of Ondonto-Stomatologie, Viet-Duc Hospital, Hanoi.

The Victims

For four days Indochinese victims and former American practitioners of war crimes testified before the Commission in Oslo. To the Indochinese witnesses, nearly all of whom had suffered wounds which will follow them for the rest of their lives, the testimony was a terribly painful experience; for it meant recounting stark detail the mutilation and destruction of their closest friends, their families, and their own bodies. Yet in their pain they were eager to pen their lives to world scrutiny in the hope that that would help bring an end to the suffering inflicted upon them every day by the war. Taken as cold transcripts, the testimonies lack much of the tone, expression, and emotion with which they were delivered, feeling which can only be suggested if the reader keeps in mind that it was a constant—and not always successful—effort to hold back the tears that underscored their words.

Nor was it at all easy for the six American veterans at the Commission to recount the tortures, massacres, and wholesale destruction in which they had all all taken part. Before they went to Indochina, none of the veterans had worked in the American antiwar movement, and most of them have only begun to speak out in the last year and a half. It is in that sense that their testimony, and the civilian work they have done since leaving the military, emanate directly from personal acts for which they feel, in the words of one veteran, "nightmarish" guilt. Thus they, too, have become victims.

Mrs. Sida

[Mrs. Sida is a middle-aged Laotian woman who watched American soldiers kill her husband and her children in the summer of 1969.]

It is a great honor for me to be able to come before this tribunal to denounce the American imperialist crimes perpetrated against my family and my village.

Since 1964 U.S. imperialism has used several types of bombers, day and night, on the neighborhoods surrounding my village, causing a great many deaths and injuries among the population, especially affecting old people, children, women, destroying and burning houses and pagodas, killing cattle and buffalos.

On January 25, 1969, many U.S. airplanes came to bomb my village, burning and razing to the ground the houses of 40 village families, killing a great number of cattle and buffalo. That is why the people of the village had decided to remove themselves to the forest in order to be safe. After having evacuated to the forest, the U.S. planes came again to bomb continuously the neighborhoods of our evacuated village. In the evacuated village I was with my family which numbered ten people: my husband's father, my husband's sister and her child, my five children, all very young, and myself.

On March 26, 1969, toward noon, that day there were nine people at home, one of my children being at school; since we heard the roar of a large number of airplanes, we ran towards a little shelter located about 10 meters from the house. The bombs exploded around our shelter causing some terrible shaking, earthslides were falling from above, and we saw some flashes passing through our shelter like we were in a storm. We thought that if we stayed in the little shelter we would not be safe and that is why we decided to move to a large shelter 20 meters away. The noise of the planes had become quiet, each of us took with himself the smallest children and we ran toward the large shelter: we had nearly reached it when the planes swept back and dropped bombs near us, killing my husband's sister on the spot and wounding the child whom she carried. My husband, running behind his sister, was hit in the chest and fell. The child my husband was carrying was severely wounded. In running behind my husband I was hit in the right thigh, in the left arm, and I had a fractured tibia, without counting many other places on my body. I fell down right there. The child I was carrying had just been hit as well and had his foot pierced through. My two other children who were running behind me were not hit. My husband's father who ran behind me was seriously hit and could no longer move himself. The noise of the bombs had subsided and my husband, with great effort, raised himself up and carried the child toward the large shelter. Not seeing me join him at the shelter, he went out to call me, but I could not move because I had a fractured tibia. My husband returned to carry my child and myself toward the shelter, but as he was also wounded he could not carry us all; he put me on the ground and taking the child that I was carrying and my dead sister's child, carried them to the large shelter. After he returned to carry me to the shelter, I was still losing blood and my husband did not have the time to give me any care for he had to go help his father. He only had time to shout to the village nurse who was near enough to come and help us, for I was still bleeding. An hour later my husband's father died from his wounds.

The noise from the planes was a little quieter, the people

and the parents had come to see us. One part of the population had helped our family to go into the hospital, another
part stayed to bury my husband's father and sister. We went
into the district hospital. My husband and one of my
wounded children stayed at the hospital for three days. He
had asked for some medicine to continue the care at home
and asked permission to go home and take care of the remaining children. I stayed at the hospital with another seriously wounded child. In spite of a great deal of care by the
hospital, ten days later my child died from his wounds. This
atrocious death of my child caused me very much pain, but
I had to stay to be cared for at the hospital. I stayed at the
hospital for seven months and toward the end of August 1969
I could walk with difficulty; my leg was not completely
healed, but as I was thinking very much about my husband
and my children and I had much concern for them, I asked
permission to leave the hospital and return to live near them.
Toward the end of the month of September the U.S. imperialists and the commando pirates of Vang Pao had attacked
and ravaged savagely our temporary commune. That is why
the people of the commune had decided to evacuate toward
a safer place. Our family, myself, my husband, and my four
children and my husband's mother—we had also left with
the others. I had a bad leg; I could not walk fast, and I could
take nothing with me. I walked slowly behind with the old
people. My husband, with his mother, walked in front with
the children carrying the supplies. At each stop my husband,
having set down the children and the supplies, after having
told the children to wait for him, came back to help me catch
up with them. Halfway there—I walked always behind with
the old people and the sick people—I heard gunshot, shrieks
and cries, and I saw many people fall in front of me. Seeing
myself in such a situation I looked for refuge on the river-

bank, hiding myself in the bushes and behind a rock, and I saw from my refuge the pirate soldiers of Vang Pao and the Americans who had rounded up the people in one place. I had seen one of the soldiers snatch a small child from the hands of his mother: the mother ran forward to grab the child, but the soldier ran her through with his bayonet. The soldier knocked the child against a tree; myself, I hid all the way through in my refuge behind the brush and the rock. I looked for my husband; I saw only one of my children near my husband. As to my husband's mother and my three children I could no longer see them near my husband. I saw the soldiers grab my child from the hands of his father, my husband jumped to take the child back, but the soldiers shot my husband and the boy. (Here Mrs. Sida had to stop for a moment, for she was crying too much to continue.) After seeing so many atrocities I passed out and was reawakened only by the noise of the bombs. I couldn't see anyone any more; I heard only the noise of the planes which were bombing those who were hidden in the forest. Before nightfall when the planes had gone, I went back onto the road to return to a safe place with the others who were dispersed and whom I met. On arrival, we knew that 40 people from our commune were missing, including my four children, my husband and his mother. Now I was a widow, without children, having lost all my children.

Thanks to the just and correct line of the Patriotic Laotian Front I was able to survive and come to this conference. Thanks to the just and correct line of the Patriotic Laotian Front, I could survive up to this day: I can no longer do the heavy work, I stay at the house to cook and watch my sister's child, since my sister goes to work in the rice paddy. My sister and her husband must now take care of all those who remain from the family. I also have a letter from the people of the village: thank you for your attention.

Nguyen Van Vinh

[Nguyen Van Vinh, 13, from the DRVN tells of how he was wounded after picking up a fragmentation bomb which exploded.]

Commission: Please tell us your name once again.

Nguyen van Vinh.

And your age?

Thirteen years old.

And you are going to school?

Yes, I am going to school.

In which class?

The fifth class.

And where is the place where you are living?

My family is living in Ha Tay Province, North Vietnam.

How big is the family?

My parents are still alive.

Have you any sisters or brothers?

I have four brothers and one sister.

We understand that you are a victim of fragmentation bombs. Can you tell me about what happened to you and when. Please tell us when it happened first.

I live in Hoa Thach village, Quoc Quai district, Ha Tay province. My hamlet is a small one. During the war of destruction, American aircraft repeatedly came to bomb our village and every time they came they dropped steel pellet bombs. I still remember once, on the 26th of December, 1966, American aircraft dropped many steel pellet bombs. As a result of this bombing, four people in my village were killed, and five others wounded.

On the 12th of February, 1970, at eight o'clock in the

morning, I was going to the school, and I saw one steel pellet bomb lying on the edge of the road. I thought that it was an exploded bomb. I picked it up and then threw it away. But then I heard an explosion, and I fell down, and I lost consciousness. I was shifted to the emergency station and then to the hospital, and I was hospitalized for 21 days, then I was treated at home. During my stay in the hospital, I am told by our aunts and uncles working in the hospital that there were steel pellets in my body and many other splinters. After I was treated in the hospital some of the steel pellets had been removed, but now there are still a number of steel pellets and small splinters which cannot be removed. It makes me painful.

Thank you dear aunts and uncles for your attention.

Phan Thi Thiem

[Miss Phan Thi Thiem, 22, from the DRVN tells of four steel pellets still imbedded in her body.]

My name is *Phan Thi Thiem.* I was a saleswoman in a state's shop. I live in Nghe An Province. I am 22 years old. I used to sell goods in Bang Ba village, Ky Son district, Nghe An Province. At 1 P.M. on March 28, 1970, myself and four of my friends were preparing goods for selling to the people. . . .

As soon as we heard the alarm the five of us ran to the air-raid shelter. We heard the planes roaring over our heads and then the bombs explode. The earth on our cover collapsed. Five of us lay down in the cover, but one bomb fell at the gate of our shelter. As a result of this, Mrs. Vu was seriously wounded and Mrs. Diem died immediately.

Another bomb exploded over the cover of the shelter. As I told you, the earth on the cover had collapsed. This made a hole in the shelter, and the bomb exploded. The result of this explosion was that myself and Miss Duc were wounded. Miss Mi suffered from the pressure of the bomb, and Miss Duc had pellets buffeting into her cheeks and shoulders. I myself lost consciousness. . . . There was much heat around the air-raid shelter . . . [which] made me and Miss Mi regain consciousness. I found the four of us wet with blood, and when Miss Mi saw this too, she again lost consciousness.

I was wounded but, as I was stronger than the other friends, I made every effort to crawl over the others and to get out of the shelter so as to look for rescue. When I got out of the shelter I had to run through the shop which was then in flames as a result of the bombs. My blood was flowing out very quickly so I again lost consciousness. When I came to, I still heard the aircraft roaring over our heads and the steel pellet bombs exploding. I could not walk anymore, but I cried for somebody to come to our rescue. My colleagues came to take me to the emergency station, and then I was shifted to the district hospital. Three hours later Miss Vu died.

Myself and two of my friends, Miss Mi and Miss Duc, were treated in the hospital. Three months later we were released from treatment. . . . I was, after that, shifted to the sanitarium, and from there to the Hanoi hospital on the 29th of August, 1970.

All medical workers and doctors have done their best to treat me, but they were unable to remove the steel pellets from my body because these steel pellets lie in very dangerous places in my body. There are now still four steel pellets in my body. One is in my neck. It often causes me to suffer a headache because it has paralyzed the nerve. I have one pellet in my left arm which causes me great pain when there is a change of weather. There is one other pellet in my right arm. It makes the arm from the shoulder to the hand invalid.

Often I feel as if bitten by ants. Even a draft of air can cause me much pain, and I feel particular difficulty when I have to do my washing. Another, fourth pellet, lies in my left buttock, penetrating nearly into my backbone. This makes it difficult for me to move my back. I cannot do labor.

I am a young girl. That is why I like to do sewing work, knitting work, but this I cannot do now because my right arm was hit by steel pellets. Now I have to ask somebody to do it for me. Even to write a letter or to sign something: I cannot do it with my right arm. I have to learn how to write with my left hand.

Before the time when I was wounded I weighed 56 kilos. I could carry as much as 70 kilograms. At present I cannot even carry ten kilograms.

Dang Kim Phung

[Miss Dang Kim Phung, a South Vietnamese woman from Gia Dinh province, related how she has been three times wounded: by a U.S. artillery shell, by toxic chemical poisoning, and most severely by napalm. Once a strong young woman, she is now a permanent invalid.]

The American GIs and the puppet troops are very savage. They have massacred the members of my family and tortured me. Two of my uncles were killed. One was shot dead, and one was decapitated. This was done by the U.S. and the puppet troops and his body was thrown into a well. One of my aunts was killed by a shell splinter. One of my little brothers was killed by toxic chemicals, I myself was three times the victim of U.S. atrocities. Once I was wounded by U.S. artillery, and the splinter is still in my leg. One time I was contaminated, poisoned, by toxic chemicals. Now the effects of these chemicals are being felt by me. My side is now blood, and my side power is only three-tenths, and my digestion is abnormal. The third time I was the victim of a napalm bomb.

I still remember the day I was poisoned by toxic chemicals. It was the 24th of June, 1968. It was at 8 A.M. A reconaissance plane whirled over and over my region. It fired a rocket. My friends and I immediately took refuge in an underground shelter. Then three low-flying helicopters went over. They dropped barrels of toxic chemicals. One barrel of these chemicals was dropped over the other end of the underground tunnel, and the size of this barrel was about 250 liters. When this toxic chemical . . . hit the end of the shelter, smoke began to enter the shelter, and we were stifling in the tunnel. We tried to get out of the shelter, but then we started coughing and spitting blood. Our skins became quickly covered with blisters. A few days later I felt very tired. Even a week later I lost my appetite and had diarrhea no matter what I ate. Now these evil effects are still being felt by me. My sight is blurred, and I have many digestive difficulties, often diarrhea.

Now I shall tell you about the U.S. artillery shelling of my commune. On October 10, 1968, at about 7 P.M., when we were having our dinner, shells began to fall on my village. The artillery came from the military post of Thien Ngon. The military post of Thien Ngon has two kinds of batteries: the ultrarapid batteries and the longer barrel batteries for long-range pounding. But the most dangerous of these was the ultrarapid. When you hear this sound of the ultrarapid battery shell, it falls immediately upon you. At that moment I had no time to take refuge. I was on my hammock, and so a bomb splinter went into my left leg. I was brought to the infirmary of the district. I was hospitalized for 20 days. Despite treatment the splinter is still in my leg. Now I have prepared to tell you about napalm.

On the 16th of February, 1969, which was the twelfth of the lunar calendar—almost two weeks after the new year Tet festival, we were enjoying the festival at that time. At about 7 A.M. a reconnaissance plane circled over and over my village and fired a rocket. Then three jet planes went over. These three bombers fired exploding bombs in a large area, at high velocity for a long time—steel pellet bombs. When the bombing was almost over I went out of the shelter and I saw that everything was destroyed and the trees were torn down. Then three more jet planes came over and began to bomb. There were incendiary bombs. One of these bombs fell directly on my house. One of these incendiary products stuck to my trousers. And to my face. Then I stripped off my clothes and took refuge. Then I fainted. I knew nothing.

More than a week later I recovered consciousness and found myself in the district hospital. For the first month after that I could see nothing. My eyes were covered with liquids. I could not open my mouth. Three months later I could eat some rice, but the rice had to be mixed with water, with a soup. I feel much pain in my wounds, and they stank. I have been often sent to the emergency hospital, the first aid hospital. Five and six months later, still my wounds could not be healed, and we had to patch up the wound with a piece of skin. At present I am not able to do anything, and when it is cold, I feel severe pains in my hands and particularly at the ends of my fingers, and I feel also much pain in my wounds. When it is hot, I have a burning feeling in my skin, and I get a headache. I cannot drop for a long time my two arms. The days I spent in the hospital were the saddest and the most dramatic days of my life because I was a young and sound girl, and it is because of the U.S. atrocities that I became an invalid and wounded for life.

Le Van Tan

[Le Van Tan, 14, from Quang Nam Province tells of life in a South Vietnamese strategic hamlet; of killing, torture, beating as well as natural disaster (floods, filth, famine).]

I am going to tell you of the savage repression by the American forces and the Saigon government forces in strategic hamlets in South Vietnam.

In the strategic hamlet where I lived was my sister, my three little sisters, and my little brother living there with me.

I remember that it was in April 1965, at midnight that American artillery from An Hoa began pounding my village. I was sleeping with my mother, my two little sisters, and my little brother on the same bed.

My mother awoke and sat up and a shell entered her chest and killed her. [Le Van Tan here begins to cry and cannot speak. He is a young man of 14 years.]

A few days later American troops came up to my village during a mopping-up operation.

These troops burned down houses everywhere, and they beat the people who refused to be brought away.

I myself, with my sisters and brother, was also brought away with other people to be exposed to the sun. Afterwards my grandmother and I were herded into the strategic hamlet of Xe Mióc. There were many people, but they gave nothing to us, and we had to sleep on the ground.

We remained there from 1965 to 1967 in the strategic hamlet. There were three walls of barbed wire. They nominated the chief of the hamlet, with the assistant chief of the hamlet, to control the entrance.

In An Hoa there are many strategic hamlets of that kind. I only know my own hamlet, but in my hamlet there are barbed wire fences, and there are also ditches, and there was only one entrance for people to go out or to come in.

In my village we go out to the field very early in the morning, at four or at five o'clock in the morning, but in the strategic hamlet they only allow us to go out into the field at eight o'clock. At five o'clock we have to come back. If we are late in coming back, we are beaten because they suspect those ones of being enemy agents—connections for the communists.

For instance, Mr. Tu, Mr. Coc, and Mr. Cang were savagely beaten. Mr. Coc had his leg broken because he came late.

In this strategic hamlet people are usually hungry. There is not enough food, and so they easily fall ill. We are living huddling together and most of the women and children and aged women fall ill and are afflicted with diseases. My own grandfather was dead and my little brother died from cholera and a number of other little children like my little brother also died.

Each family must have a card of control. If a member of the family is absent or if there is someone strange in the family, then they shoot or arrest and kill the people of that family.

If there was an explosion, people would be arrested and shot and aged people and women were given the task of sentry, of guarding the strategic hamlet.

Aged people guarded the hamlet in the nighttime. Women stood sentry in the daytime. If there was an explosion, people were beaten, arrested, or shot to death.

For instance, there was an old [man]. He was watching in nighttime. There was an explosion, and he was shot dead.

In 1968, during one month, they shut the gate of the strategic hamlet for one month. The inmates protested and struggled to go out and to return to their native places. Among those who tried to run to the gate and to go out was myself and my little sister. They threw grenades and shot at random at the crowd. My little sister was shot dead and also my grandfather on my mother's side. I escaped and I fled. When I returned again to the strategic hamlet, I saw that my little sister was killed and that many other people were killed and many wounded. Blood was shed in profusion. There were many corpses.

There are many artillery poundings over the strategic hamlets. For instance, there was the family of Mr. Thuong. All the members of his family were killed except his own wife, who had her arm broken.

In June 1968, they dropped bombs on my strategic hamlet. Many people were killed. Some of them disappeared but, due to the stinking of the corpses, it was discovered that those people had been buried by the explosion of the bombs.

In June 1970, there was an explosion near my house. The chief of the strategic hamlet began to beat the people and arrested two people and me. We were handcuffed and brought to Duc Duc. They arrested three of us and detained us separately and begun to torture us for 12 days.

They began to interrogate me. I said that I know nothing. On the 18th of June they brought me to the jail of Hoi An with my eyes covered by a handkerchief.

They detained me in the Hoi An jail for 50 days, during which time they continued to interrogate me. I said that I knew nothing. There I was savagely tortured. I was more savagely tortured in Hoi An than in Duc Duc.

When I went back to the strategic hamlet, I was very sick —very weak. I could not work. There was only my sister who worked for us. With the assistance of the neighbors I could survive.

In October 1970, there was a big flood in the strategic hamlet. Many houses were destroyed in the flood, and they were afraid that the people of the hamlet would escape to their native places, so they rounded everyone up, and they herded them into the hills, and they pounded the hills where people might take refuge, and many persons were drowned by the flood and also killed in the hills by the artillery fire. Many corpses were floating on the river and also buffalo, cows, and oxen. Many people were drowned. In the Ihn Toh family, there were five people killed during the flood and during the artillery pounding.

When people came back after the flood their houses were deeply buried into the sand. The sand was one meter high and the inmates were forced to live outside or in their old houses and were given only some pieces of straw with which to make a roof for their house and to shelter the victims of the flood.

People were suffering famine because they had not enough to eat and because their property was destroyed by the flood.

They forced the inmates to set up barbed wire, and many people were sick, and they gave no medicines to them.

People now say that this flood was due to the spraying of toxic chemicals in the jungles. [In the tropical jungles of Vietnam there are certain plants which take up large quantities of water during the raining season and store this water in their stems and leaves. The U.S. is spraying these jungles with herbicides which destroy these plants so that when the rains come the water overflows the rivers. This is only one of the harmful effects of herbicides.] The destruction of the forests, the woods, caused a water overflow, and this flood was part of that overflow.

In January 1971 when I was out farming, I availed myself of the opportunity to flee with some friends to a liberated area. The people of the liberated area cared for me.

Now there remain my big sister and my two little sisters in the strategic hamlet.

I am finished.

Commission: How many people were living in this strategic hamlet when you arrived and how many when you left?

A. When I arrived in the strategic hamlet there were about 700 families. When I left the hamlet, I think that there was the same number—700. I know only the strategic hamlet where I was living, but I know that there are many of them in the village of An Hoa—many of them.

Were many new families arriving during the time that you lived in the hamlet?

I know that in May of 1965 the whole population was hovered into the concentrated zone of the area—almost the whole population.

You have told us about killing, torture, beating, and other atrocities in the camps, and you have also been speaking about floods. Were the Americans involved in the administration of the camp or in these atrocities in any way? Have you seen any Americans in the camp?

I saw that Americans did come to the strategic hamlet. They were in uniform, and I saw them there many times.

You have mentioned dates. You have mentioned the times when certain incidents happened. How can you remember these different dates?

Those days were the days when they shot my own mother, my little sister. I will always remember those dates.

You said that you had been severely tortured. Could you say briefly what they did? Did you have the beating, water torture, electric-shock tortures?

They beat me with a stick as big as my forearm, and then they put an electrical wire to my fingers and caused me to feel an electrical shock. They also put wires into my mouth and caused shocks and also to my ears. Sometimes I fainted. Once they told me to lie on my back on two chairs. Then one of them held my arms and another held my legs and they forced soapy water into my mouth and made me swallow it, and then they jumped on my stomach so that the soapy water, mixed with blood, was forced out of my mouth and my nose.

Bui Thi Thanh

[Bui Thi Thanh, a woman, from Quang Nam province, South Vietnam, relates how 12 members of her family are killed and how she herself is arrested, tortured, and beaten.]

I am going to relate to you, to the Commission, about how the American troops and the Saigon mercenaries massacre the population in my native place, Binh Duong village.

On April 24th, 1969, at about 6 A.M. the artillery shells began to fall on my village. After a moment smoke and fire began to burst out in my commune. After this troops were landed in my commune.

In my commune was the family of Mrs. Ao. There were eight members of her family. Two of the eight members of her family were killed. Of the family of Mrs. Quang, five members were completely massacred. The daughter-in-law of Mrs. The, a woman of 21 years who had just given birth to a child, was also killed. They threw the baby on the ground and began to rape the young mother by turns.

Then, with a knife, they extricated the eyeballs of the victim. They cut off the breast of the victim and also the vagina. Regarding the baby, at that moment I was in a shelter, and together with some neighbors I went to the rescue of the baby, but the baby could not survive.

The following day the troops withdrew from my native

commune, but everywhere they go they kill people and destroy everything. On the 27th they returned to my village with 70 bulldozers and tanks. They razed to the ground all of the houses and, together with the puppet troops of Saigon —these puppet troops of Saigon came from Ha Lam—they rounded up some 360 persons, among them 23 were taken to unknown destinations.

A few days later, when the fishermen went to the high seas for fishing, they could pick up five bags which contained corpses of ten persons including women and children. Among these corpses the inhabitants could recognize Mrs. Nghinh because of a little mark she had on her cheek.

Some of the other inhabitants of my village were taken to the concentration camp of Cho'Duoc.

On September 15, 1969, at about 5 A.M. we went farming. At about 6 A.M. the artillery guns from the seaside and the guns from the military post of Tung Duong began shelling our places.

At that moment I ran to see my aunt. I could see that the artillery fire was very intense and fierce. The airplanes were circling the sky like dragonflies and dropped bombs over hamlet 2 and hamlet 5.

I was told then that hamlet 2 suffered seven deaths and two persons there were wounded. In hamlet 5, two were killed and three wounded.

When the pounding of artillery stopped, fire began to burst out and smoke was everywhere. We all took refuge in the shelters, but many of us were killed. Then puppet troops from Ha Lam were landed.

In hamlet 3, three persons were killed; among them was my uncle. He was 52 years old. The son of my uncle was also killed. He was a little boy of 15 years. Another son was also killed. He was 14.

Two men were put into a bag and thrown into a well, and then shot to death within the bag in the well.

Then 300 persons were taken away, including my own mother, my two little brothers, and myself.

Mrs. Uoc, who had been hiding in a shelter, was found and interred and asked: "Who is the chief of the guerrillas?" She said that she did not know, and they then broke her head up, killing her.

We 300 persons were brought to the hamlet of Binh Trieu. Some of us people, including myself, were brought to Mieu Ong Meo. They gave us nothing to eat and forced us to repair the roads and to dig a trench for fortification. Those persons who were not able to work were severely beaten.

Mrs. Lai was two months pregnant and had to struggle making a trench for communication and was beaten up and had a miscarriage.

The people interred in this concentration camp could not survive because they were denied all food and water, and so those interred there did struggle in order to be allowed to return to their native places, but they were severely beaten nonetheless.

One morning we were sent to cut off bamboo and to make fences of it. Those of us who were sent to do this took advantage of the situation and fled.

In November 1969, when I was going to visit my aunt after the artillery shells had begun to fire, and the American troops together with the South Korean troops were landed. I knew that the people in my native commune were killed and massacred.

In the afternoon when I escaped and ran back to my houses, I saw that my mother together with my four little brothers were killed. My grandfather and two sons of my uncle were also killed. My three aunts were also killed. A daughter of my aunt was also killed. All told, 12 members of my family were killed.

When I saw this, I fainted. I knew nothing, and the people around came to help me. Many other people were also killed in this operation in November 1969, and of my family only I remained alive.

I have been arrested 12 times and tortured twice. I have been wounded twice. Once on my hip and another time on my shoulder. It is difficult and painful for me to raise my left arm.

One day at about 7 A.M. I had gone out to farm with my friends to a place about five kilometers from my house. While we were working two aircraft hovered and circled over our place. Then four American soldiers and one puppet soldier landed. As we ran away, my girlfriend Miss Lien was shot dead on the spot.

They captured me and bound my eyes with a handkerchief. I was wounded on my hip. They brought me to Chu Lai and put me into a cell. In the evening a puppet officer began to interrogate me. This Saigon officer told me: "This evening you will sleep with an American, and this American will give you much money and gold." I said: "I am a Vietnamese girl. Why do you tell me to sleep with Americans?" Then he asked me: "Are you a Viet Cong? Do you know where the ammunition and weapon dump of the Viet Cong is? Who are the Viet Cong here?" I said: "I am a farmer, a peasant. I do not know these things."

Then they began to entice me. They said: "If you speak out, I will give you money. I will give you gold, and I will release you." I answered, "My life is in your hands for I know not what you ask me to tell."

Then, with a stick as big as an arm, they began to beat me from my head to my feet, and I fainted.

Then they tied me by my arms and hung me up with a rope so that I was swinging. After I again fainted, they took me to another room and detained me there.

On the 14th of April, after I had recovered from my fainting and beating, they again tried to entice me. They said, "Speak out and I will release you. Now please look at your body. Your body is now suffering very much. Speak out and I will release you."

I said that I know nothing, and they then began to torture me with electricity. They put wires on the ends of my ten fingers, on my nipples, and caused electricity to pass through the wires until I fainted.

For ten days in a row they tortured and beat me until I fainted and then brought me to the jail. They gave me only rotten rice to eat and never enough of that. I was very hungry after eating the little bit they did give me. My work in the jail was to clean the WC, to wash the clothes of the puppet soldiers, and to carry ammunition for them.

The cells were extremely filthy because there were over 30 persons in each cell, and we used the cell also as a WC. It is due to the lack of hygiene that the people were caused skin diseases. All the people became emaciated.

In the jail was Mrs. Hong. She was five months pregnant and miscarried through premature birth. On that day a Saigon soldier told me to go out and buy a packet of cigarettes, and I took the opportunity to flee. From the jail to my native place I traveled, begging my food along the way.

When I returned to my family, the villagers saw that I was too thin, that I was ill, and they gave me medicines and food.

In this month of November, 1969, there was a mopping-up operation by the U.S. and South Korean troops. I did not know that there was an operation in my village. As I was walking in the village an American soldier shot me, and the bullet went in my left shoulder. I fell from the shot, and they arrested me and brought me to the jail of Ha Lam.

As has happened many times and to many people, after

being arrested by them I was beaten very savagely.

They poured soapy water into my mouth, and then tramped upon my womb, upon my belly, so that the soapy water mixed with blood rushed out through my mouth and nose. I suffered many tortures and beatings and, after 15 days of being detained in the jail, I was finally released.

Tran Do

[Tran Do, 26, a law student in Saigon, tells of how he was arrested, detained, and tortured.]

My name is Tran Do. I am twenty-six. I earn my living in Saigon. After I was hurt I went back to my native place for treatment, Thu Dau Mot province, near Saigon. I lived in Saigon since my childhood, when I was eight years old, until 1969.

Now I am telling you of the Americans and their puppets in Saigon toward my compatriots in Saigon, and especially toward the students in Saigon.

Since 1965, repeated demonstrations of the students to demand their legitimate interests have been broken up . . . repeatedly repressed by the U.S. and by the Saigon governments. Now I am telling you of one or two cases in which I myself was a victim. I was arrested, detained, and tortured.

In October 1967, we were holding a press conference. It was a press conference of the General Association of the Saigon Students at the house Number 4 in Duy Tan Street. The police of the Saigon administration together with the Saigon paratroopers and American troops with the armband "M.P." came in a great number and rounded up the place where the conference was held and compelled us to disperse. When we protested against this act, they used clubs and tear gas, and they also tramped upon us. . . . Then they made use of more tear, gas so we were stifled, and some of us fell on the ground. I do not know if it was the American troops or the puppet soldiers, but they threw a grenade, and so one of my girl friends, who was a student in the Medical College, was killed and I myself was wounded. And so, for our self-defense, we threw stones and bricks and the battle lasted one hour, but, as they outnumbered us, they arrested 24 of us and brought us to police cars and sent us to the General Service of Police, Saigon. At the police station they celled each of us separately and submitted us to torture. They asked me personally: "Who was the organizer?" of the movement, and they said that if I tell them, they will send me home again to continue my studies. I replied: "Because the students have been harshly repressed and deprived, frustrated by denial of all their interests and freedoms, therefore we have to struggle. There is no one who tells us this. We see we must struggle." For 17 days in a row I was subjected to all kinds of tortures, beatings, and I fainted many times. During these 17 days I replied to them that I know nothing, and so, being unable to gain anything from me, they were compelled to release me.

In December 1967, we students organized a vigil to protest against the . . . Saigon administration's treatment of students and to militarize the university in Saigon. This vigil was held in the university city of Min Mang. At this time the military police of the Saigon administration and also American military police came in a great number and they began to crack down with their truncheons, and their clubs and sticks. They beat us up and wounded some of us in our legs so that we could only lie on the ground. Then six or seven American soldiers brought one of my fellow students whose name was Tran Quoc Chuong, a student in his second year, and they took him to a high place of the building and threw him to the ground, and he was immediately killed. After that they arrested 46 of us students, all boys. Later we learned that eight girls students were also taken away, to unknown destinations. Those 46 boys were taken to the military office of the capital city. I myself was among them.

The cases of repression, of detention, of torture by the U.S. in Saigon are inummerable. I cannot tell you everything, but I like to explain before the Commission the repression of the population in Saigon in early 1968. You know that after the beginning of 1968, when the Liberation fighters had entered the city of Saigon, American planes began to bombard several areas around Saigon, for instance, in Binh Hoa, Go Vap, and even in the Minh Mang area, which is in Saigon. They bombed heavily populated areas in the cities. They also bombarded living quarters in Saigon where many people were living. If one came to Saigon at that time, he would see many homeless people who were falling in the Saigon streets, who were lying in the Saigon streets on the pavements. So we students organized a relief committee to bring assistance to the victims. There were also many children who are homeless and who crawl about the streets in Saigon and lie on the pavements. The Saigon administration, instead of assisting or rescuing, relieving the population, concentrated its forces to carry out searches, to carry out rapes, and they also staged many military operations to arrest and detain those suspected of being connected with the N.L.F. So we had to leave our schools in order to help the victims, and we had to lodge them in the marketplaces, in cathedrals, and even in hospitals. They then ordered us to shut down the schools and universities, but we refused and we continued to lodge the victims in our school, and the crackdown continued. Afterwards they compelled all of the students in the schools and universities to go to military exercises. . . . But we continued to struggle. We resisted against the Saigon administration;

we took care of the victims so that they could come back to their former homes. Usually this was impossible because after the bombing the U.S. forces and their puppets use bulldozers to level the houses to the ground. They destroy these houses and then, if the people come back, they require them to produce certificates to prove that they were the owners of the land. Of course these papers were destroyed in the bombing and subsequent fires in the houses, so the people are unable to produce them. So they dispossess the people in order to seize the land and hold it and then rent it to the Americans.

I shall relate to you another event. One day late in April, in the area of Cho Tiep. The residents of the area were the victims of searches and plunderings, pilferings, by the U.S. troops and also by the Saigon troops. That night they looted the property, money, of the inhabitants, and the next morning American planes flew over and bombed that area. That night many women and girls were raped by the American troops and by the Saigon troops in the area. Miss Phan, for instance, who was a young girl, the daughter of a Chinese resident in this quarter, was raped by six or seven army men. After raping her they killed her and threw her body on the pavement. The people were not allowed to go out at that time, and the corpses were littering the streets. There was a curfew at 24 hours midnight, and people were not allowed to go out. The dead bodies were therefore left out on the streets because no one dared to go out and bury them. As no one went out to bury the bodies, they sent a bulldozer to go and run them over. Then they poured gasoline on the corpses and burned them.

And so, that has been the attitude and action of the U.S. and Saigon government toward the people and students. Nobody has been spared. Anybody can be freely arrested, thrown into jail, or killed. Nobody has been spared. Even doctors, students, lawyers, intellectuals, anybody, if they oppose the U.S. or the Thieu-Ky regime, was easily the prey of Saigon jails and U.S. bullets.

I am going to tell you the story of an old professor. He is a professor of philosophy. His name is Tran Quoc Khanh. He was a very experienced teacher whose behavior was very good, a very kind man. He was siding with us and opposing them, and so he was arrested, beaten up, tortured, and when he was released, he became an invalid, a disabled man. His mental capacities have decreased. He now cannot speak normally.

Regarding the material interests of the students, we have been frustrated and deprived of these rights, these material rights. For instance, we have been denied scholarships for the poor students. We have been denied the right to buy books at a cheaper price, for instance. The life of the student in Saigon is rather miserable; after our class hours we have to earn our living by selling newspapers or by teaching to earn some money.

Danny T. Notley

[Danny T. Notley, 23, served with E Company, 4th of the 21st, the 11th Brigade of the AMERICAN Division, the Division implicated in the events at My Lai. He describes a civilian massacre in which he took part.]

During [my] training there were constant references made to the Vietnamese people as gooks, dinks, slopeheads, and a number of other racist forms of reference. We were subjected to this type of language day in and day out until it became more or less common to us, and we were not surprised and are no longer surprised to hear it. I had a drill sergeant. One time I asked him what it was like in Vietnam, and he said: "It's like hunting rabbits and squirrels." That's all the more it was to him, and that's all the more it was to a lot of people.

After having been in my unit for approximately two months, we were sent on an operation into the Song My River Valley. Before we were sent into this valley we were told that the whole battalion would be airlifted into the valley by helicopter, that we were to expect very, very stiff resistance from a North Vietnamese regiment which was operating and headquartered in that valley.

Upon entering the valley there was sporadic sniper fire. But other than that there was none of the heavy resistance that we had been led to believe we would encounter. We operated in the valley for a number of days, I would say approximately a week, during which time we made no contact with an enemy except that we hit one booby trap in which two men were wounded. These men were evacuated.

My platoon was told to move up the valley about six kilometers one day. As we moved up the valley we set up a night-defensive position approximately 400 to 500 meters from the village of Trung Khan Tuo. We were to set up here because this was a major trail junction coming down out of the mountains, and we were told that there was a North Vietnamese hospital in the mountains and that Delta Company was in the mountains searching out this hospital.

We had been set up on this trail for a couple of days and had set up a booby trap on the trail coming down out of the mountains. One evening just before dark, at about six or seven o'clock, this booby trap did go off. We went up there to check it out and found one dead North Vietnamese soldier there. There were a number of old wound dressings, old bandages lying around and there were scrapings on the ground as if people were dragging a litter—possibly with wounded people on them.

We assumed that Delta Company had come so close to the hospital that the liberation soldiers felt it necessary to evacuate the hospital, and that we had blocked their route of escape. The fact that we had lost two men to booby traps thus far and that these liberation troops had tried to escape by us, created great apprehension and anxiety among the troops in that we were still waiting for this stiff resistance we were told we were going to get and had not seen yet.

A day or two later we were setting up our night-defensive position during the day, not doing anything, playing cards, and we [three or four of us] decided to go down to a stream and get water. Before we left we told everyone who might follow us: "Do not walk on the trail because we are afraid it might be booby trapped." As we were getting water, we heard an explosion. We went over to where the explosion was. Two more soldiers had followed us down, but they had walked on the trail; they had tripped the booby trap. One soldier was wounded badly. The other soldier was dead.

The dead soldier had been a very popular member of the platoon, [and] most of the people in the platoon were very upset at his death. That evening nothing happened.

The next morning our platoon leader, a second lieutenant, told one squad of my platoon to go into Trung Khan Tuo: go into this village and to search out and to destroy the liberation soldiers who were in the village. He had assumed that, because this booby trap was so close to the village, that some of the villagers in the village had set out the booby trap: that they were working with the liberation soldiers.

He sent a squad in. As the squad approached the village from a distance which I estimate to be maybe one or two hundred meters, they called back to say that they saw male personnel evading out of the village.

At this point the platoon leader stated that we should call artillery on them. They got a fire mission from Son Hoa hill which was an American forward fire support base. Artillery was called on the village: it was mostly the white phosphorous smoke rounds. The village was completely burnt to the ground, at which time the squad went on in. When the platoon leader called and asked them if they had any kills, the squad leader called back and said: "No. We only killed a water buffalo."

This seemed to upset the platoon leader because, as most people know, there is a great amount of emphasis in the army and especially in Vietnam, on body count.

My platoon leader was upset because we hadn't killed any Viet Cong, so he told this squad to return. He was unsatisfied with their performance. He told them to return to the night-defensive perimeter. They did return.

After lunch he told [my] squad to go back into the village and search the village out again. I'm not really sure exactly why he wanted us to go back into the village again. Obviously he was not satisfied with the performance of the squad which had been in the village in the morning. As we were returning to the village, I was carrying an M-79 grenade launcher.

(The M-79 is a 40 millimeter grenade launcher. I have to explain something about this. I was what we called a new man. I was a green troop. I hadn't seen any combat yet. All the new men assigned to the unit, all the replacements, were given the bad duties. In other words: to carry the radio, because that's 23 extra pounds you have to hump in the mountains. The M-79 is a very cumbersome type weapon. It is not a very secure weapon: you are dependent upon the rest of the men in the platoon to take care of you. So, because I was new, I was carrying the M-79, and a friend of mine, who came at the same time, was carrying the radio.)

I was walking about fourth or fifth back in the column of about eight to ten men, a squad patrol. Being new, and being somewhat naïve, not having seen any combat yet, I still had the mistaken idea that war was just like I had seen it in all the John Wayne and Audie Murphy movies—that we were going to make contact with the enemy and that there was going to be a fight. As we approached the village, I actually expected to see armed hostile forces in this village, and as we approached the village, there were a number of women and children standing on the near side of the village to us.

And as we walked into the village, the people who were walking in front of me, without saying a word—no one said anything—the people in front of me just started shooting people. I estimated that there were approximately ten women and children here at this time. These people were all killed.

At this time I was somewhat in a state of shock; I was very upset. I couldn't understand what I was seeing. It was completely inconsistent with what I had been told our role in Vietnam was, and I could not understand it. I was very, very upset.

The strange thing of it was that the men who were doing the shooting hadn't had to say a word to anyone. It was as if they had done this a hundred times before. They knew exactly what they were doing. I think it is very important to realize also that the men who did most of the shooting were men who had been there for 10 or 11 months, who had been involved in this over a long period of time. Therefore their reactions were somewhat predetermined. They knew what they were going to do. There was no emotion in what they did. They had been brutalized so badly that they did not realize the reality of what they were doing, and I was so upset that I couldn't understand what was going on.

After having killed the first group of people, we moved

through, on into the village, where there was a second group of people. Why these people didn't run I don't know, but they didn't. They were just standing there like the first group. I guess becuase they really couldn't believe what was happening either.

At his time my squad leader, a sergeant E-5, ordered me to fire. I had a canister round, which is a shotgun type round for the M-79, an antipersonel round. There is a great amount of debate among soldiers themselves as to whether this round is meant to kill people or just to maim. Most people who have carried the M-79 feel that you couldn't kill anyone with it. It is not an effective killing weapon, but it is a maiming weapon. The round is made out of plastic and some buckshot. My squad leader ordered me to fire. He said: "Its about time that you tried out one of those canister rounds," as if he was curious to see what it would do.

I was so upset, and I was so scared that I complied with his order. I was afraid not to comply with his order. I pointed my weapon toward the group of people. I didn't want to fire at the people, but I was afraid not to fire at the people. I realize now that I exercised very poor judgment, but its a little late now.

I fired my weapon. Whether or not I hit anyone or killed anyone I will never know because immediately after firing the rest of the people opened up with their M-16s. As I said, I did fire, and therefore I was a participant.

After that, after I had realized what I had done, I refused to take part in it anymore. I just stood there and watched. They found another group of people.

They killed this other group of people, and after that we left the village.

As we were leaving the village, there was a forward air control airplane in the area. He called us and wanted to know if we had made contact. My squad leader said yes. He asked

if we would like to have an air strike on the village. He said
yes. The forward air control pilot said, "Well, I have two
phantoms on the way."

By the time we got back to our perimeter the phantoms
were there. They made about two or three runs. They
dropped napalm. They didn't drop any high explsove; all
they dropped was napalm on the village. And then they left.

I believe that at the time we called in a body count of 13
North Vietnamese. Who determined this number I do not
know, but this is what was called in: 13. It is interesting to
note that in the official press release out of Saigon this body
count had been inflated to 21. Obviously there were more
people killed than that, but what I am trying to say is the fact
that we called in 13 and somewhere along the line they
added eight more bodies to make it look good.

Anyhow, the next day the whole platoon went back
through the village. For what reason I don't know, but we
went back through the village. I guess the platoon leader
wanted to survey the damage that was done. He got his body
count, and I assumed that he was happy with this.

Myself, I felt that this was very wrong, somebody is going
to go to jail, there is going to be an investigation, and, as I
said, I guess at the time I was somewhat naïve.

After getting into the village we found two surviving children: one male and one female. The female was, I believe,
wounded, so we called a medical evacuation helicopter and
had this girl evacuated. The boy we had with us. We called
our battalion commander who was flying around in his helicopter and told him we had a child. He said he would come
in and pick the child up. So we secured a landing zone just
to the very edge of the village. The battalion commander
flew over the village very low, circled around, and landed
right next to the village. He got out of his helicopter and
walked over to the edge of the village. From where he was

standing I am almost sure that he could see some of the bodies. If he couldn't see them, he could have smelled them because the stench was unreal. He stood there and talked with our platoon leader for a while and had the child in his arms. He got back in his helicopter and left.

I really felt that there was going to be something done about it, that there was going to be some legal action taken. To this day there hasn't been anything done about it.

People have asked me why I didn't report this when I was in Vietnam. The fact is that it is beaten into your heads when you are in basic training and in the army, that there is such a thing called chain of command, and that your immediate superior is the only person you can go to with a grievance. Everyone in my chain of command already knew about this incident, and since they didn't do anything about it, and since a great amount of emphasis among GIs—the rank and file GI in Vietnam—is survival, don't make trouble, stay out of trouble so you can go home, I didn't feel that there was anything I could do. My squad leader knew about it; he participated in it. My platoon leader knew about it; he participated in it. My battalion commander knew about it, and a Spec-4 in the army doesn't just walk up to a general somewhere and ask to file charges. I really felt that I didn't have any means of recourse. It was also so emotionally upsetting for me to have seen and participated in something like this that I completely suppressed this in my mind; I did not admit to myself what had happened. But the reality of what I saw there that day is the fact that that *is* the the war in Indochina.

I had been waiting for the war to start, waiting to see the "enemy" and not until that day . . . did I realize that we are not only destroying, as a matter of policy, the armed liberation troops, but we are destroying men, women, and children as a matter of policy.

The tragic thing of it is that people like me are caught up

in this. We are forced to do these things, sometimes to do them without even thinking. Many times we do not know what is going on until we get there, and when we finally realize what is happening, it's too late. Our training is very poor. We are told nothing about Vietnamese culture, Vietnamese history; we are told nothing about the history of their struggle. I had no idea when I went to Vietnam that these people have been waging their struggle for so long. All I was told was that Vietnam was being invaded by Communists, and I was being sent there to save them, and I can see now that this was utterly ridiculous. But this is the type of thing that you are told. This is the type of thing that you are trained with in order to get men like myself to do what the generals and the politicians want us to do. I think it is very important also to note that it is very difficult to expect low-ranking, 18- and 19-year-old GIs to make a moral distinction between right and wrong under some circumstances, when these distinctions are not even made by high-ranking generals and politicians who plot and pick targets for massive B-52 strikes, which destroy whole villages.

This type of warfare is even being stepped up because they feel that it is acceptable to the American people to withdraw all the ground combat troops but to step up air strikes. You can destroy more people, and you can lose less of your own men. This is the type of thing—this is the type of war—that Nixon is waging now. He's not slowing the war down; he's not trying to stop it. He's just changing tactics a little bit, and the end is the same for the Indochinese people, and that's just massive destruction, indiscriminate destruction.

Things like free-fire zones, recon by fire. Reconnaissance by fire is when you move into an area, say a village, or you see a tree line, and you suspect that there are enemy in that area, you fire into that area, and if there is fire returned, then you know that there are enemy there, and if there is not any fire returned, then you know that there was no enemy there, and if you just happen to kill a few civilians while reconning the area by fire, well, that's too bad. That's the general attitude of the army.

Commission: Mr. Notley, you mentioned the use of a weapon which you called a maiming weapon which had shot made out of plastic. Were you given any special instructions in regard to the use of this weapon?

The M-79 grenade launcher is a shotgun type weapon. It is breech-loading; it breaks open. You can insert one round. You can only fire one round at a time. It is a 40-millimeter weapon. It fires a grenade-type weapon, grenade type projectile, about this big around. You can fire it out and when it lands it explodes. That will kill someone. But they also have a direct-fire antipersonel round which is called a canister round. The shot is not made out of plastic. The shot is made out of some type of metal, but the shot is encased in a plastic or a hard rubber. Now, the thing about this is is that even when I was in the combat center in Chu Lai, before I ever got sent to my unit, they told us that they had had to change the canister round because of complaints by North Vietnam and the Liberation army that this weapon was in violation of the Geneva Accords because the round itself, the shot itself, caused severe infections in the wounds and that it was an unclean type weapon and that it caused infections and that it never really killed anyone unless you shot them at point-blank range right in the head—which you could do with a club. But as far as shooting at someone, it was more or less a maiming weapon, and they said that they had changed it to meet supposedly the standards, but that actually they hadn't changed it any at all—that they just said that they had changed it. I remember this very specifically. It is one thing that stood out in my mind because the man who was teaching this class laughed as if they had pulled a big one on the people of Southeast Asia, and that more or less stuck in my head. To my own thinking, in my own knowledge, it was a weapon made strictly for just maiming the victim.

You mentioned that your first contact was with the villagers. During that operation did any of the villagers fire back? Was there any fire at all directed towards you?

We received absolutely no fire from that village at all. We did find some—what we called—Ho Chi Minh sandals. They are the rubber tire sandals which we were always told belonged exclusively to the NLF, or the North Vietnamese. We also found one North Vietnamese green uniform. But this was after the killings had taken place. The people who searched these things out searched them out in an effort more or less to justify what had been done. But we received no hostile fire. They just want to have more points than the other side, and the bodies are the points, and they don't care where you get them.

Nathan Hale

[Nathan Hale, 23, was an Army interrogator in the 635th Military Intelligence Detachment, assigned to the 198th Infantry Brigade of the American Division. He describes how numerous DRVN POWs were tortured during interrogation.]

What happened to me as a soldier is the product of what the American way of life—at least as far as I am concerned—is all about.

First of all, the reason I joined the Army was twofold: I was about to be drafted; so, rather than take that route, I joined. Also I was trying to get into college, but I didn't have enough money so I decided that the GI Bill, which would give me educational benefits, would be agreeable. I went into the Army with the firm resolve to cooperate with whoever would order me to do what because I knew that if I were to act up and not cooperate that it would just be a bad time for me.

During basic training I was rather naïve as to what was going on, but I cooperated and for this reason I found military life very easy.

After basic training I went to intelligence school where I was trained as an intelligence analyst. This is a person who plots units on maps and gathers information and disseminates this information. During this training I can recall one time during a block of instruction where a sergeant, who was a Vietnam veteran, talked about shooting Vietnamese from helicopters. He was very delighted with this because he said they gave a funny twinge before they hit the ground. We all laughed, but this is an example of the attitude thus far in our military training.

After intelligence school the Army chose me to learn the Vietnamese language. I learned the Vietnamese language and gained a *slight* insight into the Vietnamese culture.

After language school I was sent to Vietnam. I was assigned to the American Military Intelligence and my job—my unit was the division level—and I was sent out to the various units as I was needed. The first thing I learned in Vietnam about the Vietnamese was that no one liked them. I didn't think too much about this, and then in the American Division compound—in the POW camp—they told me that it had recently been barbed-wired because a Vietnamese girl was taken by an interrogator into the GI barracks and raped.

After I was in the country for about a month, I was assigned to the First Cavalry which is an armored unit located north of Tam Ky.

I was shown around hill 29 by the S-2. He took me to a shack and said: "This is the interrogation shack. You can do anything in here because your job is to elicit information. You can get this information any way you want. The only thing is: don't get caught." This meant that if there were any visiting officers or visiting press or noncombatants who wouldn't understand what was going on, don't act normal.

I was then introduced to some South Vietnamese interpreters. They, in fact, taught me how to interrogate. These men used just sheer human brutality against the captives. This also instilled a kind of hate for the Vietnamese [since] the South Vietnamese didn't like them because every one we captured was a Viet Cong.

This was compounded by the GIs in the unit. Oftentimes the men would come in from the fields and literally throw the prisoners off the trucks. They would shove them, kick them; there's even times when they would scream in English at the Vietnamese and expect them to know what they were saying, and if they didn't answer, they'd probably be hit in the head or punched, or something.

Also, this unit's policy was: if you were suspected—if a hamlet was suspected—of containing Viet Cong, they would run their trucks across the hamlet. That is to say, they would line up a troop, consisting of about nine trucks. They would line up in a line and just charge straight over the hamlet, knocking down everything in sight. This would be done with tanks and armored personnel carriers.

Also at this troop, one instance: I was on the command truck—[with] the troop commander—and we passed around a grenade launcher in front of a small hamlet, a subhamlet, and we took turns with the grenade launcher knocking [them] down—it was a kind of a game to see who could hit what.

I personally used many, many things to elicit information. I personally used rifles, pistols, boards, just sheer human brutality of my own upon the Vietnamese to obtain information from them. At the time I felt I was wrong, but then, I couldn't tell anyone, and, anyway, everyone was doing it.

Here's also something about a fear that I had and it is that if you don't act—if you don't do what your superiors want you to do—then there's always the chance of reprisals. The lights are gone. Now, this is basically why I acted this way. I *think* this is why I acted this way.

As far as I know, every interrogator had done the same as I; therefore, I couldn't be wrong.

I can give you a specific incident of what happened. I went back to Division from Hill 29, and I came back, and the troops were coming in, and they were really beating on three Vietnamese men.

I made them stop, and I asked them what was going on. They said that these men were captured the day before, and they had taken them out, and they were going to show the troops where the mines, and rice, and other things were. But nothing was found, so by the time I saw these men, they were very beaten, and so I stopped them, and, at the time, I had to take the detainees to another hill to sleep because at the time we didn't have a POW compound.

The next morning a sergeant woke me up and told me that one of my prisoners had died. Well, I was really worried about this because, after all, he was my prisoner, and he died. So, I went to my S-2. My S-2 said: "Okay, we'll take care of it." We got the doctor, we went over to the compound, and the doctor pronounced the man dead. We then brought the man back to Hill 29. We put him in two 500-pound rice sacks, one over his head and one over his feet. The troops that were going out came by the interrogation location, and we gave them the body. The man was dumped, and his body was added to the previous day's body count.

The explanation for all this was that my S-2, a captain, didn't want to go through the hassle, or the bother, of the paper work.

After I arrived home from Vietnam, I didn't support the war at all. At first I tried to keep it out of my mind and pretend that it didn't happen, but it did, and it does happen, and I have to speak to let everyone know what I saw in Vietnam because I know it is true.

Commission: As I understand your story you are not particularly proud of what you were doing in Vietnam. I would like to know how you felt during the time you were there. For instance, when you used the pistol to get information can you describe to the Commission how your feelings were at that time?

It's very difficult to reflect back on emotions; however I understand your question, and I have a hard time explaining it to myself why I even acted that way. But I'm a victim of ignorance—of my own ignorance, that is—and I didn't understand what I was doing but just doing it because everyone else did. The emotional part didn't count because one of the slogans that they used was: "If it saves one American life, its worth it."

Mr. Hale, you have mentioned the use of gas grenades. Now the United States insists, I believe, that tear gas and CS have only the immediate effects of tearing and perhaps coughing or choking which last only a short time. However you said that the man hauled out from the hole was "really sick." Can you describe more fully his symptoms and do you know what happened to him?

Yes. The marines knew that this man was in a spider hole —a hole in the ground. He wouldn't come out, so I know they threw in two canisters of gas—I'm not sure of the type. However, when they dragged the man out, finally, he was unconscious, and they threw him in a rice paddy, and he stayed there for about two hours or two and a half hours, and when he finally woke up—of course, you saw his condition there. But he was so sick that he was on the brink of being delirious, and there was mucus running from his nose, and he had a hard time breathing. The only thing that he could eat was to drink a little milk, a little at a time.

I took the man back the following day, back to Tu Li— first we went to the 196th landing zone, and then we trucked him down from the 198th to Tu Li. I took him to the POW compound. The MPs decided the man was sick; they took him to the hospital, and he died during the night.

Randy Floyd

[Randy Floyd, 25, spent five years in the U.S. Marine Corps as a bomber pilot between 1964 and 1969. From March to September 1968 he served with the Marine All-Weather Attack Squadron 533 at Tu Li; he flew 98 combat missions in the two-engine A-6 jet bomber.]

In infantry training we were shown various kinds of booby traps and land mines used by the Vietnamese and were told that every Vietnamese—man, woman, child, old, or young— was our potential killer. We were told not to take chances with those we thought to be civilians because we could not effectively distinguish between a civilian or a soldier. In effect this meant that all civilians were enemy, although not always stating it so explicitly. This allowed us still to keep the rationalization that we were going over to help the Vietnamese people and fight for their freedom.

Most of my training as an officer consisted of learning the systems of the A-6 [bomber] and refining visual, electronic systems bombing techniques. Instructions were never given regarding what or what not to bomb. We were never told that we could not bomb a civilian area. We were simply taught how to bomb. I assumed, and everyone assumed, that civilian populations would be bombed when there were military targets within civilian areas. But until I reached Vietnam, I did not know that civilian targets were bombed as targets.

I arrived in Vietnam in Feburary 1968, a few weeks after the Tet Offensive. Living conditions for the pilots were very good. Two months after I arrived, we moved into air-conditioned quonset huts. We lived right there on the beach. We had access to sailboats and surfboards. For the most part it was extremely boring except for the times when we were flying missions. All that most of us ever did was either read or drink or write letters or lay in the sun. Very few of us had jobs in the squadron area that took over two hours a week. Occasionally, we could get rocketed, but normally we would sit on the patio we built and drink beer and watch it because the rockets would land about a mile away from the airstrip.

I cannot really explain to you how depersonalized the war is for pilots. You never see any blood; you don't hear any screams; you're just operating a machine, and you're doing an efficient job. I felt like I was a good pilot. I performed the job well; it was kind of a game. Most of the men I knew in Vietnam didn't really care about the politics or the policies of the war. They simply wanted to survive their tour in Indochina and go home and get out of the service.

[One] way that your unit or your Commanding Officer was made to look good was by statistics. The infantry used their body counts. We had our body counts: KBAs, that is "Kill By Air." There was great pride taken in the number of sorties my squadron flew. There was also in the tonnage of bombs dropped. We dropped more tonnage than the other three squadrons in our group which were A-4 squadrons. The number of hours flown, this type of thing—it was all a paper-statistics game: "who can look the best."

The normal load for missions in the southern part of Vietnam was either twenty-seven 500-pound bombs or twenty-seven 150-pound bombs or five 2,000-pound bombs.

Over the Democratic Republic of Vietnam or Laos we normally would carry eighteen 500-pound bombs or four 2,000-pound bombs or 12 cluster-bomb units or a mixing of 500-pound bombs and CBUs.

Most of these bombs were high-explosive fragmentary bombs. For the cluster bomblet units, I believe, we used a CBU-24, which there is a picture of out in the lobby. It is a small round bomblet that fits in a canister about six feet long and kind of flat—oval shaped. You normally release the canister above 4,000 feet. You have as speed and altitude restriction and the canister is blown open at about 2,000 feet. By looking at charts you can then see what your scattering pattern will be for the couple hundred bomblets in each canister. The bomblets are designed with grooves around them so that they tumble. They arm themselves by turning a certain number of revolutions. These bombs were designed to come apart in jagged fragments. When they enter the body of a person or an animal they will change directions and tear the insides up.

The primary mission of the A-6 is night all-weather low-level radar-computerized bombing against a fixed or a moving target that is radar-significant, such as a bridge or a factory or a railroad yard, or anything with a fairly high degree of radar reflectivity. I will explain briefly the systems that the A-6 had. We had an inertial navigation system, a track and a search radar, doppler radar, a ballistics computer, pilot and BN radar scopes, and a pilot horizontal display. The inertial navigation gave us the aircraft position and the accelerations on the aircraft for weapons release. The doppler radar gave us the ground speed. The search radar would provide a display of terrain, which allowed the BN to pick out navigational checkpoints or targets and use them to update the inertial navigation. The track radar tracked targets, giving the computer the exact distance and bearing from the aircraft to a target; it also would track moving targets, giving their speed and direction. The pilot display was a television-like affair. On this the computer would display symbology, giving the directions to steer the aircraft. It would also give me attack symbology, telling me when the computer was in the attack mode, telling me how soon release would be. Depending on the type of attack we were going to do, it would tell me whether or not we had to pull up, how many Gs to apply to keep the steering centered, things of this nature.

Once on a bomb run when the computer had stepped into attack, I would simply follow steering and pull a commit trigger on the stick. Then the computer would automatically compensate for aircraft speed and altitude, dive angle, and the type of weapon, and would release the weapon automatically whenever it reached the correct point; all I had to do was follow steering.

The missions for our squadron were ordered by the Seventh Air Force in Thailand . . . through the First Marine Aircraft Wings.

I will describe the type of missions a little bit to you. The close air support is a mission controlled by tactical air controller, airborn. This is dive bombing or visual bombing which we also had capability of. Normally we would go up and contact the direct air support center who would hand us off to a controller, and the controller would direct us into an area. Once we had established visual contact with the controller, he would normally fire a smoke rocket into as close to the enemy positions as he could get it. From the smoke he would direct our bombs—either three o'clock, six, nine, something, and so many meters. Normally we couldn't tell what we were hitting because we were bombing in relation to smoke and were out in the jungle and therefore could not see what we were hitting.

I remember one very clear case when we could see what

we were hitting. It was a small village about five miles northeast of Don Hoi, by the DMZ. In this case there was an army unit in contact with, supposedly, a North Vietnamese unit. The tactical air controller said that the North Vietnamese had gunners set up on three largest buildings, which were about two stories, in the center of town. He wanted us to aim the bomb for that. There were two aircraft. We dropped about forty 500-pound bombs in the village. I think we pretty effectively destroyed the village and the buildings, and the controller was very pleased with this. I don't know for sure, but I imagine there were civilians there in bunkers. But we obliterated that and went on to hit another target just south of there.

Another type of mission we flew was called armed reconnaissance. These were flights into Laos. There was no reconnaissance to the flights, just as there is no reconnaissance to many of the flights currently over North Vietnam. We have no reconaissance capability. We were simply flying a mission along Route Nine from Khe Sanh over to Tchepone, Laos. We were to find and destroy any kind of moving target or fixed target or, roughly, anything that was alive. One time we went in—we were supposed to do this with radar bombing if possible; it was still light—and we picked up one truck visually and tried to bomb it, and we picked up some cattle on a bridge. We bombed the cattle because we were told that anything out there was North Vietnamese-controlled, and we figured that was part of the food supply. So we bombed that, and reported it on the debrief also.

The two types of mission we flew into North Vietnam were called "rolling thunders" and "tally-hos." My squadron quit flying rolling thunders—which were in the central part of Vietnam, up through Hanoi area—just after I got there, because of the lack of experience of most of the crews. We were scheduled to resume rolling thunders April 1 of that year and the bombing halt was called March 31st down to the 20th parallel. These were single aircraft flights into some kind of fixed target. They bombed [a] Hanoi radio station right after Tet offensive; they bombed several air fields, railroad sidings, and power plants and bridges.

The primary type of mission that I flew over North Vietnam was called tally-ho. There tally-ho missions were confined to a target area between the 17th and 18th parallels, for the primary purpose of picking up with our radar moving targets: convoys or barges, anything that would reflect on radar that was moving. If we found no moving targets, we had a secondary target—one per night—which was like a suspected truck park or a ferry crossing. These were the same targets that had been fired on month after month and rebombed over and over again. If we didn't feel like it, or if we couldn't find [one], virtually anywhere in North Vietnam we wanted to drop was a free-drop zone. There was no restriction to our bombing there. We simply came back and reported the coordinates of our bomb drops and how many we dropped there. Quite a few of the pilots that I knew in my squadron would, if they found no movers and didn't want to hit the secondary target or had dropped half the bombs on the secondary target, would often drop the remainder on Dong Hoi, the principle city between 17th and 18th parallels. There was an ordnance jettison area out to sea 50 miles, but very rarely was it ever used, even though we couldn't go back with the bombs.

Kenneth Campbell

[Kenneth Campbell, 21, served as an artillery scout observer with B Company, 1st Battalion, 1st Regiment, 1st Marine

Division from February 1968 until March 1969. He lives in Philadelphia and is a member of Vietnam Veterans Against the War.]

When I was in [training] school, they directly told me to the side, unofficially, to throw away the book, throw away the manual when I get to Vietnam because it is useless. This is a different type of war.

Again there was racism, the attitude of racism in staging, and I will give you a specific instance. [In] an ambush class we had a noncommissioned officer teaching—and there were officers present on this occasion; not training officers, they were just watching. The instructor told us to wait until the Liberation troops got right in front of the muzzles of your guns. And he also instructed us, if we could, find shotguns—to use shotguns in ambushes. He said, "When they get right in front of you, fire as much and as fast as you can, and when you completely destroy the enemy, go out and strip the bodies down, take everything you can find on the bodies, take machetes with you and hack them up."

I went to Vietnam in Feburary of '68 where I was given the opportunity to use this great power, this mass-destructive power that I was taught to use. That is where I saw the racism being put into effect. I saw American troops throwing C-ration cans at little kids, little Vietnamese children, who were begging for food. They would not throw them *to* them, they would throw them *at* them. And some of these cans weighed quite a bit with the food in them.

I went to Phu Bai, where I met my officer who was in charge of my team, my forward observing team. He was a Lieutenant. I also listened to my peers—other forward observers who had been in Vietnam for several months.

My unit had just come back from the Hué city, the Tet offensive Hué city battle. They told me with great pride of the destruction they had caused with artillery. They told me with great pride of how they had blown apart Hué city to save it.

Then I went to Khe Sanh to relieve the siege of Khe Sanh which had been going on at that time, and for four months I systematically destroyed every enemy position I could find.

After that I went to Quang Tri. This was the first opportunity I had to see Vietnamese villages. In Khe Sanh there are no villages left. All the people were either moved out or killed, and their villages were destroyed. The surface area around Khe Sanh, for miles, had been so bombed-out, there are so many craters, it looks like the surface of the moon. I went to Quang Tri and here was where I saw my first villages. I thought that maybe I could fire one to the villages, thinking back to how my peers described the great destruction of villages in Hué city, and I was told I could not fire on these villages specifically because my unit, about six months earlier, had destroyed a village with ground combat troops and that there had been an investigation and that my company was in trouble and that we had to "keep it cool," so there was no firing on civilian villages then.

About two weeks later I went to Con Tien, which is just south of the demilitarized zone, about 3,000 meters. There were no villages there. Again, they had been all wiped out or moved. I spotted, with the aid of very powerful binoculars —ship binoculars, naval ship's binoculars—I looked across the demilitarized zone and spotted two North Vietnamese villages. I spotted no military action around them; we had received, to my knowledge, no fire from these villages. I saw no reason whatever to fire upon them from a military standpoint.

However, I went to my lieutenant and told him about these villages, and he said that I should fire on them—fire long-range artillery because they were a long way off, and heavy artillery to do mass-destruction. The reason he told me to fire on these villages was that they were probably supplying the North Vietnamese army with rice, and, therefore, they must be considered the enemy. I followed his instructions and for three or four hours I called in 175-mm long-range artillery and eight-inch heavy artillery using phosphorous rounds, high explosive rounds, point detonating rounds, variable time rounds which went off above the ground and exploded down end out for the purpose of killing anybody in trenches or holes, and I completely destroyed the first village.

The next day I went back and destroyed the second village and whatever was left of the first village that looked like it might be usable. In calling in this artillery on these two villages, because I was using long-range and heavy artillery which was on division level, it was necessary for me to get a clearance all the way up to division level. It was cleared by my lieutenant on battalion level, it was cleared on regimental level, it was cleared on division level. The grid coordinates that I sent in for these missions were right in the middle of these villages. These people—these officers at all levels—knew I was firing into the villages, but they cleared it anyway.

Then my unit moved south of Da Nang to an area called Duc Khe. Here, during an operation called Mead River, in November of 1968, which was a search-and-destroy operation, I witnessed Marine Corps engineers blowing up the bodies of North Vietnamese soldiers. These were dead soldiers who had been killed by Americans and the engineers, just for fun, were blowing up their bodies using C-4 plastic explosives to wire the bodies and then blow them. Again officers were present. They did not make an attempt to stop these engineers.

At approximately this time I served a short time with Marine Reconnaissance. One of the members of a Marine Reconnaissance team showed me a card. He said the First Battalion of Marine Reconnaissance use this card as a psychological warfare method. It is the card of death. These cards are planted on Viet Cong or North Vietnamese bodies to throw fear among the ranks of these soldiers. They are also used when the bodies are maimed. They are driven with a nail into the forehead of the bodies. I did not witness the nail being hammered into the head, but some of the soldiers from my unit who did this came back and told me about it. That is how I got this information. From that time on—after I bought these cards back to my unit—my unit started placing these cards on bodies. On the reverse side is Vietnamese script. The translation goes something like this: "You have only two paths from which to choose. If you stay with the Viet Cong, you will surely die. Therefore, go with the Saigon troops."

From there I went to a place called An Hoa, in Quang Nam province. In a certain operation we had in this area, in a territory designated by the Americans as "Arizona territory," we abandoned a small position on top of a hill. Approximately one half hour after we abandoned this position we stopped, turned around, and, looking through binoculars observed our position. There we observed approximately ten or 15 people walking on top of the hill. We could not tell whether they had weapons; we could not tell whether they were women or children or men. All we knew was that they were people, and they were not Americans.

My commanding officer instructed me to call in artillery. I called in the artillery with two missions, one starting from in front of the hill and working the barrage of artillery up onto the hill, the other mission on the reverse slope of the hill, walking the artillery up the reverse slope of the hill to the top of the hill. On the reverse side of the hill, at the bottom, was a Vietnamese village. This village we knew to be there because, the day before we had walked through it. There were women and children but no men in this village. The artillery barage I called in on the village and working up to the top of the hill, I used a round called firecracker, an artillery round. This round is a canister round that opens up in flight and lets out small cluster bombs which hit the ground and then are fired up into the air again by a sort of spring and plunger, and then they explode. There are approximately 15 or 20 of these little bombs in each artillery round. I called in 30 or 40 artillery rounds and worked them, up the hill from the bottom of the slope on the reverse side. I could not observe what destruction this did to the village because it was on the reverse slope of the hill and I could not see. It does not take a clever person to figure out what that must have done to the village, however.

Three months after that, in March, I left Vietnam and came back to the United States. I was still very defensive about my role in Vietnam, about what I did in Vietnam. Much of what I saw and what I did had caused doubts in my mind-caused serious doubts in my mind. And it took a long time of thinking and talking to other veterans to finally come to the conclusion that everything I had been taught, and everything I did, was wrong.

This is a hard thing to do when the only authority you have are the people who trained you to do it; this is a hard thing when throughout your life you've been trained to hate Orientals, and especially in your military training. To constantly refer to them as gooks and as slant-eyes and as zipper heads: these were all terms I learned in the military. It was a difficult thing to do. It is difficult for me to be standing here now, but I know I'm right, and I thank you people for giving me the opportunity to come forth.

Larry Rottman

[Larry Rottman was sent to Vietnam on June 1, 1967, where he was assigned to the information office of the 21st Infantry Division for the duration of his tour. He is coordinator of the Arizona-New Mexico Vietnam Veterans Against the War.]

One of the things we are trying to get at here in the Commission, in addition to the collection of raw facts, is the development and definition of U.S. military policy in Indochina—especially that type of policy which makes war crimes like the My Lai massacre inevitable. So I will try to approach the problem from a rather different direction than has been taken so far: one in which I will try to show by examining official and *de facto* U.S. military and public information policy in documents how not only war crimes are a regularly occurring phenomena, but that they are in actual reality the primary method used by the United States for its conduct of the war in Indochina.

During the period of June 5, 1967, to March 19, 1968, I served as the assistant information officer of the 25th Division, headquartered at Cu Chi, Vietnam. My duties were to be officer in charge of the division newspaper, *Tropic Lightning News; Lightning 25 Monthly Magazine,* a division magazine published in Japan; and the "Lightning 25 Radio Program" over Armed-Forces-Vietnam network. I was also officer in charge of the 25th Division press and photo releases, officer in charge of visiting newsmen including foreign and American network television crews, and a frequent briefer of Division staff and civilian news media and VIP on 25th Division policy. In this capacity I also frequently served as an informal U.S. liaison with the RVNs, Popular Forces, CIDGs, American Special Forces, Vietnamese Special Forces, and civic action teams in my area of operations.

The biggest and most frequent problem that I ran into as an information officer was what we call the nonnews. Nonnews were things which were never to be mentioned either in writing or pictures or in interviews with newsmen. Some of these taboos were explicitly stated, usually verbally by officials from the information offices in Saigon: MACOI, the Military Advisory Command Office of Information; MACV, the Military Advisory Command Vietnam; and JUSPAO, the Joint United States Public Affairs Office.

Military censorship usually came from MACOI, MACV, or the 25th Division Commanding Officer, or our Chiefs of Staff. Matters concerning policy, the overall military planning and action or special forces or CIA activities, usually fell under the jurisdiction of JUSPAO. The following is a partial list of things which were never mentioned in official Division dispatches: ineffectiveness or mistakes of the RVN; handling, processing, or interrogation of prisoners of war; U.S. use of shotguns; U.S. use of flame-throwers, hand-hold or track mounted; use of lethal or nonlethal gas, gas dispensing methods, or gas masks; female VC; very young VC; Heuy "cobra" helicopters; information on the size, accuracy, range, or effects of 122-mm rockets; M-16 rifle malfunctions or deficiencies; extent of damage and number of U.S. casualties from enemy attack; any story concerning enemy tenacity, courage, or ingenuity; marriage of U.S. personnel and Vietnamese; U.S. soldiers' use of pot or other drugs; conditions of U.S. military stockades; anything about the CIA or CIA-sponsored activities such as Project Phoenix or Air America; anything about U.S. activities in Cambodia or Laos; B-52 or other bombing errors; ambushes or defeats of U.S. units; burning, bulldozing, or destruction by other means of Vietnamese villages or hamlets; anything about troop morale, pro or con; information about captured enemy material that was of U.S. manufacture; the NLF as a term or as an organization; napalm; enemy armor and helicopters; and anything else that the officials in the Saigon information offices felt might be detrimental to the United States Army.

I will now go back through the list and present a specific example of each type.

The ineffectiveness and mistakes of RVN. During my tour there were many mistakes that took place in the 25th Infantry Division's area of operation: that's around Cu Chi, Dan H'eng, Tay Ninh, Nui Ba Den. One which happened near the village of Tau Phu Trung, approximately ten kilometers northwest of Saigon, involved a unit from the 34th RVN Ranger Battalion which, on about June 15th, 1967, ambushed an American patrol from the U.S. 25th Infantry Division. There were some casualties, but I did not know about the incident until civilian newsmen contacted me and asked me about it. I was told by the Division Chief of Staff that "nothing happened" and that is what I was supposed to say, and later investigation on my own determined that indeed an ambush of American troops had taken place, and that there were casualties sustained.

Handling, processing, interrogation, and treatment of prisoners of war. Although there was a prisoner of war compound at Cu Chi, the standard Division policy was to deny its existence to newsmen, to refuse to take them to the area where it was located even if they asked, and to respond to any questions about prisoners of war that such information was classified or not for release.

Use of shotguns, flame-throwers, or gas. No stories or photos showing GIs using shotguns, flame-throwers, or gas would be cleared by MACV or MACOI. As I'm sure you are all well aware, shotguns are prohibited by the Geneva Accords as being used as antipersonal weapons. Such releases, if submitted, would be returned stamped: "Not Cleared for Release," or we would be instructed by phone to destroy any copies of the story or negatives of the film. Stories about the VC using the weapons, however, would be cleared immediately.

Burning, bulldozing, or destruction of Vietnamese villages or hamlets. It was not an infrequent occurrence for a town to be completely destroyed for no good reason during a combat operation. During Operation Junction City in 1967, for instance, two Vietnamese villages and hamlets suffered serious to complete destruction from U.S. forces. By MACV directive no mention was ever to be made of such destruction and no pictures, especially of the burning, were to be released.

This destruction, often for no reason, happened many times during Operation Junction City, which began February 27, 1967, and concluded May 16 of the same year.

Although I arrived in Vietnam in June of 1967—a month after the conclusion of that operation—I had many first-hand opportunities to visit War Zone C, and particullarly Tay Ninh province, where the bulk of the action in Operation Junction City occurred. By June of 1967 when I arrived in country, the entire 400 square mile Elephant Ear area had been declared a free fire zone, meaning that anything that moved in it would be considered enemy and would be shot.

Flying over the area in helicopters, I could see how the defoliation had reduced the jungle to a huge waste land of barren soil and dead trees. On the Cambodian side of the Van Cau river, which separates the two countries, the jungle was lush and green, but 50 meters away in Vietnam the land was barren and lifeless. Many times during my tour I visited the area, often on combat missions; at the same time I was doing research for the official division history, and thus had the opportunity to examine all after action reports from the operation—that is, Junction City. I learned that the typical big combat operation begins with sketchy intelligence information from aerial intelligence, long range American reconnaissance patrols, Vietnamese and Cambodian agents, coerced prisoners, and just plain MACV hunches or guesses. The decision to destroy Tay Ninh province—which is, incidentally, the ancient center for the followers of Cai Dai, was based on just such inaccurate intelligence information. In the initial stages of the operation, 12 large objective areas were chosen to be attacked. These were to be search-and-destroy operations, beginning with B-52 saturation bombing. In some, but not all, cases the villagers, farmers, and wood-cutters living in the two population centers located within the boundaries of the two objective areas, were warned beforehand of the impending attacks and were told to leave the area. No one that I talked to, including the highest officers in the 25th Infantry Division or the intelligence officers of the 25th Infantry Division who were in charge of this portion of the operation, knew exactly which hamlets had gotten leaflets or loudspeaker broadcasts, or how many of the over 10,000 people in War Zone C had left or had been evacuated before the operation took off; but practically all the GIs I talked to who had been involved in Operation Junction City told me that when the attacks began, there were still many Vietnamese there—men, women, and children in the area.

The B-52 raids began with the dropping of 16,200 five hundred pound bombs. If the objectives were primarily built up—that is towns, or hamlets, incendiary bombs were used. If the objective was jungle or rice paddy, high explosive bombs dropped in a grid pattern would be used. In either event the destruction was appalling. Anything flammable was burned. All the farmlands and the teakwood forests and jungles were saturated with craters 35 feet deep and 45 feet wide. Following the bombing, the softening up went on with long-range artillery fire from 175-mm cannon and eight inch howitzers which continued the pounding objectives and destroyed the structures and individuals which had escaped the bombs. Next came 1,750 air support sorties by Phantom and Sky Hawk attack bombers. The jets expended 1,648 tons of bombs and 1,104 tons of napalm as well as countless tens of thousand of 2.75 inch high explosive rockets and tons of thousands of rounds of machine gun fire. Last to arrive and devastate the objective area from the air were helicopter gunships firing rockets, M-60 machine guns and automatic M-79 grenade launchers all in random pattern.

Following the softening up, the actual occupation began. GIs moved up by helicopter assault and set up close fire support bases. The actual searching began on the second day and was supported by artillery and on-call air strikes. The objects of this search were weapons, foodstuffs, medical supplies, bunkers, tunnels, or any other thing which could possibly be of any use to any human being or animal in that area.

Villages or hamlets within the objective area were completely destroyed. The houses were burned or blown up or run over by tanks, the food confiscated or poisoned by urination or feces, household items smashed; any livestock were killed or captured. The banana trees and the gardens were ripped up, burnt and destroyed. It was in general in this manner that the following villages and hamlets of Tay Ninh province were destroyed. . . . During Tet, 1968, the entire village of Tan Phu Trung, also known as Ap Cau, located on Highway One between Saigon and Cu Chi, was leveled. I had visited the town of nearly 10,000 inhabitants many times. It was a market center. It was one of our much-publicized model hamlets. It had a new school, a local theater company, a strong PF, and this is where we took our visiting VIPs—Bob Hope, Senator Stuart Symington, I believe, visited here—and many others. This was the ideal model hamlet. During the early days of the Tet Offensive, some sniper fire was received from the village. Units of the 3rd Squadron, 4th Cavalry, and the 2nd Battalion, 34th Armor, along with air strikes, completely destroyed the entire town. Nothing was left over three feet high. Reporters who passed through the town shortly after Tet asked why such a well-known model hamlet had suffered such destruction. One of the officers from our division chief of staff said: "We had to save them from themselves."

The NLF. According to MACV and MACOI policy, the National Liberation Front does not now, nor ever did, nor ever will exist either as a movement, as an organization, or as a semantical term. I wonder who it is that I met with yesterday if that is true.

Napalm. According to MACV and MACOI policy there is no such thing as napalm.

This testimony is but a fraction of the extent of military information control in Vietnam, which is part of a larger censorship plot—not only one to keep the truth of the war from the American people, but one to keep the truth and reason of the war from the GIs dying in Vietnam. This almost completes my testimony, and as I finish, I remember a speaking engagement I once had at a Boston high school.

It was a PTA meeting, and just before I began my talk the lady in charge took me aside and counseled me confidentially. In your talk about the war, she asked, please don't use any obscenities or discuss atrocities. Had I complied with her wishes I would have merely stood mute before the audience for my hour, for there is nothing more obscene than war. There is nothing more atrocious than war. And the Indochina war is the most obscene and atrocious in history. Only in this war do we keep public score with body counts. Only in this war do we count every living being, man, woman, child, water buffalo, or bird, as an enemy to be slaughtered. Only in this war have we condemned even the grass and trees and flowers of Indochina to death. Only in this war do we rationalize the destruction of an entire community such as Ben Tre by saying it became necessary to destroy it in order to save it. And only in this war will the underdogs—the Vietnamese, the Laos, the Thais, and the Cambodians—eventually triumph over a massively superior technological force. Not just because of military strategy, but because their cause is just.

Kenneth Barton Osborne

[Kenneth Barton Osborne entered the Army in 1966 and was trained in an Army intelligence school to handle espionage operations in Vietnam. While in Vietnam, he worked with the CIA Phoenix Program.]

I arrived in Saigon, and I attempted for several weeks to become operational in cooperation with the Army, even though I was an autonomous agent—that is, I had no real military discipline or answerability. I tried to cooperate with the Army system. I found, of course, that the Army was not capable of following through with their own regulations . . . for espionage. So I found the best way to collect information was to operate by myself with whatever facilities I could bring to my disposal.

In that effort I sought to get money, logistics, housing, and transportation from whatever agency I could elicit it. In that context I worked for several receiving or using organizations.

The kind of information I was trying to collect was of varying nature. First of all, my prime mission there officially was to establish agent nets and to receive through these nets an effective collection of combat information. That is, names of units, locations, sizes, logistics, and so forth.

This broadened over the course of the first couple of months in Vietnam to collecting information . . . on personalities who were cooperating with the National Liberation Front, who were with the local farm associations, and who in any way had an opposition or less than a complete alignment with the Saigon and American mission in the area.

In the course of collecting information on personalities, in addition to combat information, I found myself disseminating this information to an organization called the Phoenix Coordinator Program in Da Nang city. I lived in Da Nang. I lived as a civilian. I lived under cover. Not under my own name but under a false name and under a false government rating, and I was well documented. I carried official identifications stating that I was a member of the State Department US-AID Program, and I used as a cover during most of the time that I was there the programs of pacification and refugee reorientation and logistics.

Naturally, I used these to infiltrate the local economy, to contact the Vietnamese, and to spot, recruit, and train them as my agents in agent nets in what we call the I-Corps Area of that area from the DMZ down to the south of Quang Ngai.

I want you to see the analogy between my status in Vietnam and the American approach and present legal status in the area. I was sent officially with the blessing of the United States government, authorizedly but covertly, to South Vietnam to operate in the status that I have described. The whole idea and the whole mission for which I was trained and for which I later operated was to supercede any rules of international law or any agreements, either with allies or any other nation states involved in the conflict there. While I was there, I found myself collecting information and targeting allies. For instance, we collected information on the South Koreans. We collected information on whoever was available through whatever means we had, and this relates to the Phoenix Coordinator Program.

The Phoenix Program is described officially as being a collection program to gain information about personalities in the VC infrastructure. The theory being that the Viet Cong is an elusive and silent and invisible government. Obviously the troops can be dealt with militarily, but the political cadres would have to be found via more sophisticated means. If these means were developed and the personalities were arrested and "neutralized," why then the VC could not survive because their infrastructure would dry up, and without that they had no chance of operating.

That is a political theory. It is even a military theory. But in practice, this is what happens: under the capitalistic system which is there in South Vietnam now there is much competition, obviously, in a distorted economy, an inflated economy; there is much competition for whatever wealth is available. So economic competition becomes prime in South Vietnamese life, life style, and values.

If in the course of my operations one agent in my employee net somewhere would be dissatisfied with the performance of a neighbor or a friend or an acquaintance, he was at liberty by the nature of the covert methods that we used to collect information, to report this individual as a member of the Viet Cong infrastructure. For months I collected information on personalities before I realized that some of these people who were being reported as VC were in fact no more VC than I was. *But* the result of this program was that I would disseminate these personalities' names, descriptions, addresses, and so forth, to the Phoenix Coordinator in Da Nang city from whence were dispatched the PRUs (the Potential Reconnaissance Units); [the PRUs] were South Vietnamese elitist troops who would go and collect these individuals and either murder them outright or bring them back for interrogation with no real promise or chance of negative findings or eventual release or exonoration of the individual. In other words, once my agents reported anyone as a VC they were more or less practically doomed. . . .

This, when I joined it, was an incipient program. It was a young program. It had not been well developed. It was not large. It grew by leaps and bounds during the year under which I operated [in it].

At the end of the time I was in Vietnam the Phoenix Coordinator Program had gotten so out of hand and arrests and detainings were so wholesale, that I ran into a number of incidents which I think at this point would serve as a commentary on the brutality of that program.

For instance, at one point since I was collecting information on VC infrastructure personalities, it was reported to me that in a village not far from Da Nang there was an individual who was a member of the local farmers' association and who provided logistics—that is, hid in his garden and areas of his own property, guns and perhaps mortar rounds and so forth that would be used to attack Da Nang Air Base. In the interests of protecting the air base I reported this information not only to the Phoenix Coordinator in Da Nang, but also to the counterintelligence team with the 3rd Marine Amphibious Group Force, adjacent to Da Nang Air Base, an organization with which I had a smooth and cooperative rapport. They went out and found this individual and brought him back for interrogation; let me describe what they did with him.

He was reported as being a member of the Viet Cong infrastructure. Why he was reported that way I never did find out. I never did have time to investigate it, but given the fact that there was a possibility that he was not, he was interrogated in the following way by the American team there.

One first lieutenant and several enlisted men did the interrogations for this team. At the time I arrived one day with new reports and was interested in following up the report of this individual whom I had given in, perhaps a day previously, I asked the team chief there what he was doing about this individual who had been reported from the local village and he said: "We have him here now. Would you like to see him interrogated?" and I said, "Yes, I would," because I was interested in what *modus operandi* they employed. We went with the individual and another detainee who had already been interrogated and beaten and reduced to the state of an incommunicative individual. We went in a jeep to a helicopter nearby at Da Nang Air Base. In the helicopter we went up and out from the area which is empacted with houses and installations around the area of Da Nang. We flew northwest from Da Nang some 20 miles, and as we were up one of the interrogators first antagonized the individual for whom he had no use. He antagonized him, and he pushed him around, and he yelled at him, and he elicited no response from this second Vietnamese. The reason was that the Vietnamese had already been beaten down just to the point where he really couldn't respond. He was demoralized. They warned him—in English, not Vietnamese—that if he did not talk and tell them what they wanted to know, they would throw him from the helicopter. And they warned him twice. And each time that they would warn him, they would take him by the arm and run him up toward the door as if they were going to throw him out, but they wouldn't, and they would bring him back, and each time he would be more demoralized. And they would yell at him in English, "If you don't tell us what we want to know we are going to throw you from the helicopter." They did this several times, and he was reduced to crying, and that's the only way he was able to respond. Finally, in the sight of the second Vietnamese—the one whom we wanted to interrogate, they did rush him to the door and throw him from the helicopter.

This had the effect of demoralizing the second Vietnamese. He would tell then, to the interrogators anything they wanted to hear. Not necessarily what was true and not necessarily anything of value or anything accurate, but simply what they wanted to hear, because he had but one goal, and that was to return to the ground without being thrown from the helicopter.

I was taken on a second ride which had much the same format and which didn't vary enough to warrant going into detail here.

There was a standard operating procedure of the Marine interrogation unit there. At that small group of buildings . . . next to Da Nang Air Base, I also witnessed, for instance, an interrogation building, a small "hooch"—just simply a shack which is lined with screens and covered with tin and which they had subdivided into, I believe, four compartments. . . . I remember having observed a Vietnamese woman who was left in there and who was there several times as I returned to that team to observe things.

She was there constantly, and finally one time when I went back she was gone. I asked what had happened to her, and I was told that she had simply died from lack of any attention. She had not been given food; she had not been given water; she had not been given toilet facilities; all that was done was to cage her. There she was left to die, and she did die. The whole idea was that eventually she would become uncomfortable enough to talk about whatever it was they had asked her; however, she never did, and she died.

I also reported . . . a man who lived near Da Nang, and when I went back to follow up the report again, the team chief told me they were interrogating him at the time I arrived. He took me to the hooch nearby where the man was —the interrogation hooch—and as we arrived, they were bringing the man's body from the hooch. He was dead. The men who had been interrogating this man were embarrassed because they had been caught going overboard even by their own team chief, and they said that they had made a mistake in interrogating him too roughly. I noticed as they brought him from the hooch that there was a wooden dowl extending from his ear which they had used as a torture device and simply intruded it into the ear and tapped through till it finally met his brain and killed him.

This was not atypical. I must say that it was not every day in Vietnam that I saw this kind of torture method, but let me explain how much of it I saw, and why it existed.

First of all, the training which I was given was some of the most extensive training in dealing with the Vietnamese and the collection of material—intelligence data—in the context of Southeast Asia. I was never taught Vietnamese. I was never taught any foreign language, but rather went through a considerable training session to understand the necessity to operate in any way that was expedient regardless of any context of international law.

That was the main premise under which we operated. And it was the only premise. We were then documented not as ourselves or in our own status but appropriately to be maximum mobility and to have maximum access to whatever area that we need in order to collect information.

There was a total disregard for any rules, regulations, or any restrictions involved. This disregard for any restrictions —even moral restrictions—was not implicit but explicit. It was stated bluntly, more so in Vietnam than in training in the United States. . . .

These methods were reinforced from the highest levels of command from which I received instructions on collection all the way down to the lowest operation in the field.

When I got deeply involved in Phoenix, I found myself

being better financed. There came a time, soon after joining the Phoenix Coordinator Program, when I had [none of the] money problems that I had when I first started to operate with the Army. I could never elicit from the Army a feeling that they should, in fact, support by logistics and money, etc., the mission which they sent me there to do. That was not surprising considering the bureaucracy of the military. But my alternative was to work with Phoenix, which was so illegal and so covert as to have no administrative problems whatsoever. And concurrently, with having no administrative bogdowns, there was also no moral structure and no legal structure to our activities.

I feel that my status and the operation to which I can directly relate in my experience in South Vietnam stands as a commentary on the total disregard which our nation, at this point, has for any restriction which would be put on it operationally or legally or popularly, as we spoke of this morning; through the United States Senate; or internationally through a group like this, or in any way. There is no way that they will respond at this point without specific reason or specific force to downgrade the illegal nature of the war.

Commission: How could you really know whether somebody denounced to you as a Viet Cong was not simply a personal enemy of the denunciator?

If I would disseminate that information, I would later find that the combat units which received it sometimes responded to it. In other words, if I would report someone in the area of Da Nang air base who had a potential of getting mortar rounds to Thrie Bie air base, I would find a response more quickly from the marines—the 3rd Marine Amphibious Force Counterinsurgency—than from our intelligence office that I spoke of. They would respond to that because it was in their interest to protect the air base, so if I went to them and talked to them and said: "How have you followed through with that report?" and, "Has this man been guilty or not guilty?" I would find such situations as their being tortured to death. I never, at one point, was able to find anyone who had been interrogated, found innocent, and let gone off.

In the context of my net—agent nets. I was never able to find specifically how an agent determined that this man was a VC, other than what he told me in the report, and the report would go something like this: "A certain individual, name, age, description, whose wife's name is so and so, who had so many children, and who lives at this village (and then a physical description of where to find his house) has been operating as a cadre of the local farmers' association for two and a half years. His brother, so and so, went north in 1954 and is now working with the NLF in the South" or "is now a captain in the NVA. This individual operates regularly by going to this village to pick up some vegetables. This is his business: to go here and buy vegetables and to sell them along the way back home. In returning he hides money" or "logistics" or something "in his cart. He has been doing this for months or years. His additional job would be that next month there is a VC political educational session in this area at this coordinate on the map, and he will be the vice-council in charge of political education." This is the kind of format we got. Based on the reliability of the combat information which these nets as a whole produced, they were rated both formally and informally according to their accuracy. If they had been accurate by saying "this unit is here at this time" (and it was, many times), if it were more than 90 percent accurate (which these nets generally turned out to be), then the reporting of an individual as a Viet Cong infrastructure member was judged also accurate. So there was an ongoing prejudice. If an individual then were drawn in for interrogation, it was a foregone conclusion that he was in fact a VC and *naturally* he was going to deny it; maybe he would even be brave enough to deny it to death. If, in fact he were not, though, a VC infrastructure member, this situation would be not only his demise but would amount to murder.

So when I asked why, first it was based on the biography of the individual's brother who went 54 somewhere else and family relations; and secondly on the reliability of the network who produced the information its, to say on the accuracy of the former information produced by the network.

Commission: What were the criteria to assess such reliability, such 90 percent of accuracy of which you are speaking?

First of all, you have to understand the ongoing assumption that anybody in South Vietnam, be he any age, sex, political orientation, covertly and overtly, and so forth is potentially a member of the Viet Cong.

The more you get to know the South Vietnamese, the more you get to know they have a vested interest in at least cooperating with both sides; so if they cooperate with the enemy side in addition to cooperating with you, they *are* the enemy. So it is quite possible and quite plausible for someone to be accused of being a VC no matter how briefly or how incipently he has been involved with or cooperated with the enemy. Now that is an ongoing mentality as well as an assumption, and when you get someone reported as a member of the Viet Cong cadre unit, it's only a matter of drawing out of this what information you need to know. You don't approach him as potentially an innocent civilian; you approach him as a sinister agent of the Viet Cong and all South Vietnamese. Especially by the standard of the Marines or by anybody who has no cultural insights for the South Vietnamese (myself included), the conclusion is made that these people are devious, and we are lucky to find the ones on whom we can put a finger and eliminate. So there is no chance of dealing with them fairly or humanely on that basis.

Commission: So practically, the conclusion of the Phoenix

*Program when carried out in this manner would be to elimi-
nate the majority of the Vietnamese population because of
some brief contact with the Liberation units nearly every
Vietnamese peasant has had during the last years. So if this
program would be really concluded, most of the Vietnamese
population would have to be neutralized. Do I understand
right?*

The logical conclusion of the Phoenix Coordinate Program
would be to eliminate the Vietnamese population, and I
should take that one step further to overillustrate the point:
I think that if it were authorized in the world you would
naturally go and murder Ambassador Bruce in Paris because
he cooperated with the Viet Cong *to a point.* This kind of a
runaway mentality is in fact operationally a fact in South
Vietnam.

Report from Indochina

For well over a decade, Indochinese scientists, journalists, and investigators have made detailed reports of violations of international agreements and of their own territories. Only since the publication of the Pentagon Papers, which so thoroughly corroborated their work, have Americans begun to give credence to the Indo-Chinese reports. What follows are detailed accounts, compiled in scrupulously dry prose, of specific massacres, of use of illegal weapons, of territorial violations, of harsh imprisonment and generally repressive policies carried out by the American forces or their client regimes in Indochina. The reports are drawn largely from the research of special committees established in Vietnam and Laos to gather data on war crimes. For a comparison of both content and methodology, see the Commission's independent task force report in the next section.

Political Report from Laos: General Singkapo Chounnamaly

[Read by General Singkapo Chounnamaly, member of the Lao Patriotic Front Central Committee, head of the Delegation of the Committee to Denounce the U.S. Imperialists' Crimes in Laos.]

Mr. Chairman,

Ladies,

Gentlemen,

The U.S. aggressive war which has been prolonged for many years has been intensified in South Vietnam and Laos, then expanded into Cambodia and carried on by stepped-up provocations against the DRVN. Thus, the whole of Indochina is subjected to U.S. military escalation, and the crimes committed in the name of the United States have piled up since the International Committee for Enquiry held its first session.

At this second session, the Delegation of the Committee to Denounce the U.S. Imperialists' Crimes in Laos wishes to draw your attention mainly on the major facts regarding the intensification and expansion of the war in Laos by the Nixon administration and to expound some views on the U.S. crimes against our country and our people.

Despite its setbacks in Vietnam, Cambodia, and especially in its "Kou Kiet" nibbling operation against the Plain of Jars

—Xieng Khoang area (late 1969-early 1970), the Nixon administration obdurately carries on its policy of "Vietnamization" of the war, using the Saigon puppet army and Thai combat units to implement U.S. plans, "pitting Asians against Asians," intensifying, prolonging, and expanding the war in Indochina.

In Laos alone, since the end of 1970, the United States has launched bombing raids of an exterminating character, involving various kinds of planes, including B-52s, pouring on Lao territory over 3,000 tons of bombs a day, piling up untold crimes against the Lao people. A particularly serious crime was that in last February and March, when the Nixon administration mustered more than 40,000 U.S. and Saigon puppet troops supported by a huge air force, and started a massive intrusion into Southern Laos, the most brazen operation of aggression in the history of U.S. intervention in Laos, turning Indochina into a most fierce battlefield. Meanwhile, the Vang Pao special forces and the Vientiane rightist troops, established by the U.S. to serve as its tools, coordinated their actions with Thai combatant units to launch nibbling attacks against the Liberated zone of the Patriotic forces from North to South of Laos.

The open U.S.-Saigon puppet invasion into Road 9—southern Laos—was decided by Nixon, but to deceive world opinion the latter declared that it was a "restricted" operation, with U.S. support only in firepower and logistics to the South Vietnam puppet army. However, this allegation deceived nobody. In truth, before and during the operation, U.S. planes savagely bombed Laos, pouring on its population hundreds of thousands of tons of bombs of all kinds, while ground troops fired millions of shells and cartridges "at will," causing untold carnage and destruction. This laid bare the Nixion administration's crimes against the Lao people.

Thus, all the U.S. allegations aimed at defending the expansion of the aggressive war in Laos under the pretext of "self-defense" and "ensuring security" for the U.S. aggressors in South Vietnam cannot cover the U.S.'s reckless acts. As is known to everybody, the Americans and their lackeys received well-deserved blows within a very short time—40 days.

Ladies,
Gentlemen,

What are then the nature and the character of the U.S. imperialists' crimes against our country and our people?

Over the past 17 years, the U.S. imperialists have continually plotted to invade and enslave our country like neighboring Vietnam and Cambodia, in an attempt at achieving neocolonialism and turning Indochina into their military base to check the movement for independence and freedom by the peoples of Indochina and Southeast Asia. Flouting international law banning aggressive war and defending the inalienability of all nations, the U.S. administrations—the most unruly being the present Nixon one—have carried a war of aggression against our small Laos, completely sabotaging the 1954 and 1962 Geneva Agreements and brutally trampling underfoot the fundamental national rights of the Lao people and the peace and neutrality of their country. Therefore, the U.S. imperialists have violated the most fundamental principles of international law, namely the respect for the political independence and national sovereignty of the peoples of other countries, and the safeguard of peace. Thus they have committed the greatest international crime: the crime of aggression against the fundamental national rights, the right to self-determination of the Lao people and the crime against peace.

While invading Laos in the hope of subjugating its people to achieve their neocolonialist design, the U.S. imperialists have resorted to all schemes and barbarous war means in order to destroy our country and our people. They have launched their air force in indiscriminate bombings throughout seventeen straight years, devastating vast areas of Laos. Especially in 1969, 1970, and early this year, U.S. planes went all out striking at the Plain of Jars —Xieng Khouang area and southern Laos, killing and wounding tens of thousands of civilians—including old folk, women, and children—with U.S. explosive bombs, incendiary bombs, pellet bombs, flechette bombs, spider bombs, and toxic chemicals.

On the other hand with the huge support of U.S. air force and logistics, they have used Vientiane, Saigon, and Bangkok troops to nibble at the Lao liberated zone, putting to fire and sword whole villages, towns, cities, pagodas, schools, hospitals, and irrigation works, and repressing the civilian population. Meanwhile, to enforce a Machiavellian U.S. plan, these troops have compelled part of the population to leave their native places and resettle into U.S.-puppet "refugee settlements" so as to persecute them morally and materially and eventually drive them to death.

By resorting to these schemes and murderous means— which the Hitler and Tojo followers dared not use during the Second World War—and by flouting the fundamental rights of man and of nations, the U.S. imperialists have committed not only war crimes and crimes against humanity, but also an utterly heinous crime of genocide.

By these illegal and criminal acts the U.S. imperialists are not only the direct enemy of the Lao people, of the Indochinese peoples, but also the most cruel enemy of all nations in the world. Those who must bear responsibility for these international crimes before international law and human conscience are the U.S. government and individually President Nixon, as well as his immediate predecessors, and all other U.S. political and military leaders in the White House and the Pentagon.

Besides the U.S. imperialists—the chief culprits of those crimes—the Vientiane, Saigon, Phnom Penh authorities, the abject lackeys of the U.S. imperialists who betray the Lao, Vietnamese, and Cambodian peoples and nations and will fully serve the U.S. policy of aggression and expansion of the war in Laos and throughout Indochina, must also be held responsible before history and the Indochinese nations.

The Thanom Kittikachorn reactionary government has sold out Thai national sovereignty by turning Thailand into a U.S. base of aggression, against its people and the Indochina peoples. At present, it is clear beyond any doubt that the Thai reactionary government cannot deny that Thai territory constitutes a logistic base for U.S. expeditionary troops, staging base for U.S. planes, including B-52s, which daily take off to fiercely strike at the Lao liberated zone, as well as neighboring Vietnam and Cambodia. Moreover, they also sell Thai troops as cannon-fodder to the U.S. aggressors in exchange for U.S. dollars. They have introduced into Laos tens of thousands of Thai soldiers to fight the Lao people. In consequence, the Lao people sternly condemn the Thai reactionary government as the accomplice of the U.S. imperialists in the aggressive war against Laos and the Indochinese peoples.

In face of the ruthless aggression of the U.S. imperialists to safeguard their sacred fundamental national rights, and in close coordination with the fraternal Vietnamese and Cambodian army and people, the Lao patriotic armed forces people have resolutely fought off the enemy and have been smashing the "U.S. air supremacy," repelling all nibbling attacks of the Americans and their puppets.

Though in a winning posture, the Lao Patriotic Front, which symbolizes the unity and determination to struggle of the Lao people, has on several occasions expounded its just stand and fair attitude in the settlement of the Laos issue in order to end the U.S. aggressive war, restore peace in Laos on the basis of the 1962 Geneva Agreement and the present concrete situation in Laos, as put forward in the ten-point Political Program and the five-point Political Solution of the Lao Patriotic Front. This stand and good will conforms to both sense and sentiment and has been of late concretized by the Lao Patriotic Front Standing Committee and the Alliance of the Patriotic Neutralist Forces standing Committee, with a view to practically advancing toward an end to the U.S. colonialist war of aggression in Laos and creating conditions for the Lao concerned parties to discuss a rapid settlement of the Laos issue through peaceful means.

The United States is the aggressor of Laos. To peacefully settle the Laos issue, the United States must put an immediate end to its intervention and aggression in Laos in the first place; it must completely and unconditionally cease its bombing throughout Lao territory by the U.S. Air Force which is daily and hourly bombing, strafing, and slaughtering the Lao people, piling up crime upon crime.

The interventionist and aggressor must stop his intervention and aggression. The criminal must renounce his crime without posing any condition. That is a legitimate demand of the Lao people as well of the peace- and justice-loving people the world over.

In their bitter fight on the way to victory against the U.S. aggressors and their lackeys, the Lao people further strengthen their solidarity and determination to struggle until final victory with the Vietnamese and Cambodian peoples. The Lao people are firmly confident in their victory, for their fight like that of the Vietnamese and Cambodian peoples is a just one, is backed by a vast rear, the peoples of the socialist countries and oppressed nations, the forces of peace, democracy, and progress throughout the world, who extend to them their sympathy and support.

Once again, we sincerely thank the Chairman, all the delegates and friends for having spared your time and closely followed the report of our Delegation on the U.S. imperialists' intensification and expansion of the war by the Nixon administration and on the U.S. imperialists' crimes in Laos. We Lao people are daily and hourly waiting for the brilliant success of this session, and we hope that the U.S. imperialists' crimes in Indochina will be unanimously and energetically condemned at this Session.

Political Report from the DRV: Pham Van Bach

[Pham Van Bach is President of the Supreme Court of The Democratic Republic of Vietnam.]

On this tribune, at the first session of the International Commission of Enquiry, we have been given the opportunity to denounce the "Vietnamization of the war" policy pursued by the ruling circles in the United States of America, to unveil its aggressive and bellicose nature, and point out the danger arising from it, which hangs over the world's peoples who are struggling for their independence and freedom.

To Nixon and his partners, to "Vietnamize" the war does not mean to put an end to the U.S. war of aggression in Vietnam, but simply to continue it in a new, more vicious form. Through the "Vietnamization" Washington fosters the hope of realizing the U.S. military-industrial circles' unchanged goal of neocolonialist domination over Vietnam despite the unsuccessful trial of all the previous war strategies and the pressure of public opinion in the U.S. which grows more and more anxious about the disastrous effects of the direct commitment of an American expeditionary corps to the Vietnam adventure. To "Vietnamize" the war consists in gradually withdrawing a fraction of U.S. troops from Vietnam in a bid to reduce American casualties to a level acceptable for the American people and, at the same time, obstinately clinging to the Thieu-Ky-Khiem stooge clique that serves them as instrument for the continuation of the war of aggression, and beefing up the Saigon puppet army to throw it into the fighting in their place for a "change" of color in the skin of bodies on the battlefield.

We make it a point to insist this time again on this aggressive and neocolonialist policy of President Nixon before world public opinion, which is being rightly more and more concerned with what happens in Vietnam, Laos, and Cambodia: under the cover of an alleged "deescalation" and in the context of a gradual partial withdrawal of U.S. troops, in fact, Nixon is carrying on *the U.S. war of aggression* according to a new strategy, is intensifying it and extending it to the whole of Indochina.

As all those maneuvers of Washington have stumbled on the heroic and efficient resistance of the Vietnamese, Lao, and Cambodian peoples who, united in the same front, are more determined than ever to defend their fundamental national rights flouted by the aggressors, the Nixon administration, far from resigning itself to give up, pursues and increases all the more its war efforts, thus further aggravating and piling up its crimes. This, we dare hope, should constitute the object of your examination in the present session.

In the light of new events and international law, it is incumbent on us to bring here our contribution to denounce the very essence of the so-called "Nixon doctrine" and the "Vietnamization" with the crime aggravation that arises from all this Nixonian policy.

1. The Vietnamization of the war is but the continuation in another variant of the U.S. crime of aggression perpetrated for years in Vietnam.

The new aspect of the crime lies in the fact that it is performed in the framework of a doctrine named after Nixon, which amounts to a formula of action regarded by Washington as the most appropriate, under the current conditions in the world, to materialize U.S. neocolonialism in Asia. The said doctrine consists in playing off Asians against Asians under U.S. command, with U.S. support and aid deemed necessary in the interests of American neocolonialism.

Nixon never ceases to deceive the American people in asserting that "the Vietnam war is progressively declining" and "nearing its end." However, the truth is quite another thing.

Despite reiterated demands by the PRG of the Republic of South Vietnam, the Government of the DRVN, and international progressive public opinion, the U.S. troop withdrawal from South Vietnam has been rather sluggish. The Nixon administration is always reluctant to assign a deadline to the complete evacuation of the U. S. expeditionary corps and even affirms its intention to maintain the U. S. military occupation in South Vietnam by keeping there a contingent for an indefinite time. On last April 16, Nixon said the total U. S. pullout depends on two conditions, to wit: "the capacity of the South Vietnamese (i.e. the Saigon puppet administration) to defend themselves and "the release of the prisoners of war held by North Vietnam." As far as captured American army men are concerned, at the April 29, 1971 new conference, he bluntly declared: "We will be there as long as they have any prisoners in North Vietnam."

What do these new terms mean? Simply that there will be no complete withdrawal of U. S. troops, no ending of their role of occupation and participation in the fighting in Vietnam.

Indeed, it is beyond doubt that the Saigon puppets who as yet could hold on only thanks to the U. S. tutelage, aid and assistance, will never be capable of defending themselves. On the other hand, so long as U. S. forces stay in Vietnam and more GI's are captured in the continued war, how can one think of that moment Nixon spoke of when "the last American POW" would finally be released? By those highly contradictory terms laid down for the total withdrawal of U. S. troops from Vietnam, Nixon simply means that that pullout will never take place.

The Nixon administration has made great efforts to beef up the Saigon puppet army. However, the latter always remains unqualified to fight by itself. Therefore, to make up for the reduction of U.S. ground forces, Washington strengthens the U.S. firepower to excess in terms of aircraft and artillery in support of Saigon troops in their massacre-and-destroy operations. The U.S. war only assumes another form in which it would be conducted more "properly" and with less losses in American lives, according to their own words.

In addition, for all the Nixon administration's denials, a great many U.S. advisors and an important contingent of U.S. ground forces have continued to take a direct part in the fighting under various pretenses, as is confirmed by captured U.S. and puppet troops' multiple testimonies and according to many revelations by the press and trustworthy Western news agencies.

In South Vietnam, as the war of aggression goes on, fresh, horrid crimes are perpetrated every day during bloody "pacification" operations. In the first months of this year, U.S.-puppet sweeps daily averaged 80, as against 50 in late 1970. Air attacks continued and were intensified: in last April, B-52 bombing raids increased fivefold over the preceding months. . . . Following the "accelerated pacification" and "special pacification" programs, Washington has just worked out a new pacification project called "rural protection and local development" plan, the implementation of which, financed by the U.S. and put under the auspices of the U.S. Defense Department and the CIA, means the furtherance of war acts and massacres to an even greater extent.

Along with all those facts, as regards the North, brazenly trampling underfoot the October 1968 U.S. commitment to unconditionally end all bombardments, the Nixon administration has not only continued but has also intensified its war acts against the DRVN. In ten months alone, between July 1970 and late April [of] this year, over 13,000 recon flights and some 1,900 bombing raids were conducted in North Vietnam, well nigh the figure recorded in the preceding 18-month period (January 1969-June 1970). According to still incomplete statistics, over 7,000 recon missions and 600 air strikes (including 175 B-52 bombings), with almost 20,000 tons of bombs dropped, were carried out in the DRVN from January to early May of this year. Confirming this escalation move, a U.S. source reported that in the first four months of this year, U.S. bombing raids on the DRVN, cynically referred to by the Nixon administration as "protective reactions," increased four-fold over 1970 (AP-Saigon, April 29, 1971). During those air attacks, bombs and mines of all types, including latest versions of U.S. fragmentation antipersonnel weapons, were profusely used. Ground artillery from south of the provisional military demarcation line, and guns from numerous U.S. warships blockading the southern littoral, incessantly bombarded our coastal villages. Sporadic toxic chemical sprays took place over North Vietnamese localities adjoining the 17th parallel.

Following waves of massive and concentrated bombing raids on Nghe An, Quang Binh provinces, and Vinh Linh area conducted in early May 1970 in tactical concert with the invasion of Cambodia by U.S. and Saigon puppet troops in the same period, new drives of the same character were carried out on a larger scale. On November 21, 1970, over 200 U.S. planes launched almost simultaneous attacks against a still greater number of provinces, including the surroundings of Na Noi and Hai Phong. Recently, on March 21 and 22 of this year, in concert with the U.S.-Saigon incursion into lower Laos (Highway 9 front), the USAF conducted new drives of big raids against numerous civilian targets in Ha Tinh and Quang Binh provinces and Vinh Linh area. Along with these acts, the Nixon administration never ceases to threaten our Republic with new military adventures.

A crime against peace, the U.S. war of aggression in Vietnam, at the same time, constitutes in the highest degree a crime against the fundamental national rights of the Vietnamese people. As is known, it has been conducted by the U.S. for more than a decade in Vietnam with the aim to realize, through neocolonialist methods, U.S. neocolonialism in South Vietnam.

Pursued under Nixon in the form of the Vietnamization of the war, the U.S. neocolonialist Crime of Aggression is marked with characteristic features of slyness and Machiavellianism. The American imperialists, in the persons of Nixon and his associates, would like to perpetrate it henceforth at a lighter cost, with others' blood, and prolong the killing between Vietnamese endlessly in their interests. While the prolongation of the U.S. war of aggression [in] its "Vietnamized" version becomes flagrant in everybody's eyes, the culprits in Washington always try obstinately to exculpate themselves by claiming that they "want peace," that they "are going to get America out of the war," that they only want to do good to the South Vietnamese people and "are defending their right to self-determination." That is a real falsification of the truth that can deceive nobody any more.

In perpetrating fresh war acts against the DRVN, an independent and soveriegn country, Nixon and his administration declare they only practice the right of Americans to "self-defense" and to "retaliation" upon the alleged "hostile acts" on the part of North Vietnam, thus arrogating to themselves the right to fly spy planes over North Vietnam's territory and carry out recon missions and air, naval, or ground artillery bombardments with impunity wherever and whenever it suits them. All allegations advanced by Nixon as excuses for American transgressions of the DRVN's sovereignty and security are reminiscent of those talks of real gangsters who in cutting people's throats pretend that they only "defend themselves" and act within the limits of the law.

Never [has] disregard of international law, which protects peace and the people's fundamental national rights, [been] pushed to such a degree of arrogance, cynicism, and absurdity.

Under the pretext of saving the Vietnamization doomed to failure in Vietnam and in implementation of the Nixon doctrine with a view to bringing about U.S. neocolonialism in other Indochinese countries, the Nixon administration stepped up the war of aggression in Laos and extended it into Cambodia. The Lao and Khmer brother delegations to this meeting will inform the Commission adequately of the U.S. criminal acts their countries fell victim to. The application of the Nixon doctrine in Laos means the continuation of the U.S. war of aggression conducted for years on the Lao territory in the form of a special warfare, in violation of the 1954 and 1962 Geneva Agreements on Laos, and which is now further intensified and asserts itself still more conspicuously with the Highway 9 operation at the U.S.-Saigon foray into lower Laos. As regards Cambodia, in carrying out the Nixon doctrine, Washington shifted from border transgressions, neocolonialist seizure attempts, and CIA-directed subversive maneuvers under Johnson to an overt war of aggression against this country in violation of the 1954 Geneva Agreements on Cambodia. So against the Lao and Khmer peoples were committed other neocolonialist crimes of aggression which demanded their basic national rights.

Examined on the whole and on the Indochinese scale here is what arises from the application of the Nixon doctrine and the Vietnamization: the war now sets the whole of Indochina aflame; to the crime against the Vietnamese people are added the crimes of aggression against the Lao and Khmer peoples; Indochinese are turned against Indochinese, Asians against Asians in a fury of carnage and destruction which further worsens the mishap of the local populations in the interests of the Yankee imperialists.

That the U.S. war of aggression is being prolonged and aggravated is what American journalist Daniel Ellsberg confirmed in his article published in the *New York Review of Books,* March 11, 1971, issue: "If one accepts to believe Nixon's allegations in taking account only of the gradual troop pullout and the decline in American losses, one would misjudge the aspect of the war which has grown intensified: air activities, current operations outside the South Vietnamese territory, and casualties in Laos and Cambodia for which we (Americans) are responsible" (retranslated from the French). In this intensified and expanding war, not only Vietnamese are played off against Vietnamese, Lao against Lao, Cambodians against Cambodians, but people in other Asian countries are also drafted to be thrown into the pellmell butchery organized and orchestrated by the U.S. It is notorious that South Korean, New Zealander, Filippino, Australian mercenaries have been fighting by the side of Saigon puppet troops in South Vietnam, that Saigon and Thai puppet troops have been launched against Cambodians and Laotians in Cambodia and Laos. At the time of the invasion of the Khmer country last year, in his June 30, 1970, speech, Nixon called on the governments of the U.S.-dependent Asian countries to militarily intervene for Lon Nol's sake. Washington pressingly urges [its] Asian agents in SEATO to support it in its new criminal intrigues. . . . Through all those manifestations, the Nixon Doctrine turns out to be a doctrine generative of crimes of aggression against the Asian peoples, which at the same time constitute serious CRIMES AGAINST PEACE, gravely jeopardizing the security of the countries struggling to safeguard their independence and freedom and also world peace. This criminal doctrine, we must energetically denounce here to the watchfulness of the peoples.

2. The U.S. war of aggression is a GENOCIDAL WAR. The U.S. CRIME OF GENOCIDE in Vietnam goes beyond the wording of the Nuremberg Charter and the 1948 convention, because it affects all fundamental elements of the existence of the Vietnamese nation (physical, material, cultural, moral, spiritual, ideological . . .) and resorts to inhuman means and methods hitherto unknown. U.S. imperialism has knowingly behaved in this line, with its rapacious and bellicose nature, its goal of world hegemony, its role of international gendarme expansion. Indeed, obstinately longing for world domination through neocolonialism, having created to this end a war machinery endowed with mighty means of massacre and destruction, and, besides, unwilling to put up with a military and political failure that could ruin their prestige and interests, the American aggressors propose responding to the Vietnamese people's resolute and heroic resistance by the systematic use of force and the recourse to an all-out war with the most atrocious means at their disposal.

Therefore, in spite of successive defeats it met with over the past 15 years, the U.S. stubbornly pursues the crime of escalation in the hope of beating the Vietnamese people's war and, at last, securing a position of strength under the current circumstances.

The genocide taken over by the Nixon administration in South Vietnam, together with the Vietnamization of the war, grows redoubled in cruelty and sadism.

In Vietnamizing the war, Washington also tends to Vietnamize the genocide. That Vietnamese are killed and continue to be killed in the fighting, only rejoices the Nixon administration. Swedish Foreign Minister Torsten Nilsson, on May 1, told a meeting in Stockholm: "With the Vietnamization, the Americans don't care a rap for the fate of their victims. . . . Vietnamization has become a word of macabre sonority." However, on the other hand, as long as their troops stay in Vietnam, the direct active part taken by Americans in the accomplishment of the genocide against the South Vietnamese people manifests itself: by the intensified use of their firepower, in line with their "Vietnamization of the war" plan. Massacres and destruction by bombs under Nixon, in Vietnam and other Indochinese countries grow fiercer than ever. During the last period, the U.S. puppets, while maintaining old genocidal proceedings inherited from their predecessors, have bettered some of them in savageness: redoubled intensity of sweeps, removals, deportation en masse and concentration of the peasantry, increasing use of ever more hellish and sadistic *antipersonnel weapons* against the civilian population.

The consequences of the U.S. imperialists' monstrous crimes in the Indochinese countries, especially in Vietnam, are unreckonable. This atrociousness challenges all human imagination. They cause not only deaths but also inhuman and lasting sufferings to millions of survivers. Napalm, phosphorous, magnesium, termite, pellet bombs, and fragmentation weapons of all kinds, improved from year to year, maim and deform the victims' bodies, leaving behind wounds hardly treatable or even incurable. "Defoliants" and "herbicides," repeatedly sprayed at high dose and concentration and on a large scale, coupled with millions of tons of destructive bombs, lay waste the country, strike at all that live on earth: man, fauna, flora; destroy and upset the nature and the environments of living creatures. For an adequate description of these new crimes (as yet unconceivable, which, up to now, positive law couldn't provide for, and which even better the genocide in gravity and horror), anxious world public opinion has rightly spoken of *"biocide"* and even *"ecocide."*

Ever since the U.S. war of aggression, under Nixon, was intensified and extended to Laos and Cambodia, monstrous crimes have been committed there against the Lao and Khmer peoples who have also fallen victims to a genocidal war conducted by the U.S. with the same means and proceedings practiced in Vietnam: U.S. firepower intensified beyond all measure, bombs showered by millions of tons, indiscriminate massacres of civilians, searches, removals, population concentration, ill treatment and torture of prisoners; it is the U.S. genocide carried out by the hands of Indochinese turned against Indochinese, by Saigon puppets against Cambodians, by Lon Nol—Sirik Matak's troops against Vietnamese residents and Cambodian patriots, by Vientiane puppet troops and Thai mercenaries against Lao patriots.

Such are the American crimes, horrible and innumerable, in Viet Nam and other Indochinese countries, committed under the label of the Vietnamization and the application of the Nixon Doctrine.

In their process of committing crimes, Nixon and his partners cynically flout law and morality, repudiate all their signings, indulge in all arbitrariness. They trample underfoot not only all principles of international law, but also the constitutional law of their own countries, as is stated by American progressive lawyers.

The responsibility for all those crimes in Vietnam, Laos, and Cambodia, the pursuance of which flows from a national policy of the U.S. government, is incumbent upon the Nixon administration, individually upon Nixon himself and other American rulers in the White House and the Pentagon, according to the principles formulated since Nuremberg in the prosecution and condemnation of the Nazi ringleaders. It is Nixon who has fathered the doctrine named after him and the "Vietnamization of the war" policy and directed the carrying out of these. It is he and his administration who have been pursuing the war of aggression in Vietnam, intensifying it and extending it to the other countries in Indochina. And, consequently, it is they who are the authors of the crimes of aggression which generate all other war crimes, genocide, and crimes against humanity committed in those countries.

That political and military leaders in wars of aggression must be held responsible for the crimes committed by their troops and other agents on the battlefield has been unequivocally established by the principles flowing from the jurisprudence of the Tokyo International Military Tribunal, presided over by a representative of the U.S., and that of the U.S. Supreme Court. What was said and concluded at that time against Japanese General Yamashita now applies as well to Johnson, Nixon, Laird, Westmoreland, Abrams, and the likes of them. Nixon, the present Chief Executive of the U.S. and Commander-in-Chief of the American Armed Forces, is not and must not be unaware of the acts perpetrated by GIs on the battlefield in implementation of his policy, under his own leadership. The Calley affair is but a juridical comedy made up by Washington in a vain attempt to throw the blame on petty subalterns. Reacting public opinion in America has obliged Nixon to intervene (however illegally) in the penal trial of Calley. But by doing so, Nixon shows how fearful he is that a severe condemnation against Calley would disastrously repercuss on the morale of GIs who are doomed to play a similar role of Jack Ketch in Vietnam.

Mr. President,
Ladies and gentlemen,
Dear friends,

So is unveiled to the increasingly well informed world

opinion the truth about the "Vietnamization of the war" policy and the Nixon doctrine. The application of the Nixon doctrine has led to the continuation and intensification of the U.S. war of aggression in Vietnam, to its extension to all the Indochinese countries, entailing in its wake a new crime escalation which is arousing the growing emotion and indignation of world public opinion anxious to work by all possible means towards an end of this.

Since the first session of the I.C.E., along with multiple activities deployed in various international arenas by its members and Secretariat General for the denunciation of U.S. war crimes, people of all continents and different international and national organizations have raised their voices more strongly than ever against the U.S. imperialist leaders' war adventures and their criminal effects.

The American people themselves, more and more awakened to the sense of honor and their just interests, lately have also redoubled their protests against the Nixon administration's bellicose and criminal policy. This has been shown in particular during the demonstrations that raged in spring of this year throughout all the states in America, especially in Washington and San Francisco, rallying as many as one million-odd people, demanding the complete withdrawal of the expeditionary corps from Vietnam and the cessation of the war of aggression in Indochina. The entire world has followed with attention the courageous action of numerous popular and progressive organizations and large sections belonging to all American social strata, especially youths and also Viet Vets, [and] have supported it with sympathy and solidarity demonstrations. In this movement, quite a lot of people, in particular progressive lawyers, insist on a questioning the personal responsibility of President Nixon and other bigwigs in the White House and the Pentagon for U.S. war crimes in Indochina.

We are intent on expressing here once more our deep gratitude to numerous governments, peace and democratic organizations, peace-, freedom-, and justice-loving people over the world for their support to our cause and their aid to our struggle.

Despite their obduracy, the U.S. aggressors will be finally defeated for good and driven out of Vietnam and Indochina. The Vietnamese, Lao, and Khmer people, more united than ever in a common front in their struggle for national liberation, with the support of the world's peoples and the American people themselves are daily winning new successes over the enemy and are determined to bring their just struggle to final victory.

We call on the world's peoples to further step up their campaign for the denunciation of American crimes in Indochina, as well as their active support and aid to our people and the Lao and Cambodian ones, to force the Nixon administration to end its war of aggression and positively meet our just and legitimate demands.

We are convinced that the present session of the International Commission of Enquiry into U.S. War Crimes in Vietnam, Laos, and Cambodia will bring its valuable contribution to this end.

To conclude, on behalf of our Delegation and of the Vietnamese people, we express our deep gratitude for all that it has done so far and will continue to do in the interests of our cause and present it our wholehearted wishes for the best success in its work.

Report to the Commission:
Nguyen Van Tien

[Mr. Tien, a member of the NLF Central Committee, is head of the delegation from the Committee to Denounce U.S.-Puppet War Crimes in South Vietnam.]
Mr. Chairman,
Ladies and Gentlemen,

Eight months have elapsed since the first meeting of the International Commission of the Investigation of U.S. War Crimes in Vietnam, Laos, and Cambodia, held in October 1970 in Stockholm. In this span of time world opinion has come out even more strongly against the crimes perpetrated by the U.S. aggressors and their hirelings in the Indochinese countries. International actions have joined this drive of indictment, such as the gathering of World Scientists on Chemical Warfare in December 1970, and the meeting of the Centre of Information for the Denunciation of War Crimes in March 1971 in Paris. Even in the U.S.A. many American veterans back from the Vietnam battlefield have indicted their commanders for the latters' crimes or for those they have been forced to commit themselves. Evidence was produced and recorded during these meetings, while reports confirmed that the U.S. crimes in Vietnam, Laos, and Cambodia have been generated by the policy of aggression pursued by the top men in the White House and the Pentagon, a systematic policy, as pointed out by our Commission at its first session.

In the face of protest in the U.S.A. and the world, Nixon has been striving to soothe and deceive public opinion, chiefly by extolling the plan of "Vietnamizing" the war, loudly claimed to be the road leading to a "genuine peace."

But "Vietnamization" is in essence the prolongation and expansion of the war. Since Nixon's inauguration, U.S. sweeps and destructive operations have been increasing in South Vietnam, while bombings and acts of violation against the security and sovereignty of the Democratic Republic of Vietnam still continue. The U.S. war of aggression has spread to Cambodia and Laos.

In his speech of February 25, 1971, Nixon said publicly that the said policy met the U.S. objective of reducing its involvement, and that it cannot put an end to the war before a long period of time has elapsed.

Thus, it is clear that "Vietnamization" is simply *the continuation of the U.S. war with Vietnamese blood.* This has been asserted by the "Nixon Doctrine," which aims at "using the Asians to kill other Asians," "the Indochinese to kill other Indochinese" and "the Vietnamese to kill other Vietnamese," or, as [Ambassador] Ellsworth Bunker put it, to "change the color of the corpses."

While pulling out a certain number of U.S. effectives, Washington orders its Saigon quislings to frantically press-gang young men and send them to the South Vietnam, Cambodia, and Laos battlefields in furtherance of Nixon's plan.

Thieu, Ky, and Khiem, that bellicose trio of henchmen, constitute an instrument of the U.S. government for the effectuation of the war of aggression against Indochina in its neocolonialist form. These valets have shown themselves rotten and impotent, and Nixon now makes their capability of self-defense a condition for the repatriation of all GIs. U.S.

Defense Secretary Melvin Laird said on April 14, 1971, that U.S. ground forces continue to play their combat role and that the U.S. Air Force and Navy will remain in Southeast Asia indefinitely. Even with the present tempo of withdrawal, on December 1, 1971, the U.S. and satellite troops will still amount to 250,000 men, plus 20,000 GIs in the Seventh Fleet and other U.S. effectives stationed in other countries neighboring on Vietnam. This testifies to the fact that "Vietnamization" means *indefinite prolongation of U.S. military occupation so as to maintain neocolonialism in South Vietnam.*

The essential contents, mentioned above, of Nixon's "Vietnamization" of the war make it a perfidious maneuver that runs counter to the fundamental national rights of the Vietnamese, Cambodian, and Lao peoples and to the Indochinese, American, and world people's aspirations for peace. The continuation of the war in the "Vietnamization" form, far from reducing the fierceness of the conflict, simply impels *the escalation of the crimes against the Vietnamese, Lao, and Cambodian peoples.* Along with the withdrawal of a certain number of U.S. troops and the swelling of Saigon mercenaries, the White House and the Pentagon in South Vietnam have resorted to the increasing use of more lethal and destructive weaponry and means of war. The hostilities are being conducted according to the formula: native troops plus U.S. firepower. During the 20 months Nixon has been in office, *the tonnage of U.S. bombs and shells dropped over South Vietnam and the Indochinese countries has reached a high unprecedented in history.* From early 1969 to August 1970, 2.1 million tons of bombs and 2.3 million tons of shells were used by the U.S. Armed Forces,—a quantity surpassing that used by the U.S. in World War II and equalling the explosive power of 340 atomic bombs of the type released over Hiroshima. Thousands of villages and populated areas have been destroyed or razed to the ground. Napalm and phosphorous bombs have burned down vast areas (Higher U Minh, Lower U Minh) and killed or atrociously wounded thousands of people.

Toxic chemicals continue to be used, causing unpredictable damage to man and nature in South Vietnam. The meeting of World Scientists on that subject in Paris has come to specific conclusions which I don't find it necessary to recall in this report. I would just like to draw your attention to the fact that Nixon has ratified a budget of one billion dollars for the implementation of the new "pacification and development" program, which actually aims at devastating hamlets and villages, destroying all means of existence of the South Vietnamese people so as to be able to pen them up in concentration camps. During Nixon's two years in office, over 3,000 out of a total of 11,000 hamlets in South Vietnam have been shelled, burnt, and razed to the ground. More than 200,000 persons have been arrested, detained, and tortured in South Vietnam jails of the "tiger-cages" type. Thousands of them have been secretly liquidated. . . . In the cities and towns, the Thieu-Ky-Khiem junta has put its coercive machine into top gear, and multiplied arrests and acts of terror against those who advocate peace and neutrality. They flout all kinds of democratic liberties, ruthlessly exploit the laboring people, and appply a policy of obscurantism, enslavement, and deprivation, the purpose of which is to obtain money and manpower in furtherance of the "Vietnamization" of the war. According to the data of a subcommission of the U.S. Senate, in 1970 alone, the aggressors killed and wounded 125,000 Vietnamese, of which one-third were under 13 years of age. These casualties are increasing rapidly, due to the ever closer coordination between bombings, strafings, sprayings of toxic chemicals from the air, with "sweep" and "pacification" operations on the ground.

In brief, *Nixon's "Vietnamization" of the war is the continuation of aggression in a more disguised form: using perfidious methods and more deadly and destructive means of war and weaponry employed at a higher level of effectiveness, and resulting in increased crimes and greater brutality against the South Vietnamese and Indochinese peoples.* Through this policy, Nixon tries to deceive the American people and compel them to tolerate an unjust war detrimental to their own interests and to those of their country. Nixon also nurtures the hope of gaining experience from the application of this policy in order to curb the movement for national liberation and freedom all over the world. Hence, the "Vietnamization" of the war is a crime against the Vietnamese, Lao, and Cambodian peoples; a crime against the American people and against oppressed peoples in other countries.

Progressive mankind has condemned the U.S. imperialists for their crime of neocolonialist aggression, crime against peace, crimes of war, crime of genocide, and their crime against humanity. Since Nixon's inauguration, these crimes have been carried out on a larger scale and acquired greater gravity in character.

By setting Calley free, Calley who is guilty of the Son My mass murder, Nixon not only tries to whitewash the crimes perpetrated by the ringleader in the White House and the Pentagon, but also to encourage the American troops in their brutal crimes in Indochina. On April 1, 1971, Senator Fulbright, Chairman of the Senate Foreign Relations Committee, said righteously that the U.S. will not be true to itself if, in regarding the Vietnam problem, it does not abide by the principles of the Nuremberg tribunal, which stipulate that the supreme authorities and military circles are to assume the major part of the responsibility for war crimes.

Faced with vigorous protest from the American people, the Nixon administration arrested and detained tens of thousands of peace demonstrators in Washington on May 3rd, 4th, and 5th this year. It is obvious that the aggressive war in Indochina is closely tied to the fascist regime in the U.S.A.

The South Vietnamese people sympathize with and support the struggle of the American people for an end to U.S. aggression against Vietnam, Laos, and Cambodia, for the sake of the independence and freedom of the Indochinese countries, for the sake of the reputation of the U.S., and for the interests and future of the Americans themselves. We vehemently condemn the Nixon administration's crackdown on the American people and regard it as a crime that cannot be dissociated from the crimes perpetrated by the said administration against the peoples of Vietnam and Indochina, and against mankind.

Ladies and Gentlemen,

The U.S. aggressors have been causing untold devastation and destruction in the countries of Vietnam, Laos, and Cambodia. Nothing can motivate the Nixon administration's prolongation of the aggressive war in Indochina. It is high time to mobilize world opinion in favor of the U.S. government putting an end to its crimes. There is only one correct way to achieve that goal: the U.S. government must fix a time limit for the unconditional pullout of all U.S. and satellite troops from Indochina; put an end to its war of aggression; and let the Vietnamese, Lao, and Cambodian peoples settle their internal affairs themselves without foreign interference.

We are convinced that the second session of our Commission in Oslo will take active measures so as to check the criminal hands of the U.S. aggressors, thereby contributing to the victory of the Indochinese peoples and progressive mankind.

The defeat of the U.S. and the Saigon troops on Highway 9 and [in] southern Laos has illustrated the inevitable fiasco of Nixon's "Vietnamization" of the war. If the U.S. aggressors obstinately cling to their criminal policy, they will take still heavier blows from the Vietnamese, Lao, and Cambodian peoples, who are united and resolute in their struggle which will continue until complete victory is achieved.

Report from Cambodia: Thiounn Prasith

[Thiounn Prasith is Secretary of the Political Office of the United National Front of Kampuchea.]

The United National Front of Kampuchea and the Royal Government of the National Union of Cambodia attach great importance to the work done by the International Investigation Commission, under your tireless, efficient direction, on the crimes committed by the American imperialists in Indochina. We value the useful work done by the International Investigation Commission during its first session held between October 22–25, 1970, in Stockholm.

However, in spite of our interests in the work done by the International Investigation Commission, it is not possible for us to participate in a useful way in the second session which will be held from June 20–25 in Oslo. In fact, both the current situation in Cambodia combined with the difficulties in receiving communications make it impossible for us to conclude our preparations for useful participation in the second session of the International Investigation Commission in time for the date that has been set. We deeply regret not having been able to participate in the preparations for the second session and, in particular, not participating in setting the date for its convocation.

We can assure you that our offices will continue to gather all the necessary documents to show international public opinion the horrors of the innumerable crimes committed by the Nixon administration and its flunkies against the Khmer people.

The Saigon mercenaries and the Phnom Penh band of traitors, who are isolated to the extreme in this country as much as on the international level, who are surrounded by the unanimously hostile Khmer people, and who are infuriated by low morale and their troops' inefficiency, are fighting a war of the most ruthless genocide against our people, with the material and financial aid of the Nixon administration and the support of the American air force. With the exception of atomic weapons, whose plans for usage in Indochina are already waiting in the secret drawers of the Pentagon, all the most modern, ruthless weapons for mass extermination are currently being used in Cambodia, such as: giant B-52 jet bombers, pellet bombs, phosphorus bombs, napalm bombs, toxic chemical products, etc. . . . The American air force and her flunkies' planes fly 300 to 500 missions daily to attempt to symtematically destroy our liberated zones. In addition to the bombs listed above, these planes drop time bombs all over the towns, plantations, rice paddies, wheat fields, vegetable fields, and orchards of our liberated zones. These bombs are shaped like the most common little animals to be found in the countryside, like frogs, turtles, etc. . . . and explode as soon as you pick them up. These types of antipersonnel bombs have killed many old people and children in our countryside.

The soldiers of the Nixon administration, the mercenaries of Saigon and Bangkok, the soldiers of the Phnom Penh traitors led by Lon Nol-Sirik Matak-Son Ngoc Thanh have no respect for law nor religion in their attempts at massacre. These criminals who deserve to be called Nazis pay no heed to any moral code or treaty. Wherever they go, they destroy and set fire to everything: homes, monasteries, temples, plantations, harvests, livestock, instruments of production. . . .

They plunder and massacre the population without making any distinction for age or sex. They rape the women and carry away the young people to use them for their cannon fodder. Hundreds of villages and district cities have been completely destroyed, wiped off the map. Entire families have been massacred. There are numerous places where these crimes have been committed: during the month of September 1970 in Chamcar Ben, Chamcar Andaung, Tonle Bet, Snoul, Chup, . . . (province of Kompong Cham), in Taing Kauk (province of Kompong Thom). . . .

The patriots, both civilian and military, whether or not they belong to the United National Front of Kampuchea, who are arrested, have their heads cut off by the Saigonese mercenaries to be used instead of trophies, and their livers taken out of their bodies to be eaten [sic].

The Nixon administration, the mercenaries of Saigon and Bangkok, the traitor troops of Phnom Penh are proceeding in acts of vandalism and piracy to the detriment of the cultural wealth of our national heritage, thereby violating the 1954 Hague Convention (on the protection of cultural assets in case of armed conflict). Their air force is bombing and firing at the monasteries, temples and historical monuments of Angkor, causing serious damage to the national and universal heritage of humanity. The Saigonese and Thai mercenaries are ransacking the archaeolgical and artistic riches. They are removing the statues and art objects from monasteries and historic monuments as well as stone fragments sculpted during the Angkorian Period to sell them in Saigon or Hong Kong. Some people know that the bloodthirsty Saigonese puppet general Do Cao Tri, who was shot down in his helicopter last March by the armed forces of national liberation of South Vietnam, was systematically ransacking all the monasteries and temples he came across in the course of his bandit campaigns in Cambodia.

American, Saigonese, and the Phnom Penh traitors' planes and artilleries bomb the area of the temples of Angkor almost daily. Recently, at the end of February, the traitor troops of Phnom Penh, protected and financed by the Nixon administration, bombed and destroyed the pillars on the South Side of Angkor Vat (the principal monument of the temples of Angkor) and seriously damaged a part of the vast bas-reliefs which tell the story of the ancient Khmers who built the temples. These bas-reliefs are among the greatest masterpieces of the world's art. The Temple of Angkor Vat is the symbol of the grandeur of the ancient Khmer civilization. The Khmer historic monuments and, especially, the monuments of the Angkor group constitute not only the priceless national heritage of the Khmer people, but the cultural treasures of all of humanity as well.

All these crimes systematically perpetrated by the Nixon administration and its flunkies against the Khmer people, its assets, and its cultural heritage, concern all nations in the world. These crimes have produced indignant protest movements among all peoples who value peace, justice, and freedom, including the American people to whom we address our deep-felt admiration and our whole-hearted solidarity for its courageous struggle to end the aggression against the Khmer people and the other Indochinese peoples. In spite of the brutal fascist repression of the Nixon Administration, the antiwar movement of the American people is presently growing in leaps and bounds, reaching the most diverse milieus: intellectuals, students, women, lawyers, scientists, journalists, writers, workers, the clergy, sociologists . . . including the soldiers who have participated in the war in Indochina. All of them have stood up to protest the innumerable ruthless crimes perpetrated by the Nixon administration against the Khmer people and the other Indochinese peoples for the interests of the United States of America, and to struggle to end the war in Indochina. To all of them we express the deeply-felt gratitude of the Khmer people.

To all the members of the International Investigation Commission, and to all those who are participating in the second session of this commission, we express our warmest thanks for the support that they have given to our people's struggle, and we wish them success in their work, work which will strongly contribute in our just struggle against American aggression, for peace in our country as well as peace throughout the world. We are deeply convinced that, faced with the multiple, flagrant proof of the ruthless crimes perpetrated by the Nixon administration and its flunkies against the Khmer, Vietnamese, and Laotian peoples, the International War Crimes Commission will vigorously denounce and firmly condemn the aggression whose continuation and extension are a threat to all of humanity.

For the Khmer people, a victim daily, all those ruthless crimes will only end when the Nixon administration has totally and unconditionally ceased all bombing in the whole territory of Cambodia and all other acts of aggression against Cambodia, when it has totally and unconditionally evacuated all the Saigon and Bangkok mercenary troops, when it has withdrawn all support and material and financial aid from the Phnom Penh band of traitors led by Lon Nol-Sirik Matak-Son Ngoc Thanh.

As long as the Nixon administration continues its aggression against Cambodia, the Khmer people, solidly united under the flag of the United National Front of Kampuchea, headed by Samdech Norodom Sihanouk, head of State, and under the direction of the Royal Government of the National Union, the only legal, legitimate government of Cambodia, is more than ever determined to fight for its just and noble cause, without compromise nor withdrawal, for national peace, fighting alongside its Vietnamese and Laotian brothers as agreed in the Common Declaration of the Summit Conference of the Indochinese peoples.

Once again, we would like to express our sincere regret that we will not be able to usefully participate in the work of the second session of the International Investigation Commission. We extend to you, dear friends, our highest consideration.

(Translated by Judy Oringer)

U.S. War Crimes in Laos: The Cases

[Documents of the Committee for Denunciation of U.S. War Crimes in Laos.]

• *Intensification of the war of aggression while wasting the properties of the American people in Laos, thereby introducing, on an ever-increasing scale, advisers, military personnel, and U.S. as well as satellite troops.*

• *Air bombings, growing daily in savagery.*

• *U.S. Air Force-supported ground operations that take on an ever larger intensity and proportion.*

• *Confinement of part of the population to ethnic bases, in order to slaughter them, to reduce them to a precarious and degrading existence, deprived of all human rights.*

American imperialism's direct intervention in and aggression against Laos can be traced back to 1954. It has committed crime after crime against the Laotian people ever since, and particularly under the Nixon administration.

1) *American aid to feed the war.*

American aid, largely military, has become larger year by year, and it has shown a clear increase in 1969, 1970, and 1971.

a) *Before Nixon:*

From 1955 to 1968, $900 million have been supplied under the heading of aid, i.e., an average of $60 million per annum. Seventy-five percent of the total amount has been supplied for military aid.

b) *Under Nixon:*

1969: $250 million, thereof less than $60 million for economic and technical aid (declared amount) and $190 million for military aid (not revealed). Of these, $190 million "go to the special forces"; thus, military aid reaches 80 percent of the total. 1970: over $300 million, according to Senator Mansfield. 1971: Souvanna Phouma, nominal prime minister of Vientiane, declares: "American aid to Laos is being kept on its former level."

US-AID has expressed the purpose of economic and military aid for 1971 in the following terms: "To maintain the existing Laotian government and to prevent it from falling into the hands of the communists." Priorities are: to stabilize the economy, and above all the Kip (currency unit in the occupied territories); to ensure all activities connected with the war (transport and communications, resettlements of population, airlines, security, psywar, etc.); to safeguard a minimum activity of public service (transport and communications, public health, teaching, court of law, etc.); to develop the economy (rice, fishing, studies on industry, agriculture, agricultural hydraulics, etc.).

2) *U.S. advisers, military personnel, and troops conduct the war.*

In order to appease the strong opposition of the American people, Nixon, on March 6, 1970, presented the figure of 643 advisers and military [as] being active in Laos, at the same time denying the presence of U.S. combat units in that country. The truth, though, looks different. Under Johnson there were 5,000 U.S. advisers and military in Laos (in 1955, 30; in 1961, 1,500). Under Nixon their number has rapidly increased and gone up to 12,000 in March 1970. Of the total number, 1,200 are U.S. Green Berets and Air Force advisers; another 2,000 are Special Forces advisers. The rest are inserted in Vientiane's army and public service at all levels.

Apart from those 12,000 Americans who conduct the war in Laos, more than half of the 48,000 U.S. Air Force men stationed in Thailand (i.e., over 26,000) take direct part in air operations on Laos.

Advisers, military personnel, and U.S. embassy services form an apparatus deciding upon all activities of the army and the administration in Vientiane, and in practice directing all U.S. plans of aggression against Laos.

At the end of 1969 and in the beginning of 1970, U.S. Green Berets took part in operations in the region Plain of Jars/Xieng Khouang. In the beginning of 1970, thousands of U.S. Green Berets in Saigon army uniform were introduced into the Laotain lowland together with the Saigon mercenaries.

3) *The troops of satellite countries apply the policy of "letting Asians fight against Asians, letting Indochinese fight against Indochinese"; in agreement with the Nixon doctrine, they die instead of American soldiers.*

a) *The Thai mercenaries*

Under former U.S. administrations there were: in 1962, 300 Thai advisers and military in Laos; in 1968, 1,400. They were reconnaissance units, commandos introduced into the country to gather information or to point out targets for the U.S. Air Force.

Under Nixon, infantry and artillery combat units from Thailand are being poured into Laos in growing numbers. They have taken part in the fighting in many places. At present, the number of advisers, military personnel, and Thai soldiers in combat mission in Laos amounts to over 20,000. Thai units are still concentrated along the border ready to intervene in Laos. Thai combat units already in Laotian territory are concentrated in: Sam Thong/Long Cheng: 12 battalions (ten infantry and two artillery); Nha Hon: five infantry battalions; Savannakhet: four infantry battalions; Paksan: one artillery battalion; Pakse: two infantry battalions. Thai advisers and military personnel are inserted in all military zones and army units of the Laotian right wing.

b) The Saigon mercenaries

Under Johnson, only Saigon commandos operated separately along the Laotian lowland border, in order to cause disturbance and also to supply information for the U.S. Air Force.

Since Nixon took office, Saigon units together with American soldiers have often crossed the border, plundered certain localities, and retired immediately after. Specifically in the beginning of 1971, Nixon openly sent 20,000 Saigon mercenaries, along with U.S. military, into the Laotian lowland, thereby extending the war to that region.

Like Kennedy and Johnson, Nixon has never ceased to declare his observance of the Geneva Aggreements on Laos. Deeds betray the emptiness of the words. The money of the American people flows into Laos in the form of weapons and other means of warfare. More and more advisers, military personnel, U.S. and satellite troops are pouring into Laos as the war tramples [the country] underfoot and American crimes are continuously accumulating.

Exterminating Air Bombings

The air war is being intensified year by year, month by month, day by day. Particularly under Nixon, the bombing has become ten times more intense. Let us compare some figures:

1964: around 7 sorties daily; 1965: 83; 1966: 133 (beginning of B-52 bombings on the Laotian lowland); 1967: 180 sorties; 1968: 400 sorties of tactical jets and 35 of B-52's.

Since the bombing of North Vietnam was stopped, U.S. planes of all types, including B-52's, have been continuously flying to Laos from U.S. bases in Thailand and South Vietnam, as well as from aircraft carriers and from the island of Guam. The bombings, of an unprecedented savagery, are presently part of large-scale, prolonged campaigns. Aircraft attack densely populated zones of the country, supporting the operations carried out by troops of the Laotian right wing against the liberated zone.

Two large-scale campaigns took place in 1969: "Barrel Roll," against the Laotian highlands, and "Steel Tiger," against the lowland. The number of sorties (an average of 500–800 a day) went up to 1,500 a day during the spring of 1969. As a total, 800,000 tons of explosives were dropped on Laos in 1969—i.e., one thousand pounds per inhabitant of the liberated zone. Many villages have been destroyed and many civilians killed by the bombing.

1970: According to Congressman R. Ottinger's estimate, the number of sorties increased to 900, and went even higher up—to 1300—at the final stage of the operation Plain of Jars/Xieng Khouang. The bombing tonnage reached the figure of three thousand tons a day in 1971. B-52's, on the other hand, started bombing the Laotian highlands as well. These exterminating bombing raids took a high toll on the population—six hundred dead and wounded a month—and razed to the ground a number of villages in densely populated areas in Xieng Khouang, Khang Khay, Phonsavan, and Saravane, at the same time causing heavy destruction in the surroundings of these places.

In 1970, a bombing tonnage of over one million tons was dropped on Laos—an expense of one thousand dollars per annum and per inhabitant of the liberated zone!

By the end of 1970 and the beginning of 1971, certain regions of Laos—mainly in the lowlands of the Plain of Jars/Xieng Khouang—were taken as targets for ruthless bombing in order to save Vientiane troops and to prepare the invasion of the lowland. Air bombing went on relentlessly from 6 October 1970 to 8 February 1971, with an average of four hundred [daily] sorties of tactical planes and 32 sorties of B-52's. In the course of those 118 days, a total of 389,000 tons of bombs—the equivalent of nineteen atom bombs of the Hiroshima type—were dropped on Laos. During the invasion of the lowland, U.S. aircraft effected eight hundred sorties a day, and sometimes up to 1,500, in order to bomb various parts of the country mainly the lowland and the zone of Plain of Jars/Xieng Khouang.

At present, the bombing of the whole country, from north to south, goes on as ruthlessly as ever. Thus, the American air war has gone through a ceaseless escalation since 1964. Millions of tons of bombs, of every type, have been poured on Laos: explosive bombs, steel-pellet bombs, napalm bombs, phosphorus bombs, flechette bombs, etc. The most atrocious crimes have been committed against the Laotian people.

Most urban centers, villages, pagodas, schools, hospitals, and tens of thousands of granaries belonging to the population have been destroyed. Thousands of civilians have been killed; an equally large number of other—most of them old people and children—have been wounded. Vast plains, fertile ricefields, and luxurious forests have been devasted.

More than two thousand U.S. planes have been shot down by the Laotian AA defense. Several hundred pilots have died or been captured. The U.S. Air Force has lost more and more of its prestige. The number of planes shot down increases continuously:

1964:   26 aircraft
1965:   218
1966:   203
1967:   284
1968:   287
1969:   290
1970:   373

During the operation of invasion in the lowland, which lasted 43 days in 1971, 496 planes and helicopters were shot down or captured.

Air Force-supported Ground Operations that Destroy the Lives and Property of the Laotian People

Since 1955, American imperialism has been using U.S.-armed Laotian mercenaries to fight against Laotians. Under Nixon, there are also Thai and Saigon puppet soldiers, carrying U.S. weapons and equipment, involved in ferocious combat against the Laotians. Under preceding U.S. administrations, from 1955 to 1967, 25,000 men of the Laotian right wing army have been used in the attempt to destroy the patriotic forces regrouped in Sam Neua and Phongsaly and to bring to heel the population of the other ten provinces. From 1959 to 1962, 44,–57,000 of these troops were thrust against the liberated zones in Vientiane, Xieng Khouang, Nam Tha. In [the years] 1963–68 the troops were increased to 63,–67,000 (one-third of them "special forces") and employed to "pacify" the occupied regions or used in "mopping" operations throughout the country. Certain operations, such as those against roads No. 8 and 9, Xieng

Khouang, Nam Bac, etc., mobilized up to ten or twenty battalions.

Under the Nixon government, escalation of the air war has
run parallel to a widening and intensification of Air Force-
supported ground operations. Dozens of operations have
been carried out against the liberated zones since the beginning of 1969. The "Special Forces," organized and led by
American officers, served as spearhead at the beginning.
Then added to them were Thai and Saigon troops equally
used as shock forces. U.S.-Laotian operations against the Laotian lowland are typical examples.

U.S.-LAOTIAN OPERATION "KOU KIET" AGAINST THE PLAIN OF JARS/XIENG KHOUANG (END OF 1969-BEGINNING OF 1970)

The new formula of the Nixon doctrine was applied. Important amounts of troops were mobilized: twelve thousand
Laotian mercenaries, mainly "Special Forces," plus five thousand Thai mercenaries, all supported by hundreds of helicopters and combat planes, including B-52's, from seven U.S.
air bases in Thailand and aircraft carriers of the Seventh
Fleet. They applied the "scorched earth" policy in the Plain
of Jars/Xieng Khouang: "burn all, destroy all, exterminate
all." From the beginning of the campaign (August 12, 1969)
until its complete failure (February 22, 1970), the most horri-
fying crimes were committed against the population of
Xieng Khouang:

• More than five thousand civilians—mainly old people,
women, and children—killed or wounded by the air force
and ground troops;

• Over 3,500 dwellings, 147 pagodas, and 3,500 granaries of

the population destroyed or burned down by aircraft and ground troops;

• 44,650 buffaloes, 30,420 oxen, 9,372 horses, 55,600 pigs, and a large amount of other domestic animals stolen or killed;

• The towns of Khang Kay, Xieng Khouang, and Phonsavan, as well as densely populated areas of the surroundings, razed to the ground. Many square miles of green forests and fertile plains in the Plain of Jars/Xieng Khouang destroyed by bombing and shelling.

• Thirty thousand civilians forced by gunpoint and bayonet to leave their native villages to be resettled in concentration camps around military posts and bases.

OPERATION OF INVASION OF THE LAOTIAN LOWLAND BY U.S.-SAIGON TROOPS

At the beginning of 1971, Nixon pretending "to cut the supply roads of the communists," sent into the lowland 45,-000 U.S.-Saigon troops which had at their disposal enormous amounts of equipment and means of warfare, including two thousand planes of all types (1,500 combat planes, 52 B-52's, 800 helicopters), over five hundred pieces of artillery, five hundred tanks and armored vehicles. The plan was a massive invasion of the Laotian lowland. Those troops coordinated their actions with the Vientiane troops and also with units of the Thai army previously introduced into Laos.

The invasion had been prepared long before by the White House, the Pentagon, and the U.S. headquarters in Saigon. As a forestage of the operation, U.S.-Saigon units had crossed the border and carried out *blitz* attacks in the lowland. Also a ruthless 118-day-long bombing campaign had preceded the invasion.

Apart from 100,000 tons of bombs and shells, U.S. aircraft sprayed chemical toxics on Laotian territory during the operation, destroying the vegetation and poisoning civilians, and obliterated villages, schools, pagodas, and hospitals in the lowland.. During the past 17 years, Nixon and his predecessors have waged thousands of large-scale operations of encroachment on the liberated area, and search-and-destroy operations in the occupied regions. Crimes of growing atrocity accumulate more and more as new military operations are effected. By using violence, U.S. and puppet troops have not succeeded in their attempt to subdue the Laotian people, nor have they annihilated Laos patriotic forces. On the contrary, their violence has brought them well-deserved punishments:

• They have lost five thousand men in the encroachment, operations on the liberated area and the search-and-destroy operations between 1959 and 1962.

• Other casualties: 118,000, including thosuands of U.S. and Thai military men, from 1963 through1970, and

• 27,700 men since beginning of the dry season 1970–71. In the invasion of the Laotian lowland, 19,000 men of the U.S.-Saigon forces (including more than five hundred GIs) were disabled.

Transfer of Part of the Population to Concentration Camps

Through demagogic maneuvers, air bombing, and scorched-earth operations, U.S. imperialists and their agents have forced part of the population in the liberated zone to leave their villages, to abandon the land they have tilled through many generations in order to live in concentration camps called "refugee camps," located around military posts and bases.

Such "resettlement" is a vast project, put in practice in coordination with air bombing and ground operations. Its aim is to prevent part of the population from living in the liberated zone, where it could resist U.S. aggression and construct a new society—a society in which all men are equal and enjoy self-determination. That part of the population is concentrated around military posts and bases to prevent attacks from the patriotic forces. In the long run they are doomed to a slow death or to kneel down before the invader. US-AID has supplied four million dollars a year for the "resettlement" project from 1968 through 1969, and the funds for the same purpose have increased considerably since. In 1970 only, the transfer of people from one camp to another costs no less than five million dollars. Senator Kennedy has remarked: "That shows clearly that we are prepared to pay any price to remove the whole population from the zone controlled by the Pathet Lao."

Here are some examples of concentration camp zones:

—Around the military base of Sam Thong/Long Cheng (a CIA base), there were eight thousand people from regions north of Luang Prabang, from the Plain of Jars, and from Sam Neua. Since the base is surrounded and threatened with destruction by the patriotic forces, the prisoners have been moved southwest from the base or to the plain of Vientiane.

—Northwest and southwest of the Plain of Jars were concentrated 45,000 people from Nakhang, Hua Muong (Sam Neua) and the border region of the two provinces of Sam Neua and Xieng Khouang. In February 1970, the U.S. and puppet forces, threatened with annihilation in the Plain of Jars/Xieng Khouang, transferred the prisoners to concentration camps in the Plain of Vientiane.

—In Nam Huoi (Hua Khong province): twenty thousand people from Muong Sinh and Nam Tha.

—In Ban Keun, Tha Ngon, Tha Bat, Tha Dua: sixteen thousand people moved over from the Plain of Jars in February 1970.

—Near the town Luang Prabang: five thousand people transferred from Nam Boc, Phongsaly.

—In Nam Tan, Nam Huoi (Sayaboury province): two thousand people from Muong Say and Muong Hum.

—Near Savannakhet and Pakse: six thousand, all transferred from liberated zones in the Laotian lowland.

—In Attopeu: three thousand, brought from liberated zones in the lowland. In the meantime they have been liberated by the patriotic forces.

According to US-AID, the people resettled in concentration camps belong to ethnic minorities in the following proportion: 40 percent Meo, 30 percent Lao Theung, 10 percent Lao Lum, and the rest members of other minorities. How many crimes committed to put into practice the confinement of the people: slaughter, death threat, pressure, mistreatment, brutality! Here are some cases of crime against ethnic minorities, a few examples chosen among thousands of them:

—In order to compel the Meo living in liberated zones (Sam Neua and Xieng Khouang province) to move to the surroundings of the "Special Forces" base Sam Thong/Long Cheng, U.S. and puppet troops sent their agents into the villages with flashing promises: The American would give lots of money to those who were willing to go to live with the Meo "king," Vang Pao—promises that were accompanied by threat with destruction of villages by bombing. Once gathered, only those families are provided with rice that send their sons to the Special Forces and their daughters to the military posts. The rest are left to their fate.

—With the aim of forcing the Lao Theung settled around the posts in Muong Sinh, Nam Tha, and Nam Sac to move back to concentration camps nearby Luang Prabang and Nam Muoi (Hua Khong province), mercenaries were sent to the villages to sack property, to kill people, and by those means to obtain the abandonment of the places. At the end of 1968—to cite a typical example—a mercenary Laotian company commanded by U.S. advisers burst into Nong Chuc village, burned all dwellings and the paddy, killed the cattle, and forced 270 inhabitants who had not been able to flee, to follow the company, either on foot or by helicopter, to concentration camps near Luang Prabang. Four villagers who were reluctant to obey were bound and killed by bayonet on the spot. On the way, when the mothers and their babies were exhausted, the soldiers murdered six children and tore others from their mothers to throw them immediately after down the precipice on the edge of the road. Among the people transported by helicopter, two old men, 60 and 70 years of age, were dropped from the helicopter, for otherwise they would have been "useless mouths to feed" in the camp.

—In order to compel the inhabitants of liberated zones in the lowland to return to concentration camps near Savannakhet, Pakse, Saravane, and Attopeu, U.S. planes bombed the villages. Along with the bombing, Vientiane troops carried out search-and-destroy operations and forced all those who could not flee to follow them. Thus, in the beginning of 1967, U.S. planes dropped burst bombs, steel-pellet bombs, and napalm bombs on the villages of Da Xia, Vang Nhao, Ban Dong, and Ban Nong Chua (Lao Ngam), killing or wounding 67 people, destroying 231 dwellings, nine pagodas, 31 granaries, and many farming tools. Four battalions were sent to raze the region and to force two thousand people to move to concentration camps near Saravane.

—During the operation against Plain of Jars/Xieng Khouang (end of 1969, beginning of 1970), 30,392 people were compelled to settle around military posts. Whoever refused to obey was killed on the spot: it was the case of Luong Tba, Xieng Phan, and some women like Bun, Pun, Duong Xi, in Pha Tang Phun Khon and Xom Xon villages. Once in the camps, all young people over fifteen had to carry weapons and were used to repress their own fellow countrymen. Young girls had to satisfy the desire of U.S. advisers and puppet officers. Old people, women, and children were reduced to atrocious conditions: penury, hunger, and disease. Of the eight thousand people gathered in Na Luong, one thousand (among them four hundred children) died a month later.

When their campaign against Plain of Jars/Xieng Khouang was running to disaster, U.S. imperialists gave orders to fly by helicopter the people imprisoned around their posts to the concentration camps of Tha Ngon, Ba Keun, Tha Lat, Tha Dua, etc., in the Plain of Vientiane. The first three months they distributed rice of the "American help to refugees": a daily ration of seven ounces per person. Later on, the prisoners were abandoned to their fate.

Those who are still able to work are hired for construction in Tha Lat, Nam Ngum, etc., where they are employed to build roads and barrages. Old people, women, and children have to cultivate maize, potatoes, and manioc. Their living conditions there are by far worse than they are used to in their native villages. Some of them have no other way out than to beg in neighboring villages, but they are brutally beaten by guards when this is noticed. Several western journalists who have visited the camps have declared that those people "live in misery and meet many difficulties." Whenever a prisoner demands assistance, he is brutally beaten and labeled "communist" or "enemy" of the government.

Such is the reality of the U.S. imperialists policy towards the Laotian people. Hundreds of thousands of Laotians are presently confined to concentration camps, deprived of all basic human rights. Day after day they meet with moral humiliation, mistreatment, penury. Living in misery and humiliation, they are condemned to material and moral degradation.

Exterminating air bombardments, "scorched earth" operations on a large scale, the transfer of the population to concentration camps surrounded by military posts and bases— they all constitute the crime of genocide, no less grave than the crime of aggression and the war crimes U.S. imperialism has been committing in Laos for many years.

Wholesale Massacres in South Vietnam Since the Son My Case

[Testimony of the Committee to Denounce U.S. Puppets' War Crimes in Indochina.]

The massacre of civilians is generated by a policy of the U.S. imperialists and their henchmen in South Vietnam aimed at repressing the patriotic South Vietnamese people's struggle against U.S. aggression. Contrary to Nixon's contention that the Son My case was an isolated one, slaughters by U.S. puppet and satellite troops have since then continued to occur incessantly in South Vietnam in various forms; using extremely savage methods. A number of major massacres since the Son My case, now preliminarily investigated and recorded, follow:

"Massacre all, destroy all, burn all" Operations

Massacres, first of all, come as a result of U.S. puppet, and mercenary troops' random killing activities in sweeps in South Vietnam.

Wherever they go, they kill everything, destroy everything, and burn everything, leveling villages and hamlets, herding people into concentration camps, then selecting many of them for secret execution.

1. The massacre of over 500 people in Son My, Quang Ngai province. On March 16, 1968, American troops belonging to the 82nd Brigade raided Son My, Son Quang, Son Hai, and Son Hoa (Son Tinh district), burning houses, butchering people, raping women, and looting properties all along their way. In Son My especially (Tinh Khe), they applied the "burn all, destroy all, kill all" policy in a most atrocious manner. They blew up shelters, mustered the population, and gunned hundreds of people to death. They also drove the population into their houses, fired at and grenaded them, then burned the dwellings. They threw children into the fire, stabbed even suckling infants, raped many women to death, finished off those in agony and hurled their corpses into wells or into the river.

In this terror operation alone, the GIs slaughtered 380 people in Lang hamlet, 87 in My Hoi, 35 in Xuang Duong, all part of Son My village; and in all 502 people, mostly old people, women, and children.

2. Massacre in Rach Gia. From July 30 to August 7, 1968, the U.S. puppets launched a mopping-up operation code-named "Dai Thang," supported by naval aircraft, B-52 strategic bombers, and artillery, to savagely raid a number of villages in Go Quao, Vinh Thuan, and An Bien districts. They killed 227 people, wounded over thirty, abducted more than fifty, and destroyed and plundered many properties.

3. Massacre in Quang Nam. From November 7 to 17, 1968, in the so-called "accelerated pacification" campaign, the U.S. puppets sent motorized and infantry units to raid many villages of Thang Binh, Tam Ky, and Que Son districts. They killed 190 people in Binh Dao village (Thang Binh), took away ninety inhabitants of Ha Tan district capital to liquidate them, slew 35 persons in Phu Phong (Que Son), and killed and wounded 118 others in Binh Duong (Thang Binh). In particular, in Binh Duong, they tortured 35 old people and

children in a most savage manner, then buried them alive. In all they slaughtered 476 persons.

4. Massacre of over three thousand people in Ben Tre and My Tho provinces. From December 1, 1967, to April 1, 1968, the U.S. Ninth Division launched a raid code-named "Express" on Ben Tre and My Tho provinces. For four months they mopped up many areas, slaughtering people and burning down thousands of houses, hundreds of hectares of fields and orchards.

5. Murder and liquidation of 1,500 people off the coast of Ba Lang An (Quang Ngai province). From January 18 to February 3, 1969, more than eight thousand American, puppet, and satellite troops commanded by U.S. General Cooksey raided Ba Lang An area, comprising Binh Chau, Binh Phu, Binh Tan (Binh Son district). They used 130 tanks, 80 helicopters, 18 guns, and 23 warships to land troops. Thousands of tons of bombs and shells were poured on the villages. Wherever they went the raiders destroyed, killed people, and raped women. A small hamlet of eighteen households in Tinh Son village was hit by over one thousand shells. In many hamlets no houses were left.

After twenty days of this operation, Binh Phu, Binh Chau and Binh Tan were wiped out, and others like Son Hai, Son Hoa . . . were heavily destroyed. Over three hundred people were slaughtered on the spot. Nearly 11,000 were marched off to Van Thanh concentration camp. Of this number, 1,200 were singled out for solitary confinement, then liquidated one by one off the coast early in March 1969.

6. Massacre in Ty Sé, Phuoc Son, Quang Nam province. From January 15 to 27, 1969, four U.S. battalions mopped up Ty Sé, Phuoc Son area. They herded the population together in groups of twenty or thirty, then machine-gunned them. The survivors were shipped to Nong Son. As the boats sailed along, they fired at people aboard from the banks, killing

many of them, whose corpses were then thrown into the river. In all, the raiders killed two hundred civilians and burnt down nearly one hundred houses.

7. Massacre in Dau Tieng area, Thu Dau Mot province. From March 17 to 31, 1969, over ten thousand U.S. puppets mounted a raid on Dau Tieng area, code-named "Atlas Wedge," comprising villages 14 and 15 in the Michelin rubber plantation. Thousands of tons of bombs and shells were poured on the area, over one hundred people were killed and about three thousand beaten black and blue and then herded into concentration camps. Agence France-Press, on March 24, 1969, wrote of the damage to the Michelin rubber plantation as follows: "The villages were burned and about three thousand people were penned up. . . . The damage was hard to estimate, but according to specialists, it would take about ten years' peace and hundreds of millions of Vietnamese piastres to restore the plantation to its 1969 level."

8. Massacre in Thang Binh district, Quang Nam province. From March 31 to April 4, 1969, U.S. puppet units, supported by 54 armored cars, raided Binh Sa, Binh Dao, Binh Hai, Binh Nam, Binh Duong, Binh Phu, Binh Dinh, and Binh Quy villages, all in Thang Binh district. They killed 93 people, wounded 18, and abducted 33 others. In Binh Sa alone, they slaughtered fifty people at one go and burned 103 houses.

9. Massacre in Loc Phuoc, Loc Hoa villages, Quang Nam province. On May 9, 1969, the American aggressors launched three battalions of the Fifth Regiment, First Marine Division, supported by air force and artillery, against Loc Phuoc and Loc Hoa villages (Dai Loc district), Quang Nam province. Wherever they passed, the GIs burned houses down and slaughtered people. In coordination with the infantry, U.S. artillery from Bo Bo, Nui Ho, and Ai Nghia positions subjected the villages and hamlets to intense pounding; in a single night, Quang Doi hamlet was hit by

thousands of shells. The raiders massacred 301 people, mostly women and children.

10. Massacre in Binh Duong and Binh Phu villages, Quang Nam province. From April 25 to May 13, 1969, the U.S. puppets mustered over two thousand troops, supported by 72 military vehicles and many planes and guns, to mop up Binh Duong and Binh Phu villages, Thang Binh district. As a result, 145 people were slaughtered; hamlets 1, 2, and 6 of Binh Duong were completely razed; the population was driven into concentration camps like Nui Que, Ha Lan, and Tam Ky town.

11. Massacre in Thang Binh, Quang Nam province. From April 24 to May 23, 1969, many U.S. puppet battalions, supported by hundreds of armored cars, planes, and naval craft, combed the eastern part of Thang Binh district. Hamlets 3, 5 and 6 of Binh Duong village were razed to the ground.

On April 27, the raiders entered hamlets 1, 2, 4, and 6, searched every house, drove out all the occupants, lined them up, and butchered 75 people, all old people, women and children. On April 28, 29, and 30, they searched hamlet 5, killing 73 people.

All told, they slaughtered over three hundred people, liquidated 23 others, and marched nearly four thousand off into concentration camps. More savage still, they scattered the corpses to hinder their burial and terrorize the population.

12. Massacre in Rach Gia province. In June and July 1969, the U.S. puppets mounted many raids against a number of villages in Rach Gia province. They slaughtered 169 people, injured 198 others, burned down more than 328 houses and over 3,000 gia (1 gia = 20 kg. = 44 lbs.) of paddy. In Vinh Thuan, Vinh Binh Nam, and Vinh Binh Dong they killed over one hundred people. On July 15th and 26th they arrested seventeen peasants of Khmer origin in Canal 1, Binh Minh

village, cruelly beat them, and disembowelled them or lined them up and machine-gunned them.

13. Massacre in Upper U Minh and Lower U Minh forest areas. From September 23 to October 29, 1969, the U.S. puppets carried out a big sweep in Upper U Minh and Lower U Minh areas. They killed and wounded more than 250 people, mostly women and children, and destroyed over two thousand houses. Many families were wiped out down to the last member.

14. Massacre in Thoi Binh district, Ca Mau province. Late in October 1969, the U.S. puppets raised Bien Bach and Tri Phai villages and one hamlet of Tan Phu village, Thoi Binh district, killing and wounding 115 people.

15. Massacre of over one thousand people in Quang Ngai province. In October and November 1969, U.S. puppets razed four villages (Son Loc in Son Tinh district, Tu My in Tu Nghia district, Pho Loi and Pho Xuan in Duc Pho district) and fifeteen hamlets in Tu Phuoc, Xuan Pho, Son Nam and Son My villages. They killed and injured over 1,000 people, burnt and destroyed ten thousand houses and tens of thousands of hectares of crops, upturned thousands of tombs with bulldozers, and looted many properties to a sum of over two hundred million Vietnamese piastres.

16. Annihilation of A-Yun hamlet and Ho village in Darlac province. On October 20, 1969, and January 17 and 19, 1970, puppet Battalion 2, Regiment 45, under U.S. command, raided, looted, and completely destroyed A-Yun hamlet of Ede nationals in Darlac province.

17. Massacre in Kien Phong. From October 23, 1969, to January 1, 1970, over one thousand U.S. and puppet troops carried out a sweep code-named "Mekong Sacred Waves" in Kien Phong province. Wherever they went, the raiders gave themselves over to killing and looting. Two girls, Nha, aged 15, and Phung, aged 13, were raped until half-dead by four

GIs. Le Thi Loi, aged 17, was ravished to death by thugs who then threw her body into the river. Mrs. Thanh, aged 67, was violated by three GIs until she lost consciousness. More than seven hundred hectares of fields and orchards and fifty civilian dwellings were destroyed and leveled with bulldozers. On January 15 and 21, 1970, the raiders slaughtered 36 people, mostly women and children, in hamlet 4, An Long village.

18. Massacre in Kien Tuong. From February 5 to 14, 1970, the U.S. puppets launched an operation code-named "Mekong 2/4" against Kien Tuong. They slew over three hundred persons, tortured and took away for execution many others.

19. Massacre in Bien Bach and Tri Phai villages, Ca Mau province. For four months running, from September 29, 1969 to February 6, 1970, over one housand U.S. and puppet troops mounted a long-run sweep on Bien Bach and Tri Phai villages, Ca Mau province. They massacred 162 persons, mostly old people, women, and children; wounded 52 persons; beat to incapacitation 36 others; burnt and destroyed nearly one thousand houses and ravaged over seventy hectares of fields and orchards.

20. Massacre in Mo Cay, Ben Tre province. From February 22 to 25, 1970, U.S. and puppet troops, under U.S. advisory command, mounted a pacification operation in Mo Cay district, Ben Tre province. In the two villages of Hung Khanh Trung and Tan Thanh Binh, the raiders killed fifty civilians and wounded fourteen, and tortured and took away 82 others to an unknown destination.

21. Massacre in Son Thang and Son Thach, Quang Nam province. On February 19, 1970, a unit of the Seventh U.S. Marine Regiment combed the two villages of Son Thang and Son Thach. The raiders slew eleven children and five women in three houses in Son Thang. In Son Thach they beheaded eight old people and children with bayonets.

On June 19, 1970, Krichten, a GI who had taken part in this sweep, confessed that his unit had murdered sixteen women and children; a surviving baby was also finished off as it cried.

22. Massacre in Khan Lam village, Ca Mau province. From September 1969 to March 1970, the U.S. puppets sent a continuous stream of aircraft, including B-52s, to bomb and strafe Khan Lam village, Ca Mau province. In January 1970, in a bombing raid against canal 5, hamlet 2, they caused 24 civilian casualties. During sweeps wanton slaughters occurred. In hamlet 5, the raiders raped 42 women in the one raid. Mrs. Nguyen Thi So and her two daughters were violated to death and their bodies thrown into the sea. On February 24, 1970, the U.S. sprayed toxic chemical poisoning over six hundred people; then planes came to bomb the village again. In all, from September 1969 to March 1970, 333 civilians, among them 117 children, were killed or wounded.

23. Massacres in Ca Mau province. From March 6 to 26, 1970, many U.S. puppet sweeps took place in Duyen Hai, Song Doc, and Thoi Binh districts. Wherever they went, the raiders slew, burned, and destroyed: they butchered over three hundred persons, mostly women and children, wounded fifty others, ravished 320 women, of whom a 15-year-old girl was raped to death; they burnt three hundred houses, over four thousand gia of paddy, and plundered much property.

24. Massacres in Vinh Son and Khan Son, Khan Hoa province. From April 1 to 6, 1970, U.S. and Pak Jung Hi troops launched a sweep against the two districts of Vinh Son and Khanh Son, Khan Hoa province. They burned and destroyed large numbers of houses and killed over thirty people. Three families were exterminated, like Mr. Ma Han's. Ma Han's father had his head cut off and displayed; six other villagers were wounded by gunfire and 84 taken away.

25. Massacre in Quang Ngai. Throughout the month of April 1970, a U.S. battalion of Brigade 198, Americal Division, and a puppet battalion of Regiment 6, supported by hundreds of tanks and armored cars, carried out many sweeps in the eastern part of Binh Son district, Quang Ngai province. Armored vehicles leveled fields, orchards, and houses; flame-throwers and incendiary bombs dropped from helicopters occasioned great fires in Binh Hoa, Binh Phu, Binh Tan, and Binh Thanh villages. The U.S. and puppets subjected hamlets and villages to intense shelling, then sent infantry to round up civilians whom they savagely tortured and herded into concentration camps. In a single raid on the said village, they massacred 36 persons, wounded 11 others —mostly old people, women, and children, killed seventy buffalo and oxen, and burned and leveled two hundred houses.

26. Massacre in Tra Vinh. On April 1, 1970, two regular battalions, six companies of security guards and police, and one detachment of armored cars with air and artillery support raided Tam Phuong hamlet (southwest of Tra Vinh provincial capital). Prior to the actual raid the U.S. and puppets bombarded the hamlet with one thousand shells and sent ten helicopters to strafe it for hours on end. Then the infantry troops broke in and began to kill the people in an extremely brutal manner. They murdered and injured 140 persons, of whom the bulk were of Khmer descent, and demolished almost all the houses in the hamlet. The day before, planes had bombed the same locality, causing eighty civilian casualties, including 27 Buddhist priests. In total, over 220 people were killed or wounded.

27. Massacre of pupils in Vinh Hoa village, Rach Gia province.In early April 1970, in a sweep in Vinh Hoa village, Rach Gia, the U.S. and puppets slew at one stroke 45 school children who were sheltering in an underground shelter.

28. Massacre in An Bien and Vinh Thuan (Rach Gia-Ca Mau). From April 1 to 19, 1970, the U.S. and puppets continuously combed and strafed Dong Yen, Dong Thanh, Dong Hung, Dong Hoa (An Bien district), and Vinh Binh village (Vinh Thuan district), causing 109 civilian casualties, mostly women and children.

29. Massacre in Le Bac hamlet, Quang Nam province. On April 15, 1970, a company of the Fifth U.S. Marine Regiment broke into Le Bac hamlet, Xuyen Loc village, Duy Xuyen district, Quang Nam province. Wherever they went, U.S. troops killed, burned, and destroyed. They captured 38 people, mostly old people, women, and children (13 of the latter were under 12), whom they gathered together, and then machine-gunned them: 37 were killed. A child who clung to its mother frightened was snatched away by GIs who then poinarded it and smashed its skull with rifle butts. Only a little girl of 11, Hoang Thi Ai who was seriously wounded in the gunfire, survived because she was thought dead.

30. Massacre in Dam Hoi, Ca Mau province. On May 7, 1970, thousands of U.S. and puppet troops raided the three villages of Tan Tien, Tan Thuan, and Nguyen Quan, Dam Doi district, Ca Mau prvince, killing and wounding over seventy people. Many women were raped to death, among them a 14-year-old girl and a sexagenerian.

From July 12 to 20, 1970, the U.S. puppets dispatched four air-supported battalions to comb the surroundings of Dam Doi township. The toll: over one hundred houses burnt and 125 people slain, mostly women and children.

31. Massacres in Vinh Loi village, Soc Trang province. In June 1970, the enemy mounted numerous raids on Vinh Loi village in Soc Trang province, killing large numbers of civilians. From 1968 to June 1970, enemy troops stationed in Vinh Loi alone slaughtered 105 persons, wounded 127, and

took away 219, burned more than one thousand houses, and robbed the population of much property.

32. Massacre in the western part of Da Nang. On July 19, 1970, 1,500 U.S. Marines and 5,000 puppet troops mounted a raid code-named "Pickens Forest" to the west of Da Nang city. They broke into, and wantonly fired at, civilian dwellings as people were sleeping, causing many casualties. According to western sources, over forty persons were killed or beaten black and blue.

33. Massacres in Mo Cay and Giong Trom districts, Ben Tre province. On July 24, 1970, enemy troops stationed in Mo Cay district capital bombarded Thanh An village, wiping out Mr. Nguyen Van Tien's family of 13 members.

On July 26, 1970, enemy planes strafed people at work in the fields of Binh Khanh village, causing 22 casualties.

After, from July 26 to 30, 1970, troops were unleashed to comb villages in Mo Cay and Giong Trom districts. The raiders massacred 78 persons, wounded 25 others, burned 320 houses, and killed over one hundred head of cattle. In all, the enemy killed and wounded 138 people, mostly old people, women, and children.

34. Massacres in Long My, Can Tho province. In early August 1970, the U.S. puppets launched successive raids against the southern part of Long My district comprising Xá Thien, Luong Tam, Vinh Vien, Thuan Hung, and Vinh Thuan Dong villages, killing and destroying at random. Over one hundred people were massacred, and much property was plundered.

There is no complete account of the massacres of civilians committed daily and hourly by the U.S., puppet, and satellite troops throughout South Vietnam; these are only some typical cases. In 1969, the Nixon administration's first year, in Quang Nam province alone, ninety major massacres occurred, resulting in 4,700 persons killed, among them 1,959 women and 1,579 children; over six thousand buffalo and oxen slaughtered; 12,400 houses and 97 churches, pagodas, and Buddhist temples burned down or destroyed. Ben Tre province alone was subject to nearly 4,000 sweeps, during which over 2,200 persons were slain, mostly old people, women, and children.

Mass Killing by Means of Bombardments

Along with ground raids, the U.S. and puppets have also resorted to intensive bombardments by aircraft of all types, and ground- and warship-based artillery to massacre people with maximum effect. The amount of ordnance used by them in South Vietnam is monstrous. In 1969, the Nixon administration's first year, they dropped on South Vietnam 1,571,000 tons of bombs (twice the yearly average under Johnson), i.e., equal to the tonnage dropped in Europe during the Second World War. Most vicious antipersonnel weapons have been used, such as steel-pellet bombs, flechette bombs, napalm, phosphorous bombs, bombs which explode in the air or at ground level or only after penetrating deeply into the earth, and even ultraheavy-calibre bombs have been used. On March 3, 1969, 15,000-pounders were used. Besides guns based on warships stationed in rivers and at sea, there are about 2,500 pieces of artillery in military installations on land, including ultrapowerful and ultrarapid guns capable of firing nuclear warheads. Almost all the populous areas in South Vietnam are in the range of enemy artillery. Hai Lang district, Quang Tri province, with its 80,000 inhabitants, in 1968 and 1969 alone was hit by over 1,028,000 bombs and shells.

The following are a number of major massacres:

1. Massacre of more than eight hundred people in the vicinity of Chau Doc provincial capital. On May 6, 7, and 8, 1968, U.S. helicopters and jets made hundreds of sorties to drop napalm, fragmentation, and steel pellet bombs to bombard and machine-gun populated areas in My Duc, Khan Hoa, Chan Phong, and Vinh Le around Cahu Doc provincial capital, killing and wounding over eight hundred Hoa Hao believers and Cham nationals and destroying hundreds of houses.

2. Massacre of 109 people in Vinh Khanh, Chau Doc province. On May 8, 1968, the U.S. and puppets concentrated the population of Vinh Khanh in a school ground, then called on helicopters to come and fire on it, killing and injuring 109 people. One seven-member family was exterminated. Then the raiders looted the population's property, which they loaded onto armored vehicles to carry away.

3. Massacre in Tam Hoa, Da Nang. On October 29, 1968, U.S. planes bombed Tam Hoa village. United Press International admitted that the U.S. Air Force had dropped four 200-kg. bombs on the populated village of Tam Hoa, 30 km. southwest of Da Nang, murdering and injuring more than one hundred people.

4. Massacre in Thai Hiep, Bien Hoa. On the evening of February 26, 1969, U.S. planes bombed the Catholic village of Thai Hiep (Ho Nai), Lo Than area, and Bia Binh camp, destroying over two thousand houses, two churches, and a school and causing more than two hundred civilian casualties.

5. Massacre of 350 people in Kong H'ring, Kontum province. From late 1968 to early 1969, by means of continual bombings, strafings, and sweeps, the U.S. puppets drove over ten thousand Christian believers of Sedang nationality in 47 villages into Kong H'ring concentration camp and subjected them to ill treatment, forced labor, and privations.

To wrest back their freedom, on the night of February 22, 1969, the internees struggled for their release. The U.S. puppets bombed and shelled the camp, then trooops, supported by armored cars, broke in firing wantonly. After nearly four hours, 350 mountaineers were slaughtered and thousands of others injured.

6. Massacre in Tay Ninh province. On June 19, 1969, the U.S. puppets dynamited the Tay Ninh jail, killing and wounding nearly one hundred people detained there. Meanwhile U.S. planes bombed Vuon Dieu strategic hamlet, one km. from Tay Ninh provincial capital, demolishing three hundred houses, and killing and injuring many people. Earlier, on June 6, 7, and 8, they had shelled the place, destroying thousands of houses and killing and wounding one hundred people.

7. Massacre in Vinh Xuong strategic hamlet, Chau Doc province. On June 18 and 19, 1969, aircraft and artillery bombarded Vinh Xuong strategic hamlet, wrecking seven hundred houses and killing and injuring more than 160 persons.

8. Massacre of two hundred fishermen in Phan Ri, Binh Thuan province. On August 10, 1969, several flights of U.S. planes attacked a fleet of fifty fishing boats from Phan Ri village, Hoa Da district, Binh Thuan province. Out of two hundred persons aboard, only one survived.

9. Massacre in the Chau Thuat strategic hamlet, Ba Lang An area. On November 11, 1969, guns from U.S. warships and from positions on dry land subjected the population concentration area in Chau Thuat, Ba Lang An area, Quang Nam province, to intense shelling, killing 45 persons in the hamlet.

10. Massacre in Bau Binh market, Quang Nam province. On December 12, 1969, U.S. helicopters and infantrymen fired at Bau Binh market, Quang Nam, for two hours running while it was in full swing killing 210 people, mostly women.

11. Massacre at the Gia Kiem church, Bien Hoa province. On Christmas Eve, December 24, 1969, U.S. puppet artillery fiercely shelled the Gia Kiem church, Bien Hoa province, as believers were attending mass, causing 103 casualties, mostly old people, women, and children.

12. Massacre in Binh Dinh. On February 4, 1970, U.S. troops stationed in Vinh Quang hamlet, Phuc Son Village, Tuy Phuoc District, Binh Dinh province, fired at a puppet detachment which was conducting a sweep, causing 10 puppet casualties. A skirmish followed and helicopter gunships were called in to strafe the hamlet, killing fifty Vietnamese civilians.

13. Massacre in Bay Nui, Chau Doc province. On March 10, 1970, in a raid on Thoi Son village, Tinh Bien district, the U.S. ordered its aircraft to strafe puppet troops to urge them to go forward, killing 74 puppet soldiers. On March 25, 1970, U.S. planes again bombed puppet troops in Trac Quang, killing and injuring over twenty of them. Besides, more than one hundred Khmer nationals were killed near Trac Quang post during the same raid.

14. Massacre carried out by B-52 bombers in Ben Tre. On March 1 and 20, 1970, the U.S. sent B-52s to wantonly carpet-bomb densely populated areas in Luong Hoa, Luong Phu, and Long My villages, Ben Tre province, killing 85 civilians.

15. Massacres in Khanh Binh and Khanh Lam, Ca Mau province. On June 1, 1970, the U.S. puppets mobilized armed helicopters and artillery to attack Khanh Binh and Khanh Lam villages, Ca Mau, on fifty occasions, causing 43 civilian casualties.

On June 1 and 2, 1970, enemy aircraft fired missiles at fishermen along the coast of Khanh Lam village, sinking a boat and killing and wounding ten persons.

16. Air strikes against fishing boats off the coast of Rach Gia. On June 20, 1970, U.S. planes attacked a fleet of civilian

fishing boats off the coast of Rach Gia, killing over seventy persons and wounding over two hundred others. Many corpses went to the bottom of the sea.

Massacre and Annihilation by Means of Toxic Chemicals

The U.S and puppets have also conducted chemical warfare on an ever-increasing scale for the purpose of extermination and long-term effects. The following are only some typical cases:

1. In Quang Tri, Thua Thien. In July 1969, successive high-dose chemical sprayings were carried out over a large area in Huong Thuy, Hai Long, and Trieu Phong districts and along the DMZ, ravaging all fruit trees and crops and poisoning hundreds of persons.

In December 1969, the U.S. puppets treated Hung Loc, Hai Thuy, Minh Thuy, My Thuy, Hong Thuy, and An Thuy villages and the vicinity of Hué city with toxic chemicals, killing a great deal of tea and jack-tree plantations, withering up hundreds of mau (1 mau = 3,600 m.) of rice sprouts, and contaminating over one hundred persons, of whom thirty died on the spot.

2. In Quang Nam. On January 31, 1970, the U.S. puppets released one hundred CS bombs and CS-filled drums on the two villages of Ky Phuoc and Ky An, Tam Ky district. The gas envelopped all the five hamlets of these villages, spread to hamlets of other villages, and still remained a week later. Two hundred fifty persons were seriously affected.

On February 28, 1970, for the second time, fifty CS-filled drums were dropped on the said villages, contaminating over one hundred villages.

On February 4, 1970, the enemy fired one hundred gas shells from the Tuan Dong position into Binh Dao and Binh Duong villages, Thang Binh district, poisoning 130 persons who then vomited, shed tears, felt oppressed, coughed. . . . Many of them fainted away.

3. In Quang Ngai. In early October 1969, the U.S. puppets combed Nghia Tho, Nghia Lam and Nghia Thang villages. They killed 77 persons, most of whom were women and children. They drove 27 others into underground shelters and threw hand grenades in to finish them off: among the victims were many old people—Thuy, Nhan, Sau, Cuu, Mrs. Luu, Mrs. Tinh. . . . The survivors were herded into the Go Su concentration camp in Nghia Thang village. Exposed to the inclement weather and attacked by disease, the internees demanded to be taken back to their native villages and their normal life. The cruel agent, Nguyen Hiep, ordered them to take a poison that he said was "detergent." As a result, many suffered violent colics or were affected by beriberi, others became deaf, dull-sighted, and some died on the spot. In all, the poison killed 197 persons.

Faced with this monstrous crime, the inmates of the camp struggled for compensation for the lives taken, and demanded to be returned to their villages and to normal life. The U.S. puppets savagely shelled and machine-gunned the camp to repress them, killing another 21 people on the spot and wounding seven others.

On April 10 and 14, 1970, the U.S. puppets dropped twenty gas-filled drums on densely populated areas in Vuc Liem, Truong An (Duc Pho), and forty on Khanh, Giang and Truong Le (Nhgia Hanh). As a result, 250 persons were contaminated, forty of them seriously: the victims were suffocated, coughed blood and some died on the spot.

4. In Binh Dinh. On February 11 and 12, 1970, toxic chemical sprays took place over Binh Thanh, Binh Giang

villages (Binh Khe district), and along Highway 19. Many fields and orchards were blighted, 250 people were poisoned. In Phu Lac hamlet alone, thirty inhabitants were seriously affected, and 19 oxen, 85 pigs, and hundreds of poultry were killed.

From May 5 to 15, 1970, in a sweep against Phuong Ha, Phuong Phi, and Vinh Hoi villages, Phu Cat district, the enemy attacked civilians with gas-mines, gas grenades, and gas insufflators, causing many persons to be suffocated and cough blood. More than ten of them died on the spot.

On July 3, 1970, in Gia Duc hamlet, Hoai An district, U.S. aircraft sprayed toxic agents over the fields and released twenty gas-filled drums on the hamlet, causing many people to lose consciousness. Twelve of the victims had violent nervous fits and had to be taken to hospitals.

5. In Khanh Hoa. On April 2, 1970, three U.S. planes released thirty gas-filled drums on the mountain areas of Chu Ma Bat and Chu Gay, poisoning many woodcutters. Twenty of them became delirious from serious contamination.

6. In Ninh Thuan. In late July and early August 1969, toxic chemical sprays were continuously carried out over the northern part of Ninh Thuan province, ravaging many ricefields and killing 72 people.

7. In Kontum. On April 19, 1970 six C-123s sprayed more than twenty tons of toxic agents over Dac Bo and Dac Ring, devastating an area 25 km. long by three km. wide, poisoning hosts of persons.

8. In Darlac. On January 4, 1970, enemy artillery fired gas shells on an area 12 km. east of Ban Me Thuot, contaminating twelve persons who then vomited or fainted away.

9. In Tay Ninh. On July 18, 1969, the enemy released one hundred gas-filled drums and fired gas shells on the northeastern part of the Tay Ninh Palace, poisoning hosts of persons. On July 20, 1970, toxic chemicals were sprayed from

Trinh Minh The Canal to Phung mountain. In those two days, over one thousand civilians were contaminated, among whom thirty children died on the spot.

In the last twenty days of September 1969, the U.S. dumped thousands of gas-filled drums on the two villages of Ninh Thanh and Hiep Ninh, belonging to the Tay Ninh Palace. Besides, hundreds of gas shells were fired on the said localities. More than one thousand persons were poisoned, and thirteen children died on the spot.

On September 7, 1968, Go Dau market was treated with toxic agents as people were gathering to buy and sell. A large number of people spat blood as a result of contamination, and a nursling died immediately in its mother's arms.

10. In My Tho. In November 1969, on sixty occasions, enemy aircraft sprayed toxic chemicals over twenty villages, especially Long Tien, Long Trung, Long Khanh (Cai Ly), Binh Minh, Thanh Thuy, Hoa Dinh (Cho Gao), and villages along Nguyen Van Tiep canal, damaging thousands of hectares of orchards, contaminating over eleven thousand people, of whom many died.

11. In Gia Dinh. In May 1968, high-dose chemical sprays took place over Long Thoi, Nhon Duc, Phu Xuan, Phu Loc, Tan Quy, and Phy My villages, Nha Be district, resulting in hundreds being poisoned and, among those, two hundred killed.

12. In Vinh Long. For nearly a week beginning February 9, 1970, enemy aircraft repeatedly sprayed toxic agents over and dropped gas grenades on Hoa Tan, Phu Long, Phu Quoi, Phu Khanh, Phu Huu, An Khanh, and Phu Thuan (Binh Minh district), affecting over one thousand persons (of whom two hundred vomited blood or lost consciousness from serious contamination) and destroying hundreds of hectares of rice-fields and orchards.

Similar cases have occurred in all the provinces of South Vietnam.

Massacres Carried Out by Pak Jung Hi Mercenaries

Not contenting themselves with committing mass murders by their own hands in South Vietnam, the U.S. puppets also engaged a number of client countries to send mercenaries to participate in their blood-revels there. Among U.S. satellite troops in South Vietnam, Pak Jung Hi mercenaries appeared to be the most helpful hirelings. The following are some typical massacres conducted by them:

1. Massacre in Dong Bo, Khanh Hoa province. From October 28 to early November, 1968, Pak Jung Hi troops mounted a raid code-named "White Horse" on Dong Bo area, Khanh Hoa province. Wherever they went, they killed people at random. They slaughtered 320 persons, mostly women and children.

2. Massacres in Thang Binh, Que Son, and Duy Xuyen districts, Quang Nam. From November 11 to 16, 1969, eight puppet and Pak Jung Hi infantry battalions, in coordination with four armored regiments and 350 "pacification" cadres under U.S. command, launched an "accelerated pacification" operation, code-named "Sea Tiger," against more than twenty villages in the three districts of Thang Binh, Que Son, and Duy Xuyen, in Quang Nam province. Wherever they went, the raiders massacred people wantonly. In Lac Can market, Binh Duong village, they marched 75 civilians onto a dune, then killed them all, apart from a three-month-old baby which survived owing to its being covered by its mother's corpse.

In Bau Binh Thuong and Bau Binh Ha hamlets, they killed 54 villagers, who had taken refuge in Tho and Phung's shelters, with hand grenades. Mr. Su's ten-member family in Phu

Son hamlet, Binh Hoa village, was completely exterminated, including seven children under 7 years of age. Mr. Pho, 70, in Phu Haa hamlet, Binh Hoa village, after being savagely tortured, was finished off by the thugs who twisted his neck. Miss Hoa, 20 years old, of Binh Thuy hamlet, Binh Duong village, was beaten to death and her body crushed to pulp. The raiders rode armored vehicles over Mrs. To Thi Chin, 80, Hien Luong hamlet, Binh Hoa village.

According to still incomplete statistics, on November 11 and 12, 1969, the aggressors and their henchmen killed over seven hundred civilians in Binh Duong, Binh Giang, Binh Trieu, Binh Hoa, and Binh Dao villages.

3. Renewed Massacre in Quang Nam. From July 27 to 30, 1970, Pak Jung Hi troops mounted a raid code-named "Golden Dragon" on certain coastal areas in Quang Nam, killing over forty people, mostly women and children.

On September 16, 1970, the "Green Dragon" Brigade conducted a sweep against Binh Duong village, Thanh Binh village, slaying over one hundred persons in a most savage manner.

4. Massacre in Binh Dinh. From July 15 to 31, 1970, Pak Jung Hi mercenaries conducted sweeps against coastal areas in Binh Dinh province. In a single raid code-named "Ho," slew 103 persons, mostly women and children.

5. Massacre in Suoi Che and Ca Lui, Phu Yen province. From October 8 to November 2, 1970, Pak Jung Hi troops combed Suoi Che area, Phu Yen province. Massacres took place all along their way. On October 18 and 19, 1970, alone, the raiders butchered 147 persons in Suoi Che and six others in Ca Lui. Many victims were beheaded, disembowelled, or had their eyeballs extracted. In Ma Tuy, Maphuong, and Maxam hamlets, only three children survived.

Previously, from September 9 to October 2, 1970, GIs from Division 4 had also raided the area, killing and wounding 33 persons in Manham hamlet.

In 1970, in six major operations of regiment-size upward alone, Pak Jung Hi mercenaries massacred 1,392 civilians in Central Trung Bo.

No mountain can match in height the towering crimes piled up by the U.S. aggressors and their henchmen in South Vietnam; no ocean can best them in depth; earth and heaven are angry, vegetation too resents them, entire mankind indignantly condemns them.

Crimes against the Townspeople in South Vietnam

[A document from the Committee to Denounce U.S.—Puppets' War Crimes in South Vietnam.]

In trying to explain away their war of aggression, the U.S. aggressors have tried to present themselves as defenders of an outpost of the free world against communism. They have in this way tried to deceive the South Vietnamese people in the urban areas as to the character of the war. But the townspeople, who have now lived for years in areas controlled by the U.S. and the puppets, have come to realize the nature of the war, and their realization has led to opposition. This opposition has gradually gathered force and has inspired a mass movement which is supported by people from all sections of society: not only have workers and students joined in protesting against the puppet regime and its supporters, but invalids of the Saigon army and even members of the Saigon parliament have joined forces with them.

In defense against this movement, the U.S. and the puppets have resorted to fascist methods in order to try and control the urban movement against them. All shades of opposition are mercilessly suppressed, as one can see from the development of the situation.

282

In the Pre-Nixon Period

The U.S.-dependent junta in South Vietnam has established "anticommunism" as "national policy" to put down
those who struggle for independence, democracy, peace,
and neutrality. As early as November 1954, the puppet administration imprisoned leaders of the Saigon-Cholon
"movement for the safeguarding of peace" because this organization stood for peace, freedom, democracy, and the
peaceful reunification of the country through free general
elections as stipulated by the 1954 Geneva Agreements.
Among the arrested were Nguyen Huu Tho, Trinh Dinh
Thao, and many pharmacists, lawyers, engineers, bankers,
industrialists, Buddhists, priests, professors, etc. . . . In the
following months, they continued to arrest many others and
ordered the organization to be dissolved.

On July 10, 1955, the U.S. puppets arrested Mrs. Nguyen
Thi Dieu, a teacher and a former participant in the Resistance against the French colonialists, who was then teaching
in the Duc Tri college in Saigon, and tortured her to death.
Mrs. Dieu was five months pregnant, and she left behind her
three young children.

Along with the repression of intellectuals, the U.S.-patro-
nized puppet administration feverishly cracked down on students and pupils in towns and cities who struggled for an
improvement of the education program, and against deprav-
ing culture and U.S. enslavement, and who advocated peace
and neutrality. Besides persecution of individuals, massive
crackdowns sometimes took place; for instance: on September 10, 1963, 2,400-odd students and pupils were arrested;
on August 25, 1963, a girl-student Quach Thi Trang was shot;

on May 23, 1962, the death sentence was passed on teacher Le Quang Vinh and a number of students.

Buddhists with democratic and peace tendencies were also mercilessly repressed. On May 8, 1963, in Hué, armored cars were dispatched to fire 37mm shells on a demonstration, killing 12 Buddhist believers and injuring many others. In Saigon, on June 16, 1963, armed police cracked down on a 700,000-strong demonstration of Buddhists, wounding many people and arresting others. Numerous Buddhist priests and followers immolated themselves in protest against the puppet administration's savage policy of repression of Buddhism.

As regards the Saigon working people, the puppet authorities, acting under the slogans of "town decongestion" and "town trimming," ordered dwellings in the workers' quarters cleared of their occupants, destroyed, or surreptitiously set on fire. As a result of the U.S. policy of enslavement, foreign goods flooded the South Vietnamese market, causing the national economy to stagnate, the working people's conditions to grow ever harder, with wages constantly lagging behind the cost of living. In 1957, the puppet junta forbade over three hundred Saigon trade unions to carry on their activities by virtue of Bao Dai's 1954 Edict No. 23.

To silence public opinion, the puppet administration bullied the press in a most brutal and totalitarian manner. Numerous newspapers were closed down or subject to vandalism many journalists imprisoned or deported for having voiced the people's legitimate aspirations or having partly disclosed the rottenness of the stooge administration. The latter, on the one hand, imposed a harsh censorship upon the press and, on the other hand, appealed to rules dating from colonial and feudal times as excuses to persecute it. For instance, the press in towns and cities have always had to abide by the July 29, 1881, law on the press, enacted by the French colonialists and the June 26, 1928 and December 4, 1928, decrees, put into effect by the French colonialists and Bao Dai.

From giving "anticommunism" as a pretext to repress the population, the puppet junta went to the length of brazenly and overtly ordaining laws aimed at stifling the people's yearnings for peace and neutrality, such as the February 1, 1964, Decree 93 and May 17, 1965, Decree 4/65, which outlaw those who advocate neutrality and peace.

This is not to mention the U.S. puppets' encouragement of prostitution (in Saigon alone, 300,000 girls and women have become whores), the hooliganism, the analphabetism, the drug habit . . . in South Vietnamese towns and cities.

In 1968, the U.S. perpetrated a crime of more extreme gravity against the townspeople: the bombing of over two hundred cities, towns, townships, and district capitals. In Saigon, several areas in the center and other districts were demolished by U.S. bombs. Over 85 percent of Hué city, a time-honored cultural and historic center of the Vietnamese people, was destroyed. Forty-two provincial capitals and townships in the Mekong Delta alone had one hundred thousand houses wrecked and more than ten thousand civilian casualties as a result of U.S. bombings.

To sum up, the U.S. and puppets' crimes against the South Vietnamese townspeople are comprehensive, encompassing all political, military, cultural and social fields. They have flouted the national spirit, degraded the mentality of the people, and caused great losses in terms of property and lives to different strata of the towns' people, entailing serious long-term consequences.

Since Nixon's Inauguration

In execution of Nixon's "Vietnamization" plan (the aim of which is to continue and prolong the war of aggression in

South Vietnam) since 1969, the puppet administration has intensified the repression of the townspeople in a most atrocious manner.

On February 5, 1969, Nguyen Van Thieu openly used foul language against those who stand for peace and neutrality and threatened to shoot or behead them before he was finished, to smash all organizations which demand the formation of the coalition government, the restoration of peace, and the ending of the war. This line has frequently been reiterated by Thieu.

Pursuant to this policy, the puppet junta arrested, imprisoned, and sentenced en masse people of peace and neutralist tendencies who oppose the U.S. war of aggression, stand for coalition, and demand that the Vietnam problem be settled by the Vietnamese themselves without foreign interference. Among those were Reverend Thich Thien Minh, deputy head of the Saigon Buddhist Institute; Mme. Huynh Tan Man, chairman of the Saigon Students' Union; Pham Van Nhon, editor of the French-language *Le Nouveau Vietnam (New Vietnam)*; Nguyen Lau, director of the English-language *Saigon Daily News*; Nguyen Van Thang, secretary general of the Saigon Students' Union; thirty intellectuals in the "Committee for the Formation of Progressive National Forces," etc. . . . On March 17, 1969, in sentencing Reverend Thich Thien Minh, the puppet tribunal emphatically stated that all movements for peace will be severely punished.

Since 1969, almost all the demonstrations, meetings, and teach-in organized by students, intellectuals, and other strata of the townspeople to voice their yearnings for peace were suppressed by means of gunfire, truncheons, tear gas, missiles, etc. . . . U.S. MPs took part in many crackdowns, and on August 30, 1970, helicopters manned by American pilots fired missiles and dropped gas grenades on a student demonstration in Saigon. Quite a lot of students of both sexes were tortured so savagely that, on being summoned to trial, they could not walk by themselves and had to lean on each other and finally lay sprawling over the floor, as was the case on April 29, 1970. The students' General Union, a number of deputies in the Saigon "National Assembly," and the advocates representing the students raised protests against the torture of students by the puppet authorities.

Also subject to brutal treatment were all Saigon newspapers that voiced the people's aspirations for peace and neutrality, demanded the ending of the war, stood for a coalition government, opposed U.S. involvement or denounced U.S. crimes against civilians, or exposed the Thieu-Ky administration's rottenness. In 1968, there were over thirty cases in which Saigon newspapers had their editions confiscated or were closed down or fined. In 1969, over forty such cases were recorded. In 1970, the Saigon press went through more than 230 cases of seizure, close-down, fining, suing; in 1971, as of mid-May, over 250 cases. The *Tia Sang (Morning News)* alone, from March 13, 1970, to May 8, 1971, was subject to over 130 confiscations and fines. At times, as many as a dozen different editions were confiscated or a score of newspapers prosecuted in a single day (March 18, 1971). In February 1971, seizures took place on eighteen out of the twenty-eight days of the month. March 1971: more than one hundred confiscations and fines. Several publishers and authors were fined or imprisoned, among them the Christian priests Truong Ba Can and Chau Tin, [who] had to serve a nine-month term of imprisonment each.

Since 1969, the puppet administration has intensified searches in towns and cities to an extent never before experienced. In 1969, in Saigon, the police carried out over seven thousand searches; on the night of January 20, 1969, over 9,700 people were arrested or searched. On April 6, 1969, as many as nine thousand "civil defense guards," under

U.S. command, mounted a search operation into Districts 7 and 8. From April 30 to May 5, 1969, they arrested over 4,200 people in Binh Chanh district for interrogation.

In 1970, from September 15 to December 28, the U.S. puppets searched and apprehended over 280,750 people in Saigon. In Can Tho provincial capital, from September 15 to October 20, 1970, more than 7,850 persons experienced the same ordeal. In early November 1970, Tra Vinh provincial capital had over one thousand of its inhabitants arrested.

From February 12 to April 12, 1971, nearly ten thousand people in Saigon were subject to arrests and searches. In early February 1971, over one thousand people were rounded up and arrested in Tra Vinh provincial capital. In January 1971, Hué city saw hundreds of its inhabitants apprehended, among them over thirty Buddhist priests, professors, students, and pupils [who] were seized on January 13, 1971.

In the interests of the war, the puppet administration has increased taxes to extort more money from the townspeople —some of them multiplied tenfold. According to the Saigon paper *Cong Luan (Public Opinion)*, October 14, 1970, edition, the small silk merchants in Binh Tay market (Saigon) on whom previously an annual tax of 80,000 piasters had been levied, now had to pay 700,000 piasters yearly. Income taxes of 2,–4,000 piasters rose to 50,–200,000 piasters. For a dwelling in Phan Dinh Phung Avenue, Saigon, one must now pay 600,000 piasters of land tax, as against 60,000 piasters last year (*Tia Sang*, Saigon, January 9, 1971).

The townspeople's conditions have grown harder and harder, due to the terribly sharp rise of the cost of living. In 1958, a quintal of best quality rice could be obtained at the price of 500 piasters: now it costs 10,000 piasters; the price of a duck egg climbed from one piaster up to 22 piasters, that of a shirt from 80 piasters to 1,500 piasters (*Cong Luan*,

Saigon, October 15, 1970). The U.S. review *Look* of August 11, 1970, reported that since 1965, the cost of living in Saigon had increased by 600 percent.

According to an *Agence France Presse* dispatch on March 25, 1971, there were fifteen thousand lepers in Saigon, and two-thirds of the sick people in Hué were suffering from tuberculosis. The house-, land-, and market-clearance campaign continues to rage in Saigon (*Cong Luan*, Saigon, April 22, 1971).

This document reflects only some of the U.S. puppets' crimes against the South Vietnamese townspeople.

The repression by the aggressors and traitors whips up increasing opposition by the people in the South Vietnamese towns and cities, and the struggle has therefore grown more implacable with every passing day. Of late, being routed on the battlefield, the U.S. and puppets have stepped up massive terror campaigns all the more. This fact shows that they have been obstinately resorting to their criminal acts to carry out Nixon's "Vietnamization of the war" plan, opposing the Vietnamese people's basic national rights, damaging the American people's legitimate interests, and running counter to the aspirations of progressive peace-loving people the world over.

International Law and American Policy

As illustrated by the foregoing reports and testimonies, American pursuit of its war in Indochina has transgressed countless international legal conventions. Yet those transgressions only take on a coherent perspective when discussed in terms of America's political commitments and goals in Indochina. The interrelationship between international law and American policy is explored in these concluding statements and reports from the Commission's second session.

International Law and the U.S. War in Indochina: Hans Göran Franck

From the point of view of international law, the United States involvement in Vietnam may historically be said very briefly to have developed as follows:

The United States has intervened in Vietnam with the aim of preventing the Vietnamese people from freely controlling their internal and external affairs, in conflict with the Geneva Agreements of 1954, the general principles of international law, and the spirit and letter of the Charter of the United Nations. By making use of junta regimes in South Vietnam, the United States has subjected the Vietnamese people to brutal and unlawful oppression. When this oppression resulted in popular uprisings, the United States intervened with military power in violation of Article 2, paragraph 4 of the UN Charter, which provides that the members of the organization shall refrain in their international relations from the threat or use of force against the territorial integrity or political independence of any state.

Since that initial illegal intervention in the internal affairs of Vietnam, the United States involvement has now moved into what is a purely military intervention characterized as a war of aggression.

The aggressive military actions of the United States have continuously increased in scope and have been extended to the Democratic Republic of Vietnam (North Vietnam), Laos, and Cambodia. The Democratic Republic of Vietnam has been subjected to bombings, artillery bombardment, and chemical warfare by the military forces of the United States.

Laos has been subjected to bombings, chemical warfare, and ground actions by U.S. military forces as well as its allied and mercenary troops. An attempt to invade Laos has been undertaken by the South Vietnamese ground troops and the American air forces, with massive American logistic support. For years Cambodia has also been subjected to repeated military violations by United States air and ground forces and the forces of its allies, and in 1970 these violations culminated in an American military invasion of Cambodia.

All of these aggressive actions are in conflict with Article 2, paragraph 4 of the UN Charter.

There has been no deescalation of the aggressive policy of the United States in Indochina during 1971. In South Vietnam the war continues on an undiminished scale. The bombing of the Democratic Republic of Vietnam, Laos, and Cambodia continues. The Saigon administration's American-controlled forces are still in Cambodia, and efforts to break into Laos have continued after the unsuccessful invasion. The threat of a direct military invasion of the Democratic Republic of Vietnam has increased as President Nixon's government continues to conduct a markedly aggressive military policy in Indochina without regard to the rules and principles of international law or to the contents and aims of the UN Charter.

As the United States has escalated its aggressive war, its military methods have become more brutal and indiscriminate. U.S. leadership has completely abandoned the principle that belligerents shall distinguish between combatants and the civilian population, even though, according to the rules of international law, the civilian population must under no circumstances be the object of military actions. In fact, the military actions of the United States in Indochina have come to be the very antithesis of this principle, exposing a policy in which the civilian population is considered to be a legitimate target for hostilities. Furthermore, U.S. military training bears a racial stamp. A deep contempt for the Indochinese people is inculcated in the military personnel during their training period and is strengthened by the command's tolerance or encouragement of atrocities against civilians and prisoners of war.

Categories of Crimes

We can distinguish the following categories of crimes on the basis of the rules of international law:

• *Bombing and artillery bombardment of civilian targets* in violation of the 1949 Geneva Convention Relative to the Protection of Civilian Persons in Time of War and the Fourth Hague Convention of 1907 which prohibits the bombing of towns, villages, dwellings, or buildings which are undefended.

• *The utilization of prohibited methods of warfare* such as antipersonnel bombs containing splinters, pellets, or darts, napalm and phosphorus bombs—i.e., such means of warfare as are designed to cause "unnecessary suffering," as defined in Article 23 of the Fourth Hague Convention of 1907.

• *Chemical warfare* in violation of international conventions and declarations, primarily the Geneva Protocol of 1925. Hundreds of thousands of people have been afflicted by injury directly due to poison. However, investigations also appear to indicate that the poisons cause injuries to coming generations.

Biological-chemical warfare confronts coming generations in Indochina with a frightening perspective as the natural premises for human life have been subjected to a systematic destruction whose effects are impossible to ascertain. The natural ecological balance, the relationship of living organisms to their environment, are threatened by a devastating disturbance of extremely long duration. The immediate effects of chemical warfare are to some extent covered by provisions in various international legal conventions. Article 55 of the Geneva Convention of 1949 establishes, for example, the obligation of an occupying power to guarantee the civilian population's food supplies. Yet the entire scope of the problem with its more long-range effects has still not been covered by international law.

• *The use of gas* is in conflict with the so-called Washington Treaty of 1922 and the Geneva Protocol of 1925 which prohibit the use of asphyxiating, poisonous, or similar gases, as well as bacteriological warfare. The objection which states that under normal conditions the gases used cannot be considered fatal is irrelevant, since the manner in which they are employed causes both death and serious injury.

• *Massacres of civilian populations* constitute self-evident criminal actions in violation of the laws of war, particularly the principles of international law recognized in the Charter of the Nuremberg Tribunal and in the Judgment of the Tribunal unanimously affirmed by the General Assembly of the United Nations and the 1949 Geneva Convention Relative to the Protection of Civilian Persons in Time of War. Massacres such as that in Son My are not isolated occurrences in the course of military actions, but an integrated part of the military strategy of depopulating areas which are liberated by national liberation forces. The training, the battlefield conduct of the commanding officers, and the general tactics of the warfare—i.e., the conscious forms of the sanctioned military policy—furnish the basis of explanation for the frequent occurrence of these atrocities.

• *Mass deportations of the civilian population* were criminalized in the Charter of the Nuremberg Tribunal as a crime against humanity. In Indochina numberless people are driven to camps or strategic areas where they encounter poverty or death as a result of undernourishment and disease.

In addition, the American bombings and chemical warfare cause millions of people to flee to the burgeoning slum areas in the cities, to hunger and disease, to misery and accelerated oppression. The living conditions in the camps, the strategic areas, and the slums do not meet even the absolutely minimum demands for sanitation, medical care, and food supply. A large proportion of the people there are even denied the right to work. All these conditions are in direct violation of the obligations of an occupying power, as established in Articles 55 and 56 of the Geneva Convention of 1949 Relative to the Protection of Civilian Persons. These articles require the supply of food and medicines to the population to be guaranteed and that prophylactic and preventive measures to combat the spread of contagious diseases and epidemics be initiated and enforced.

• *The regime in the prisons* of South Vietnam serves a criminal purpose in conflict with the Nuremberg Principles, which criminalize political persecution in connection with crimes against peace or war crimes as a crime against humanity. The prisons are an instrument for the suppression of political opposition to the military policy. Tens of thousands of people who oppose the United States aggressive war are cast into prison arbitrarily and without formal charges or previous judgments pronounced by regularly constituted courts; these actions are in full disregard of the legal protection prescribed under the 1949 Geneva Conventions. Thousands of people die or are crippled by brutal torture, and tens of thousands more die of intentional malnutrition and a lack of medical care.

Not only does the government of the United States invest enormous sums in the police force and the penal system of South Vietnam, but the prison system is even administered under the supervision of American advisers. New constructions and the expansion of existing prisons take place in collaboration with American experts. The prisons are furnished with advanced torture equipment—for instance that for electric torture—from the U.S.

Statements of witnesses and reports show that brutality in the South Vietnamese prisons does not consist of excesses by some individual criminals; rather, terror has been systematized as a phase in the military conduct of the war.

• *Torture and other inhuman treatment* of civilians and prisoners of war is in violation of several provisions of the Geneva Conventions of 1949 which undertake to protect the inviolability of life, health, and personal dignity of civilians and prisoners of war. The Nuremberg Principles also give an authoritative expression in general form for this basic legal premise as do the terms of the Hague Conventions of 1907. The regularity of the atrocities of the American troops and the troops of their allies in Indochina as a result of direct orders, encouragement, or conscious tolerance from their superiors is significant. The aim is often to exact revenge for purely military operations or to spread terror as a part of the psychological warfare.

Immeasurable Material Destruction— "Military Necessity?"

The material destruction caused in Indochina by the massive American bombings and artillery bombardment from ground and naval positions is without comparison in the history of the world. Whole cities have been wiped out. Small peaceful villages, individual dwellings and farms, all kinds of human places of abode have been leveled to the ground. Distinctively civilian buildings and institutions such as hospitals, nursing homes, schools, child care homes, churches, pagodas, and cultural and historical monuments and buildings have been mercilessly attacked by the American military forces. The economic, social, and cultural losses caused by this total warfare are immeasurable in scope. The American leaders have systematically and consciously utilized their military resources to totally crush civilian production capacity within large areas of Indochina. All types of industrial and agricultural installations, from factories to plant nurseries, have been attacked and destroyed. The immediate and long-range damage to the civilian production capacity cannot be determined more exactly. It has become impossible to live and produce anything in certain regions; others have resisted at the price of serious deterioration in their production capacity.

The prohibition against bombing or shooting at civilian targets which was discussed above not only protects the lives and health of civilians, even if this may be considered its primary goal; the protection also concerns man's material resources, the prerequisites for the creation and maintenance of social life.

The rules of international law criminalize plundering— destruction or devastation of material resources which is not dictated by military necessity. The "military necessity" concept is unclear and disputed within the doctrines of international law. However, it cannot be extended indefinitely. Its nature of exceptional rule, which justifies otherwise illegal actions under especially compelling circumstances, cannot be denied. The government of the United States is not capable of presenting any legally acceptable premise which makes it possible to refer to "military necessity" as the reason for its military strategy, since the relevant criteria for such a claim do not exist. The destruction and devastation are not an exception but a rule.

As the aggressor in Indochina, the United States cannot excuse the method of warfare which its leaders have chosen themselves on the grounds of "military necessity." It is not "military necessity" in the legal sense which dictates the military strategy pursued by the United States. The American leadership calls a "military necessity" whatever is required to crush the will to resistance among the Indochinese peoples.

Is the United States Committing Genocide?

At its first session, the International Commission of Enquiry concluded that the nature and scope of the crimes which are being committed by the United States and its allies can be deemed to fulfill the legal prerequisites of the 1948 UN Convention on the Prevention and Punishment of the Crime of Genocide.

There are certainly experts on international law who consider [that] the United States has committed war crimes and crimes against humanity on a wide scale in Indochina but who hesitate to go so far as to characterize the war as genocide. A legal analysis with attention to the Genocide Convention offers certain difficulties. There are no guiding precedents. When the trials against the war criminals of World War II took place, there was still no Genocide Convention. Actions of the type which were criminalized in the

Genocide Convention were largely defined legally and judged under the definition "crimes against humanity." The overall view which permeates the Genocide Convention was, however, still not introduced in the concept "crimes against humanity."

In addition to a more exact definition of the descriptions of the criminal acts, the Genocide Convention implies such a significant change in the general character of the construction of the crime that there is reason to devote attention to it. It did not say, as the Charter of the Nuremberg Tribunal had declared, that the various actions must have been committed *with the intent* to destroy in whole or in part a national ethnic, racial, or religious group as such. The implication of this change conveys us directly into one of the problems which may cause hesitation in applying the genocide concept to the United States war in Indochina. The question is: "Is there 'intent' in the meaning of the Genocide Convention?"

We shall not make the answer to the question more subtle than circumstances demand. Let us first eliminate any misunderstanding with regard to the motive of the persons committing the acts, on the basis of a comparison between the Charter of the Nuremberg Tribunal and the Genocide Convention. As distinguished from the Charter, the Genocide Convention does not place any demands for specific motives on the person committing the action. The legal judgment is therefore in principle not affected by the nature of the motive. It is judicially irrelevant if the motive is economic, strategic, or racial, even if evidence can be presumed to be stronger if the motives are expressly racial.

The concrete execution of the United States military policy in Indochina is permeated by a manifest racism. During the training period, strong racial prejudice is intentionally instilled into the troops. The ruthless methods of warfare and the military command's macabre incitement to competition between troop units to report the greatest possible number of enemy dead undermine the morals of the individual soldier and create a racial attitude toward the Indochinese people. Racism becomes a method to facilitate the execution of the military strategy which is sanctioned by the American leaders.

Since, in technical meaning, the motive is irrelevant for the determination of whether genocide is committed or not, we are not required to proceed from any presumptive motives when we limit and characterize the group which is subjected to the criminal acts. The nature of the groups is determined on the basis of the criteria which characterize it in relation to the aggressors. In relation to the United States, the national identities of the Indochinese peoples constitute the determining factor. The American attack on the Indochinese people is directed at their nationality as such. In relation to the United States, the Vietnamese, Laotians, and Cambodians are killed in their character of representatives of their nations. They are killed because they refuse to renounce their national rights. The liberation struggle against the American invaders is national, and the leaders of the United States cannot escape their responsibility by placing a political stamp on their victims.

If foreign troops invaded the United States and indiscriminately began to exterminate its population, with the motivation that they could be presumed to support one of the large political parties, would the American government then not consider that this constituted aggression against the American people? The persecution of political groups within a country's own area of jurisdiction may be presumed to fall outside the limits of the Genocide Convention's definition, but not an attack on putatively political groups in a foreign country, however distasteful the invading power may consider such a group to be.

But is, then, the United States' aggressive war in Indochina based on an intention of the type proscribed in the Genocide Convention? We do not have any official statement by the leaders of the United States which clearly reveals such an intent. But the rhetoric employed by the American leaders is not proof which denies the truth of our statement that the American war of aggression in Indochina is based on the kind of conscious intent that was criminalized by the Genocide Convention. At most, statements which directly express the intention to exterminate a specific group of people constitute proof of criminal intentions. On the other hand, contradictory statements are not evidence that there is no criminal intent.

The intent is revealed by the formation of the systematic extermination policy as it is manifested in concrete actions—and not in statements made by President Nixon, Secretary of Defense Laird, or General Westmoreland.

The legal presumption which applies is that the natural consequences of consciously undertaken acts are intentional, insofar as the opposite cannot be proven. It cannot be denied that the United States military policy is likely to cause significant decimation of the civilian population of Indochina. Millions of people have already been killed or maimed. Millions of others are threatened by physical annihilation as a result of the living conditions forced upon them by the leaders of the United States.

Some may perhaps feel that this still cannot be a question of genocide, since the population statistics in Indochina do not show a marked decline. Legally, this objection is not of decisive importance. The *natural* consequences of the military policy of the American leaders is the primary consideration, not the factual effects. The responsibility of the leaders is not mitigated because the subjects of the attack avoid a greater degree of decimation because they manage to protect themselves.

We cannot penetrate the thoughts and deliberations of the American leaders. We must proceed from what they must reasonably realize and have knowledge of. From this starting point, we can clearly establish that they must have realized the devastating effects of the methods of warfare which they have sanctioned. But in any case, the guilt of the American leaders is not decided by whether they have themselves realized the criminality of their acts.

If we summarize the United States military policy on the basis of Article 2 of the Genocide Convention, the following picture is obtained: massacres, bombings, artillery bombardment, gas warfare, and executions in prisons and camps cause mass death among the civilian population. These actions, together with the chemical warfare, torture, and extreme conditions in camps and prisons, cause serious physical and psychic injury to millions of civilians. The destruction of cereal grains and other vital resources, as well as the devastation of the natural environment, mass internments, mass deportations, concentration measures, the intentionally instigated refugee situation, and the collapse of the entire social structure threaten enormous sectors of the population with gradual physical destruction.

In the latter case, the logical relationship between intent and effect is perhaps not equally self-evident. But consider this colossal process of destruction which is mercilessly driven forward. Consider the gigantic organization system behind this destruction, which is administered by enormous numbers of people and massive technological resources.

Consider, then, the enormous flood of information which must flow into the White House and the Pentagon concerning every aspect of the military situation. The American leaders have every opportunity to determine the effects of the policies they sanction. The responsible leaders must realize that the devastating effect of their military policy is, in the final analysis, the end result of the guidelines they themselves have established.

The individual soldier does not master the war. This does not mean that the individual soldier should be relieved of all responsibility for cruelty and inhumane acts against civilians and prisoners of war. Every criminal offense which can be prevented is a gain for justice and humanity. It is the soldier's self-evident duty to act in accordance with the humanity prescribed by the laws of war. But it is difficult for the soldier to resist the influences of the war, the dehumanization of his military training, and the false ideals which are imprinted in him.

It is also our self-evident duty to support him in his difficult situation. It is our self-evident duty to tell him that this war is criminal. It is our self-evident duty to support every refusal or obstruction which contributes to the prevention of criminal acts, which helps to bring the war to an end.

A whole generation of young American men are threatened by destructive brutalization and by deep moral and psychic destitution. The brutal deeds of violence they are forced to commit in Indochina must be indelibly etched in their minds.

Physically and socially crippled, they are cast out into a reality to which they may never be able to adjust. This self-destructive plague cannot be combatted by silence, by pushing the returning soldiers aside into inadequate care institutions and hospitals, by silencing or ignoring their experiences.

Only by converting the paralyzing passivity and silence into positive and extroverted action can assistance and aid be given to the war veterans in the United States.

The soldiers who stand up in the United States and bear witness to the brutalities are making a significant and important contribution to peace and justice. They arouse their comrades from a malignant and painful silence. They give other young men the courage to refuse to participate in this criminal war. They strengthen the large majority of the American people in their efforts to end the war. They reveal the rhetoric and phrasemaking of the American leaders to the whole world. They undermine the position of those elements within the American society who with grotesque sentimentality praise the most brutal actions and call them heroic deeds.

The aspects which we have developed from the starting point of the Genocide Convention convey us straight into the heart of the question of the legal responsibility for the criminal war policy which is being pursued in Indochina.

Let us conclude this legal discussion about whether there is an intent, in the meaning of the Genocide Convention, with respect to the United States conduct of the war in Indochina.

We have noted that in a technical sense the policy pursued in Indochina corresponds to the definition of acts described in the Convention; that it is conducted in an organized, systematic manner and on a very wide scale; and that the United States's political and military leaders and the economic lobby groups which support and influence military policy must reasonably be deemed to realize the consequences of their political measures in Indochina.

According to the legal criteria, the war therefore clearly has a genocidal character. The American leaders have the power to stop the extermination process, but they do not do so. They have the power to rescue millions of people from death and suffering, but they do not do so. We can trace the political decisions and orders which result in this mass annihilation back to the top echelons in and around the leaders of the American government.

The American military strategy in Indochina is carefully

planned with the conscious realization of its effects on the civilian population. It is intentionally planned without consideration for these results or with the aim of attaining these very results. What is the difference between intentional extermination and intentional extermination if the victim does not surrender? The Jews were exterminated by the Nazis irrespective of whether they submitted or not. The Indochinese peoples can free themselves from the effects of the genocidal war if they surrender on the terms of the American leaders. But is this a meaningful distinction, legally and morally? No. For we know that the Indochinese peoples refuse to submit. They refuse to surrender their national rights.

If the extermination of a people constitutes an instrument of blackmail, or if the extermination of a people only constitutes a means to another final end which it is desired to attain, it is still the intentional extermination of a people— i.e., genocide.

Rafael Lemkin, the originator of the Genocide Convention, characterized the Nazi genocidal actions in eastern Europe as "a new occupation technique with the aim of winning the peace even if the war itself is lost." This definition could equally well have been written to define the military policy of the United States in Indochina.

By decimating the population and driving it from the rural areas to the cities where it can be more easily controlled, the American leaders endeavor to "pacify" Indochina. Confronted with the unsuccessful effort to conquer the Indochinese peoples with a gigantic American army, and [confronted with] the growing pressure from opinion at home, the American leaders are now following a new policy which, with seemingly reduced military efforts, endeavors to maintain American influence in the area. President Nixon is endeavoring to carry out the impossible task of simultaneously escalating and deescalating the war. In order to counteract the prolonged and gradual American troop reductions, the bombing is escalated and the forces of the local vassals are equipped at an accelerating rate. The net result is continued genocide, although to a greater extent by proxy. The combined pacification and Vietnamization strategy means "merely changing the color of the bodies," as the American ambassador Ellsworth Bunker is said to have expressed it. The profile of the war changes, but it does not become less criminal—only more subtle and cynical.

The fate of millions of Indochinese still rests in the hands of a few men in the White House and the Pentagon. The principal responsibility for the policy of genocide also rests here.

The Legal Responsibility

Legal responsibility for crimes against international law has two aspects. On one hand, there is the responsibility for crimes which can be attributed to the state as such, and, on the other hand, there is personal responsibility. The state responsibility is primarily civil. A state cannot be punished, but demands for economic compensation can be raised in the form of war damages, for example.

When establishing state responsibility, no psychological guilt criteria are employed. The obligation to pay compensation exists as soon as a crime against international law can be attributed to a nation. It is apparent that the United States war of aggression in Indochina can be attributed to the United States as a nation.

Personal responsibility for crimes against international law is subject to criminal jurisdiction. The legally punishable responsibility for crimes against international law has been formulated by international and national judicial practices and by international codification and national legislation. The foremost precedent within the field of international law is constituted by the judgments at the war crimes tribunals after World War II. The principles established by the Nuremberg Tribunal have later been codified in the so-called Nuremberg Principles, which were adopted by the General Assembly of the United Nations in 1950. The Nuremberg Principles establish punishment for *crimes against peace, war crimes*, and *crimes against humanity.*

According to the United Nations Convention on Genocide, genocide constitutes a crime under international law. According to the Convention, genocide, conspiracy to commit genocide, direct and public incitement to commit genocide, attempt to commit genocide, and complicity in genocide are all punishable offenses. The Genocide Convention expressly prescribes that the contracting parties shall legally establish effective punishment for genocide.

According to the Nuremberg Principles, national legislation does not constitute a prerequisite for establishing legal responsibility for violations of international law. The absence of such legislation does not free an individual from judicial responsibility.

The United States assumed a leading role in the trials in Nuremberg and Tokyo against war criminals. More than any other nation, the United States worked to bring about a generalization of the principles which were the basis of the sentences in Nuremberg. Also, the U.S. Department of the Army Field Manual 27–10, covering the rules of warfare, recognizes the principle of legal responsibility for crimes against peace, crimes against humanity, and war crimes.

We can, therefore, consider it established that the United States is clearly bound by the Nuremberg Principles.

The United States has also pledged that it will respect, among other things, the five Hague Conventions of 1907, the 1929 Geneva Convention Relative to the the Treatment of Prisoners of War, the 1929 Geneva Convention for the Amelioration of the Conditions of the Wounded and Sick of Armies in the Field, as well as the 1949 Geneva Conventions for the Amelioration of the Conditions of the Wounded and Sick in Armed Forces in the Field and at Sea, the Treatment of Prisoners of War, and the Protection of Civilian Persons in Time of War.

The United States has also signed the so-called Washington Treaty of 1922 and the 1925 Geneva Protocol containing prohibitions against asphyxiating, poisonous or similar gases, and bacteriological means of warfare. The United States also participated in the formulation of the so-called Hague Rules for Aerial Warfare of 1923 with a prohibition against terror bombing of civilian populations.

The United States has signed but not ratified the Genocide Convention. Also, the United States obligation under the Briand-Kellogg Pact against wars of aggression should be pointed out, as well as its obligations under the Charter of the United Nations.

The United States has thus surrounded itself with a comprehensive network of international legal rules concerning war and warfare. The United States has exceeded these legal boundaries in its aggressive war against Indochina. Humanity demands that the injustice cease and that justice be established.

Both judicial logic and the moral commandments demand that the question of the legal responsibility for these state-organized crimes be raised. Not because humanity demands scapegoats for the horrors which afflict it; not because we demand revenge for suffering and death; not because we demand that evil shall be punished. We raised the question of legal and moral responsibility in order to break the rule of violence over law and justice. The International Commissions have neither the power nor the competence to exact legal responsibility in the individual cases. However, the Commission can take the principles of these practical and legal questions under consideration.

We cannot find any valid objections to taking up the legal side of the individual responsibility for a discussion of principles.

By drawing attention to the individual responsibility for the United States war of aggression and criminal military actions, our analysis will serve a practical purpose. We place it at the disposition of the forces striving for peace who are calling for the political and moral responsibility of those who form, influence, and effectuate the military policy.

There are no definitely fixed boundaries for personal responsibility for violations of international law. The Nuremberg Principles and the precedents from Nuremberg and Tokyo establish the starting points, but the fixed framework for the personnel categories to be tried for alleged war crimes can only be determined by a competent national or international court which tries the conditions in the case.

The Nuremberg Principles establish that superior orders do not relieve anyone from responsibility under international law, provided a moral choice was in fact possible for him.

Thus, we must proceed from the premise that even the subordinate person can, within certain—perhaps narrow—limits, reach morally just decisions in conflict with illegal orders, in spite of the psychological pressure inherent in being under command. However, the pressure exercised by a surrounding environment comprising widespread criminality and brutality can, in combination with twisted, imprinted ideals and the very fact of standing under the command of a superior whose judgment is assumed to be reliable, make it very difficult for the subordinate to retain what we consider to be sound moral values. But it is important that we maintain the principle of personal responsibility on all levels, chiefly to counteract all of these negative factors and to make it clear to the individual that he has the right and the duty to refuse to carry out orders which are in violation of international law.

The question of personal responsibility has been given burning actuality by the exceptional judicial measures taken in the United States after the massacres in Son My. The hysterical wave of sympathy for those responsible which followed the processes has aroused dismay and abhorrence. If we are to follow our principles, we cannot take a stand on individual responsibility in concrete cases. However, let us emphasize some reservations on the basis of principles. It is, for example, very doubtful if the court-martial in question could be considered to have jurisdiction over the offenses of the Son My massacre, as superior officers in the U.S. Army are potential codefendants under the Nuremberg Principles.

It is possible, but in no way certain, that the processes already conducted can lead to some positive repercussions in the form of more law-abiding behavior on the part of men and officers for fear of judicial punishment—in any case as long as only a few individuals are tried. The sense of justice is not satisfied with the fact that some few military persons of low rank are charged and held responsible, while those who are ultimately responsible for the entire war go free form every form of judicial measures.

It cannot be denied that the trials as such have contained elements of real moral courage through the upright conduct of individual persons, but, regardless of whether the intention behind the processes has been the best, they have still served as spectacular processes whose implications we cannot clearly foresee. At the worst, they can serve to conceal the real responsibility for the war and its brutality. At the best, they can give rise to a more conscious direction of the charges against the very highest political and military levels.

The tribunals in Toyko and Nuremberg reflected the idea that responsibility for illegal battlefield practice rests with the military and political leadership. This formula for criminal responsibility was clearly shown in the Matter of Yamashita. The Japanese general Yamashita was tried and sentenced to death for extensive war crimes committed by troops under his command in the Philippines. Significant for this decision, which was upheld by the Supreme Court of the United States, was that Yamashita was condemned even though he claimed that he did not have specific knowledge of the alleged crimes.

The basic motive for the upholding of the sentence is well explained by the majority opinion of Chief Justice Stone in the Supreme Court. He said, among other things:

> It is evident that the conduct of military operations by troops whose excesses are unrestrained by orders or efforts of their commands would almost certainly result in violations which it is the purpose of the law of war to prevent. Its purpose to protect civilian populations and prisoners of war from brutality would largely be defeated if the command of an invading army could with impunity neglect to take responsible measures for their protection.

The Yamashita case sets a precedent which has particular bearing on the U.S. warfare in Indochina with respect to the responsibility of political and military leaders for crimes which have been committed under their command, especially when no continuous measures have been taken to investigate and punish crimes in order to prevent their repetition.

In the case of individual violations and massacres, this pattern for the distribution of responsibility would certainly appear to be adequate with respect to the responsibility of the military command next to the top echelon. However, the general conduct of the war, the bombing strategy, the policy for the moving of the people, and the application of "free fire zones" can obviously not be characterized as violations which were not sufficiently effectively stopped or which are tolerated. This is criminality on a gigantic scale which is directly initiated and sanctioned by the highest political and military leaders. Here we have the heart of the responsibility complex. The American Chief Prosecutor in Nuremberg, Robert H. Jackson, named, in general, the circle of persons who should primarily be considered for trial and judgment for crimes against international law as "the planners and designers, the inciters and leaders," characterizing them as "men of a station and rank which do not soil their own hands with blood." In order to avoid compromises with this morally and judicially self-evident basic principle, it is expressly stated in the Nuremberg Principles that a position as head of state or responsible government official does not relieve anyone from responsibility under international law.

The legal responsibility for the political and military leadership may in principle be presumed to be collectively shared by the members of government and the Joint Chiefs of Staff. Passiveness is not sufficient reason for evasion of responsibility. At best, it may be considered a mitigating circumstance with regard to the punishment. This attitude is concretely exemplified by the War Crimes Tribunal in Toyko, which stated, in connection with the question of responsibility for the treatment of prisoners of war, that a member of the government who had not resigned from a government that could be said to bear collective responsibility for the prisoners of war should be regarded as coresponsible for the maltreatment of the prisoners.

The United States participated directly in the development of a broad concept of criminal jurisdiction for national leaders during time of war. A leading decision-making official must take specific measures to prevent crimes against internatioal law or resign from the government. If he did not do one or the other, he became—by remaining in the government of a state which was guilty of war crimes—a war criminal.

Responsibility for war crimes and crimes against humanity can in varying degrees be ascribed to persons from the very highest ranks of leadership and down to the lowest military personnel. The responsibility for the policy of genocide and the most severe of all crimes—aggressive war as such—may, on the other hand, only be attributed to the highest political and military leaders.

At the Nuremberg trials, the chemical company of I.G. Farben was tried for the manufacture of Cyklon B, which was used for liquidations in the concentration camps.

I.G. Farben's counterpart in the United States is the supplier of war materials, Dow Chemical Company, which has —among other things—been responsible for the manufacture of napalm for the American military forces. The different producers of war materials, together with other strong capital interests, have actively worked for an uncompromisingly aggressive war policy in Indochina. The responsibility of the industrial leaders and holders of capital deserves to be noticed and studied very carefully from the judicial standpoint.

The Imperfection of International Law

The preamble to the 1907 Fourth Hague Convention contains the following declaration of principle:

> Until a more complete code of the laws of war can be drawn up, the High Contracting Parties deem it expedient to declare that, in cases not covered by the rules adopted by them, the inhabitants and the belligerents remain under the protection and governance of the principles of the law of nations, derived from the usages established among civilized peoples, from the laws of humanity and from the dictates of public conscience.

This so-called Martens Clause expresses the idea that, in addition to the pacts and conventions, there are general principles which must not be violated.

As a system of rules, international law is incomplete. It is constantly changing as a result of the development of the internal conditions and external relations of the nations. It therefore never contains an exhaustive list of what is permissible or not permissible in war at any given point of time. The general formulation of the Martens Clause is intended to establish an outer limit for what is permissible during war. The underlying purpose of these laws must always be the guideline for our interpretation of the laws of war—to limit unnecessary suffering. We do not reject the crimes committed by the United States in Indochina because they constitute violations of abstract principles which have been agreed upon and confirmed. We reject these crimes because they imply suffering for numerous people of flesh and blood.

The codification of the international laws of war has taken place in stages. The conventions and agreements which are in force reflect varying conceptions from different points in time. With the rapid development which has taken place in military techniques, many of the older rules appear unappropriate today. There are also considerable gaps in international regulations governing warfare—for example, the use of chemical weapons against nature and people.

Even if the system of rules for war and warfare are imperfect, they would still offer a relatively good degree of protection for civilians and prisoners of war if they were loyally followed by the belligerents. If the rules were followed to the full, the United States would not conduct a merciless war of aggression against the Indochinese people. If the American leaders really took the conventions and pacts which the United States has agreed to respect seriously, they would not conduct a ruthless policy of extermination in Indochina.

The organizational form of the United Nations and the reigning power structure in the world make the United Nations powerless when confronted by the fact that the greatest military power in the world brutally attacks three smaller and more weakly developed nations.

The imperfections in the rules for the conduct of warfare do not concern the supervision and control of conformity with the rules so much as the lack of a real possibility of presenting complaints about violations before a competent organ. Ultimately, it is naturally also a lack of ability to apply effective sanctions against violations. In practice, these functions are nonexistent today.

The existence of legal regulation of the conduct of warfare does not automatically mean that the law will be observed. There must also be an insight concerning the advantage of such regulation. This is absolutely necessary as long as there are no means of punishing violations. Between equal military parties, it may be presumed that the motivating force for refraining from violations is strong.

Neither of the parties can overstep the existing rules without running the risk of retaliation.

The leaders of the Axis Powers ignored this risk in their military arrogance. The ruthless conduct of the war by the Axis powers was followed by military retribution which, if seen as an isolated phenomenon, would probably be considered to be an offense against the rules of international law. These excesses on the part of the Allies were understandable, however, and can to a great extent be historically justified. The struggle concerned the survival of a whole civilization when confronted with Fascism and global oppression.

In Indochina the situation is totally different. Bearing in mind their enormous military resources, the leaders of the United States have abandoned all legal and moral scruples with respect to warfare. The cynical attitude revealed by the American leaders is very shortsighted, however. The American leaders are certainly concerned over the lack of military victories, but they probably feel certain that they will not be punished for their excesses. The rule of violence which the United States has established in Indochina may, however, recoil on theUnited States itself. Potential opponents to the United States must naturally ask themselves if the war policy in Indochina should be considered to be genuine American state practice. Such an evaluation may lead to strategic redistributions to counteract the form of warfare these potential enemies have reason to anticipate from the United States by the use of corresponding means.

In purely general terms, the American war policy means that a dangerous precedent has been established which may bear results in military situations where a situation of short-term balance does not exist.

It is important that the American people come to a clear realization of the legal and political implications of the American military policy in Indochina. It is necessary that the American people forcefully reject and work against the military policy which violates the treaties and conventions the United States has pledged itself to respect and which, according to the American constitution, constitute "the supreme law of the land."

International Law and the Liberation of the Colonized Peoples

The legal analysis of the United States war in Indochina would not be complete if we did not also take up the international legal aspects of the sweeping changes which national states have gone through since World War II.

The great colonial empires have been broken up. The people in the colonies have liberated themselves from foreign political domination and constituted themselves as sovereign states with a demand for equal rights and complete political independence. This process of liberation is still not complete. In the Portuguese colonies, for example, an armed liberation struggle for national independence and the right of self-determination is still in progress against the Portuguese colonial forces. The demands that every people shall be able to determine its own political, economic, social and cultural development have been given stronger emphasis continuously as more and more nations have liberated themselves from colonial oppression.

Several significant resolutions have been adopted in the United Nations which confirm the right of all peoples to self-determination and political independence. It has been maintained that all dependent peoples have the right to struggle for independence and that in accordance with the Charter of the United Nations, they have the right to seek and receive support in their struggle for independence. United Nations resolutions have expressed strong concern in view of the growing threat to world peace presented by armed interventions and oppressive measures undertaken with the aim of preventing the liberation process.

All measures which are undertaken with the purpose of undermining the national unity of a people or to gain advantage from such dissension are considered to be contrary to the purposes and principles of the United Nations. There is nothing which entitles one nation to intervene in the internal or external affairs of another. Armed intervention is to be considered equivalent to aggressive war and thus to constitute a violation of the United Nations Charter.

The struggle of the Indochinese people for political independence can be seen as a part of the global liberation process which has taken place since World War II. The defeat of the French colonial power in Indocina implied a new phase of development for the Indochinese peoples. The first phase toward self-determination and independence had been won. In this situation, the United States government stepped in to upset the Geneva Agreement, which was intended to guarantee the Indochinese people against interference in their internal affairs.

By political maneuvers, the government of the United States succeeded in obtaining a firm grip on the national government of South Vietnam. The Diem regime in South Vietnam was made completely dependent on the United States by means of massive economic and technical assistance, as well as military assistance in direct violation of the stipulations of the Geneva Agreements.

South Vietnam was militarized under the supervision of the United States. The police system and the prison system were expanded to enable the suppressing of all opposition to the Diem terror regime. By the American intervention, Vietnam was forcibly divided into two parts in conflict with the terms of the Geneva Agreement.

After years of continuous escalation, the government of the United States has also drawn Cambodia and Laos into its efforts to stop the liberation process in Indochina. With its mighty military resources, the United States has attacked the severely exhausted Indochinese people in order to prevent their just effort to determine their own development.

The leaders of the United States have been eager to maintain that the war in Indochina shall not be seen as a mistake or an isolated instance which will never recur. According to the notorious domino theory, the American leaders have seen it as their duty to combat liberation in Indochina. Ultimately, this strategy is said to concern the United States' own security. America's self-assumed role as the judge over peoples' welfare and future has no foundation in international law. The United States government has not been furnished with any international powers to force its political ideals upon other countries. The right to achieve social changes in parliamentary or revolutionary order must be considered to belong sovereignly to every people individually.

In 1954, Richard Nixon, who was then Vice President of the United States, declared that "the Vietnamese lack the ability to conduct a war by themselves or to govern themselves." Since that time, this concept has been the guiding principle for America's Indochina policy, with the difference that over the years the American governments have discovered that the people of Laos and Cambodia are not capable of conducting wars and managing their own governments either.

The American war policy in Indochina has, however, not successfully proved that President Nixon's thesis is true. In spite of an overwhelming military strike force, the United States and its marionette regimes have not been able to achieve even the primitive legitimacy which, in accordance with traditional international law, is accorded to a military occupant who can effectively control an invaded territory. The American troops have not succeeded in defeating the national resistance forces which in concrete form defend the principles of international law and their right to self-determination, political independence, territorial integrity, and national unity.

The Political Economy of War:
Douglas F. Dowd

It is as easy to deride those who argue that the United States went into Vietnam for economic reasons as it is to dismiss as naïve those who plead that we got in there by miscalculation and will get out as soon as time and circumstance permit. It is considerably more important to know why and how we did enter the lists in Indochina, for that set of actions was part of and consistent with a larger pattern that goes beyond Indochina in both time and space. And perhaps of greatest immediate importance is to understand that as matters now stand, the United States does in fact have an already large, and potentially immense, economic stake in getting its way in Indochina. We must come to grips with such matters if we are to assess the meaning and persistence of the war. Nor shall we be able to find the appropriate means to end the war if we mistake the nature of the task.

The United States became formally involved in the Indochinese war no later than 1949, when President Truman lent support there to France, in return for cooperation in the development of NATO—which, implying as it did a strengthened Germany, made the French uneasy. The United States was then indisputably the foremost economic and military power in the world; but our consciousness of the nature and meaning of that role—whether in business, political and military circles, or in the minds of the attentive public—was, by comparison with what we know today, quite limited. Before very long, in the Dulles era, consciousness caught up with fact and, in so doing, expanded and accelerated a process that earlier took place in an almost casual manner—usually in the name of "filling power vacuums." Neither the full range of needs nor all the beckoning possibilities were envisioned, except by a tiny group of steely-eyed and experienced dwellers in the higher reaches of power, men like Acheson and Harriman and Dulles. Their more or less hidden views in the Roosevelt and Truman periods became overt only in the 1950s. In the 1960s they were codified and institutionalized.

Was America's entrance as a major actor in the Indochinese theatre a result of direct economic interests? Not originally. But now, after more than twenty years of growing political and military involvement, direct and serious economic interests for Americans and the United States do exist; and if they continue to grow, they will become compelling.

The magnet that pulled us into Indochina under Truman was marked "global strategic concerns"—which, in Southeast Asia, meant especially a concern for restoring stabilitity to Indochina. But involvement is a process, not a condition; and over time the process has meant not only a greater *strategic* importance for success or failure, but, as well, the addition of a strong economic interest. The latter, unless the war ends soon, threatens to overtake the more general concerns that first prompted the relationship with Indochina.

If all that is true, far from preparing to leave Indochina alone, the United States is less likely to do so now than it was five or ten or fifteen years ago. And flowing from that appraisal is a set of probabilities that has already achieved all too much reality: although opposition by Americans to the war has now reached overwhelming proportions, it does not follow that the Nixon Administration will bring the American presence in Indochina to an end. Instead, it will be forced to seek innovative means of camouflaging our intervention there, while isolating and repressing *active* domestic opposition to the continuing operation. Thus it is that American ground casualites are reduced and troops withdrawn, while bombing and shelling have more than doubled under Nixon; and thus it is that Nixon embraces (if a bit stiffly) large demonstrations like those of April 24, while his Attorney General instructs the police and the general public to view the nonviolent disruptions in May as the work of *Hitler Jugend.* Thus it is, as Senator Eagleton has recently discovered, that the American military leaders in Vietnam expect to maintain a residual ground force and a bombing capability for a period of time unspecified.

Explaining U.S. involvement in Indochina in "strategic" rather than "economic" terms does not conflict with the notion that economic elements are intrinsic to the very existence of a geographic strategy for a capitalist society. As the capitalist power without serious competition after World War II, the U.S.A. could not afford to develop a global strategy moving in the simple terms that equate substantial military-political presence with substantial economic presence.

Imperialism is a matter not only of economic gain, but of politico-military expansion of the frontiers *within* which that gain can be made, while also pushing or holding back rivals (whether capitalist or socialist). Within the frontiers, and especially at the periphery—where, after all, the greatest resistance is likely—are areas that require heavy expenditures with little attendant direct economic gain—at first, or even in reasonable prospect. Indochina was such a place in 1954. A decade later, when we began to bomb North Vietnam, the larger strategy was already joined to profit, and the clear prospect of growing economic gain. In Indochina, as so

326 INTERNATIONAL LAW AND AMERICAN POLICY

frequently happens, the manner in which a social process began was deflected and transformed by the workings out of the process itself.

One must retrace the path of American involvement, then, in order to appreciate why it is that both our military and our economic penetration, and our devastation of the land, the society and the people of Indochina, have increased over the years. Seeing that, we may see also why the political life of the United States itself—echoing and mirroring the deadly struggle in Indochina—becomes ever deadlier. Nixon, Agnew, and Mitchell, in such light, are doing their jobs very well indeed.

The story begins much further back in time than I shall penetrate. Suffice it to say that, as William Appleman Williams and others have shown, the American war with Japan stands as eloquent testimony to the longstanding American interest in Asia, an interest which in one form or another goes back to the first decades of our nationality. However, a full examination of the actual and potential resources, markets, and investment outlets in Indochina (not Asia) would tell us little about the *initial* involvement of the United States in Indochina, under Truman.

What was decisive for Truman's (and, later, Eisenhower's) moves were three major problems, all requiring that Indochina be kept under Western hegemony.

The first, the French *quid pro quo* with NATO, has been mentioned. The second concerned the Chinese Revolution, and the hopes and fears American policymakers developed in that connection as they dwelt on the prospects for a successful and revolutionary war for independence in Indochina. Whether the domino theory was valid or not, it was taken seriously by those who espoused it; and Indochina was a very wobbly domino.

The third problem was Japan. Very much in our pocket

after defeat, Japan was groomed to be a junior partner in the American empire, the Asian bastion of a global system. [See "Captial's Last Frontier" by Jules Henry, *The Nation*, April 25, 1966.] As an industrial power, Japan had to find sources and uses for its industrial strength. Among other things, this meant finding viable alternatives to resuming its historic economic relationships with China. Southeast Asia, although it could not fully satisfy those needs, was an essential condition for their satisfaction. In turn, that meant that Southeast Asia had to be stabilized, and most of all at its hot center: Indochina (From 1945 on, the other hot spot, the Philippines, had similarly occupied American arms and money, and success had ensued with deceptive ease.)

So it was that the political-military side of American involvement in Indochina began quite simply as providing financial and minor political assistance to France—money, reticence mysterious for an anticolonial power, and support for the ludicrous Bao Dai. By 1952, the United States was supplying the French with more than three-quarters of the money for the Indochinese war. By 1954, Bao Dai was ensconced on the French Riviera, and the French were no longer in Indochina to be supported. Our next step was to become directly involved politically, when we set up the Diem regime. Swiftly, this required political and police advisers and the weapons of terrorism, to render effective a regime that could be sustained in no other way—nor, as it turned out, even in that way. And so American military forces, wearing diverse costumes and labels, began to find themselves in Indochina (not just in Vietnam), in numbers exceeding 20,000 by the time JFK was assassinated—and who knows how many more on the lands and seas surrounding Indochina.

And just as political involvement was increased by an ever

deepening military *and* political involvement, so these relationships in turn had an economic element added to them. The economic involvement had two faces, which require separate comment. First, the war, which steadily (and by now, almost totally) disrupted the economies of South Vietnam, Laos, and Cambodia (in that order), placed the United States in the position of becoming a growing supplier not only of military stuff but of construction equipment, of industrial (both capital and consumer) goods, of foodstuffs, and of the required and profitable financial apparatus that went along with what has now become an American economy abroad. The Indochinese economies are now thoroughly displaced, disrupted, and corrupted, and the peoples of the area provide degraded services for the American needs—services ranging from mercenary soldiers, pimps, prostitutes, and black marketeers to obscenely cheap labor for production and consumption. The top layers of the economy, the layers where the large and growing profits roam, are controlled by American and Japanese interests; but, of course, the usual *compradores* in the upper strata of the kept Lao, Cambodian, and Vietnamese military and bureaucracy get a fat slice of the action.

The second aspect of our growing economic involvement in and with the Indochinese war overlaps the first but also has some distinct (and more substantial) meanings. The relationships *in* Indochina entail the subjugation and vicious exploitation of the Indochinese peoples; but there is much that has to do with the American economy as well, and with its position as *the* world powers.

In Indochina itself, there were for all practical purposes *no* American economic interests as of, say, 1954. For years we had been much interested in the Philippines and in Indonesia, and more than once we had poked our fingers into the pies of Burma and Malaysia; but not, economically, into

Indochina. The French would have put a stop to that, had there been the impulse. What was true in 1954 was likely to remain so for the years just after that time—given one additional matter. That is, when the United States first entered Indochina as an agent, whether to support France or Diem, it was quite generally believed that our efforts would be crowned with swift success; at the start, we foresaw no substantial quantitative involvement of any sort. Indochina was judged to be a strategic piece of geography that could be secured with minor effort, not as an area in which to make substantial economic gains. But soon the process began to be transformed.

In this instance, as in others, once a strong political position was established, other relationships began to multiply. On the most general level, there can be no doubt that the military expenditures made by the Department of Defense from the early 1950s on came to have an ever more stimulating effect on what was a weakly growing domestic economy. That effect came to be quite substantial in the early and mid-sixties; so much so that it became inflationary after 1966 —though disguised by Johnson, so as to keep the war disguised. Now we can all see that the economic blessings from the war have been mixed and may on balance even be negative (especially when balance of payments matters are taken into account, as they must be). Still, one would like to know just what would take up the slack if the $15 billion to $30 billion a year for that war were to be cut down significantly.

Less generally, but more to the point, the war began to be a significant and conscious source of gain to particular economic interests in this country. At first that meant the corporations supplying the goods and services of the war itself— construction firms, and firms producing the weapons and equipment and supplies of the American and Vietnamese military. But, as with the spread of the Roman Empire (among others), activity at the frontiers soon came to require and suggest associated commercial, industrial and financial activities. Somewhat later, the area began to promise good returns for investment.

Already by 1966, South Vietnam had become a significant source of profit not only to ordnance, weapons, and aircraft (especially helicopter and fighter bomber) producers, but for the construction consortium RMK-BRJ and heavy equipment (bulldozers, locomotives, tractors) suppliers such as American Trading Company and Engineco, companies whose existence had depended upon the growing war for a number of years. Foremost Dairies moved in to supply milk and ice cream for American troops; Parson & Whittemore of New York had invested $5 million in a paper plant and would double that soon after, as it met the bureaucratic needs of the cancerous U.S. establishment in South Vietnam. Esso and Caltex were selling over half of all the oil and gasoline used in the area in 1966. Pan American had dozens of regular and chartered flights to and from the States every day carrying cargo and whole soldiers one way, coffins the other, and its counterparts on the sea—Seatrain and Matson and President Lines, among others—rediscovered the meaning of the word prosperity. Johnson International of New Jersey had its textile mill going in South Vietnam in 1966, and a whole range of predators were selling autos, stocks, and real estate to GIs as they planned to return home. By 1968, Philco-Ford and IBM were doing their part in South Vietnam for the electronic war, as was National Cash Register. Pfizer, Sterling Drug International was installed to heal wounds, and both Bankamerica and Chase Manhattan were present to lubricate the growing American and *comprador* economy.

More recently, South Vietnam has become dependent upon imports of rice from agribusiness in the States (although it was historically a rice exporter); in 1970 and 1971, larger-scale investors such as Ford Motor Company were beginning to join the ranks of one hundred or more corporations counting on the success of Vietnamization to make South Vietnam, Laos, and Cambodia into new and lush pastures—up to and including plans for a Holiday Inn in Phnom Penh.

Americans are nothing if not businesslike and sensitive to the needs and possibilities of a new big chance. Thus it was that, standing behind the growing activities instanced above and making it possible for much more to join the game, was a rapidly and consciously developed infrastructure, as noted by Nation's Business, in February 1968 (written presumably, before Tet):

> American businesses being established in Vietnam, through investments, acquisitions, partnerships or subsidiaries, will find an expanding network of communications, highways, waterways, docks and airports, every one of which could be useful to industry or commerce.
> In the past few years, six new deepwater ports have been built, eight shallow draft ports, eight jet air bases with 12 new 10,000-foot runways, 80 smaller fields, scores of bridges and hundreds of miles of roads, oil tanks and pipelines, storage and maintenance facilities and housing for 325,000 soldiers, much of it convertible into housing for industrial workers.

In short, all sectors and functions of the American economy—business, agriculture, industry, commerce, finance, labor, and our economic rhythms—now connect somewhat or greatly to our little economy in South Vietnam; and all have some significant interest in seeing the Saigon regime maintained.

Add all that up, and it probably does not approach a critical point; not just yet. But add in something else that has only now come to light, though its reality goes back a decade: I refer to the offshore oil deposits of Southeast Asia. It is now believed that the long-exploited deposits of Indonesia and Borneo are only a fraction of the oil reserves of the region; and it is now understood that the offshore resources of South Vietnam, and of the whole curve extending east from Burma around through the Gulf of Thailand (which includes offshore Cambodia) and into the South China Sea, constitute an oil pool which, as one petroleum expert has said, make the Louisiana oil resources "look like a postage stamp on an elephant's ass." The elephant's ass has South Vietnam at its strategic center. So it is vividly true that strategy and economics combine into a very precious mix, located in South Vietnam.

Just because of oil? For contemporary economies, and for contemporary warfare—excluding the total nuclear type— no resource runs even a close second to oil as being vital; and in the structure of business power in the world, the oil corporations (and, among them, the Americans) stand at the very peak of power. The major American, European, and Japanese oil corporations have already leased a good part of the offshore areas throughout Southeast Asia for exploration and development. The leases for the regions offshore from South Vietnam are to be bid for some time this year, probably this summer. All this takes place when underwater exploration and drilling techniques have just become adequate to the task, when Middle Eastern oil countries have become tough bargainers and when the leading Western powers all anticipate the doubling of their oil needs in the next decade or two.

It all takes place at a time, too, when our presence in Southeast Asia, and most especially in South Vietnam, has come under universal attack. There is no question but that the Nixon Administration is doing what it can to induce American oil companies to take up the eighteen South Vietnamese leases; nor is the welcome from Thieu-Ky anything less than enthusiastic, for both financial and military-political reasons.

The economic promises developed for Americans in Indochina in the past few years and, even more, those of the past two or three and those yet to come, cannot be made good if the United States withdraws from Indochina—for in that case Indochina would not be favorably related to us, least of all as regards oil. So new investments make no sense—unless, unless. . . . Nixon knows he has a better chance to continue his policy of securing a "stable government" in South Vietnam if he can also induce politically powerful corporations to tie themselves even more than they already have to the destiny of South Vietnam. Oil counts heavily in that equation. If Nixon and the oil companies move together on this front, as David Gelber has said (in *Liberation*, Spring 1971), "then we might have to consider the possibility that the war in Indochina has just begun."

Concluding Statement

The International Commission of Enquiry into U.S. Crimes in Indochina has, during its session in Oslo, June 20–24, 1971, been faced with a long line of witnesses who together have given a remarkably consistent overall picture of the U.S. warfare in Indochina. We have listened to U.S. soldiers, formerly attached to different branches of the military in Indochina, revealing what they did to the local population—acts often influenced by racial bias acquired during the course of their upbringing and military training. We have listened to detailed statements from victims—from men, women, and children—about what they have experienced of torture, imprisonment, attacks from the air, or deportation. Whole villages and vast areas of their country have been destroyed. In addition to all this, we have received information from medical doctors, scientists, and journalists concerning what they have seen. It all adds up to the same picture. The witnesses and their testimonies have been considered by a medical expert, the Norwegian Dr. Mons Lie, and also by an expert in witness-psychology, Professor Arne Trankell of Sweden. Their conclusion was that the witnesses gave reliable evidence.

Important information has been provided by National Commissions for Investigation in the Indochinese countries.

A delegation that was sent on a mission to the Democratic Republic of Vietnam on behalf of our Commission gathered a considerable amount of material and analyzed facts that confirm documentation from the National Commissions of Investigation in Indochina. The Commission can state that the facts that have been revealed by testimonies during the session give accurate examples of the general character of different types of violations.

The Commission has also had the opportunity to scrutinize a considerable number of scientific reports (for example, we have read reports on chemical warfare and its effects, including the use of gas) as well as other evidence such as weapons, films, photographs, and maps.

It is, of course, very hard for individual members of the Commission to evaluate every detail of the information received during the session, but since we also found the material presented in Oslo very consistent with information we have received earlier from other sources—especially from U.S. correspondents as well as those from foreign countries, we feel convinced that, on the whole, we can rely on the material we have received.

The Commission has not the capacity of a court. It does not possess the power, competence, or means of sanction of a court. It consists of individuals from different cultures who hold to some extent to different basic values. We do, however, agree on the need to expose what is going on in the war in Indochina. We are deeply disturbed by some of the information which has been brought before us, and we feel an urgent need to bring this information to the attention of the world.

The material, both oral and written, which has been presented to the Commission will later be printed and published. Readers of this material will then be able to draw their own conclusions from this overwhelming documentation. Our conclusions are as follow:

• The policy of the U.S. Government has lead to an extension of the war in Indochina. While implementing its "Viet-namization" program, the United States has openly attacked Cambodia and Laos and resumed its bombing of the Democratic Republic of Vietnam.

• In this process, the United States has been using its highly developed industrial technology to create even more sophisticated methods of destruction. The Commission was shown several new types of fragmentation bombs which evidently have been used for attacks on civilians. It was provided with evidence relating to the chemical warfare in Indochina which destroys the ecological balance in this part of the world. Fields have become sterile and water poisoned. In large areas there is almost no animal or plant life left. Places where people once lived have become incapable of sustaining human life. These effects, and the social breakdown as a whole, will cause serious difficulties for coming generations in Indochina. Chemical warfare remains one of the most serious features of the U.S. warfare. It causes damage primarily to the civil population, especially to its weaker members such as children, women, the aged, and the sick.

• Evidence also revealed that gas is being used against the civilian population, frequently with lethal results. Over and above the application of the most modern technology of warfare should be added the whole pattern of destruction that is created by the "pacification program." This program is designed to control the civilian population. Millions of civilians have been forcibly deported, to be concentrated in camps and city slums.

• Probably more than one-third of the population of South Vietnam have become refugees as a consequence of mass deportation, search-and-destroy missions, the bombing of hamlets, and the privation of villagers of food through crop destruction. This forced movement of people has led to the breakdown of the family structure, the very basis of Indochinese society. The same pattern of social destruction has followed the U.S. terror bombing of Laos. It seems clear to the Commission that mass deportation is official U.S. policy. We received evidence about indiscriminate use of incarceration and cruel forms of imprisonment. Prisons bulge. Arbitrary imprisonments are extremely common and prisoners live under the most deplorable conditions. Mr. Don Luce of the World Council of Churches in Geneva gave testimony to the Commission concerning wretched conditions in the so-called "tiger cages." New jails and tiger cages are being constructed under the supervision and financial support of the U.S.

There are strong indications that torture is a common feature of the U.S. and Saigon interrogation of prisoners of war and of civilians. Witnesses maintain that in certain prisons or prison camps almost all inmates have been subjected to torture at least once.

• Air attack is the major means of indiscriminate killing of the civilian population. Exterminations of the Son My type, as well as the murder of individual civilians, also seem to be much more common than supposed earlier. The massacre in Son My was reported more than one year before its confirmation in the United States. Several cases of similar events were brought to the attention of the Commission in Oslo. During the invasion of Cambodia, Vice President Agnew openly admitted that one of the objectives of this U.S. operation was to attack legally protected targets such as hospitals.

The acts mentioned above violate the five Hague conventions of 1907; the 1925 Geneva Protocol, containing prohibition against asphyxiating, poisonous, or other gases and bacteriological means of warfare; the 1925 Geneva Convention for the Amelioration of the Conditions of the Wounded and Sick of Armies in the Field; as well as the 1949 Geneva Conventions for the Amelioration of the Conditions of the

Wounded and Sick in Armed Forces in the Field and at Sea, the Treatment of Prisoners of War, and the Protection of Civilian Persons in Time of War. The United States has pledged itself to respect these documents and conventions. According to the Constitution of the United States, they are parts of "the supreme law of the land."

All these crimes can be categorized as war crimes and crimes against humanity, according to the Nuremberg Principles of International Law.

Taking all this into consideration, it is also the conviction of the Commission that the conclusion of its first session that the United States war in Indochina amounts to genocide was correct. The peoples of Indochina are attacked because they maintain their fundamental national rights. The juridical basis for these rights is also embodied in the Geneva Agreements of 1954 and 1962, which granted the rights of political independence, territorial integrity, and national unity to the peoples of Vietnam, Laos, and Cambodia.

The United States is violating the United Nations Charter that prohibits the use of force against other nations. U.S. aggression is directed at the very foundations of the society of nations. It implies a denial of every people's right to self-determination.

The peoples of Indochina must have the right and the possibility to settle their own affairs withour foreign interference in accordance with their fundamental national rights. Only in this way can peace, law, and justice be established in Indochina.

The Commission is convinced that the crimes committed in Indochina are not only the results of actions of individual soldiers and officers. Clearly, these crimes are the results of the long-term policy of the United States in Southeast Asia, and the main burden of responsibility must lie with those who have been making this policy.

The "Vietnamization" is a means to prolong a war that already is lost and that can only be continued at a heavy cost to the peoples of Indochina.

The Commission appeals to all men, women, organizations, and governments to work for an immediate cessation of the U.S. war of aggression against the Indochinese peoples and the complete withdrawal of U.S. and allied forces without delay.

Unanimously adopted, Oslo, June 24, 1971

Index